Spring in your Step

Discover and Celebrate the Magic of Springtime

Gillian Monks

Spring in your Step

ISBN 978-1-9163396-7-5

HERBARY
BOOKS

Published by Herbary Books
Caernarfon, Wales

www.herbarybooks.com

For Rachel Walker,
without whom I might never have become a published author,
with my love.

And for
Carol and David Walker,
for all their loving support.

Contents

The Yarrow at Drybones

Sing muse, of Drybones, loveliest of places
With ugliest of names;
Sing, till each passer-by his steps retraces,
And hails its beauties with profound acclaims.

I sing the Yarrow, not the stream
Of Scottish tale and sonnet,
Yet one as beautiful, I deem,
As fit to be a minstrel's theme,
Although no Scott has shed a gleam
Of his own glory on it.

What charms thy varying banks display!
Here, bordering on the level,
There, rising most abruptly, they
Are clothed with trees whose branches sway
Above thy rock-strewn, devious way,
Fit scene for fairies revel!
Man's hand with thee hath meddled much,
Oh stream with charms entrancing -
Man's hand, that oft (his blindness such),
Fair Nature's face doth smear and smutch,
But light and mild with thee his touch,
Thy beauties e'en enhancing.

His cotton mills by thee arise,
Huge buildings, unromantic,
But when 'neath winter's gloomy skies
Their lighted windows greet our eyes,
They show in quite another guise,
As by some fairy antic.

Duxbury mill, most weatherworn
And picturesque of places,
Doth still thy pleasant banks adorn,
And with thine aid still grinds the corn,
As in the days ere steam was born,
How pretty its mill-race is.

Birkacre! Woodland scented word,
A human hive discovers;
Where work-days, nothing else is heard
Save sound of engines, steam-bestirred,
On Sundays, nought save song of bird
And laugh of rambling lovers.

Here mankind hath done his best to make
Thee do a servant's duty;
But, though contrived for his own sake,
Each sluice, each artificial lake,
And you fair falls, thy course that break,
Add something to thy beauty.
But Drybones is the sweetest spot
Thy passest by, O Yarrow.
Though noble's hall adorn it not,
No dwelling sav a poor man's cot,
Who beareth Adam's arms, I wot,
The gardener's spade and barrow.

Here, sheltered from obnoxious blast,
Fair flowers and fruit are growing;
Here, whilst our English summers last,
Roses abroad their fragrance cast,
And thou, sweet Yarrow, murmurest past,
'Neath breezes blithely blowing.

The woodland paths whence one discerns
Thee flowing on for ever,
The wild ravines, overgrown with ferns,
Such as concealed Clan-Alpine's kernes*
Enough, if from my song one learns
To love thee, little river.

John Wilson, 1903

*The 'Lady Of The Lake', Canto V

Introduction

There is an energy, an optimism about springtime which is quite unlike any other time of the year. Perhaps it is more distinct because of its juxtaposition to the seemingly dark, drab, lifelessness of winter? Out of all the death and decay, the exigencies of months of severe weather and the lowering of spirits imposed by lack of daylight and sunshine, there begin to appear tiny, imperceptible signs of new life which grow unnoticed. By the time the dark green elder buds have semi burst upon their branches, the lamb's tail catkins are merrily dancing from every twig, birds have coupled and are building their nests, ewes have quickened and given birth and the snowdrops and crocus are in colourful bud, spring is actually well under way. The natural world has been quietly beavering away for several months – in some cases, since well before the Winter Solstice – gathering its strength for another season of birth and growth. As humans now so frequently segregated from the natural rhythms of the Earth we do not notice until after the fact. In reality, our 'signs' of spring are the culmination, not the beginning.

What we tend to miss in our modern existence is the fact that the natural world is like any other living organism. It does things in its own time and in reaction to a thousand other contributing factors. All aspects of life are on a never-ending continuum; as one form of plant life germinates and begins to push up through the soil, another will have just bloomed and a third will already be sere and withered as it fades back into the ground. The seasons do not conform to calendars and begin on a certain date. They rise and fall and roll and roil around the yearly cycle, opportunistically pushing forward towards new life and fruition yet mutually supportive and necessary to all that has gone before or will come after.

Humanity has chosen to separate itself from these natural cadences of life. We have built homes and communities which maintain the same temperature and have access to synthetic daylight all year round, regardless of what the season is or the weather chooses to do. We have been callously shoe-horned into unnatural and painful forms of existence in the name of convenience, commercialisation and 'progress'. It has been demanded of us that we deny our natural instincts and needs… and then we wonder why so many of us are ailing and sick.

In Spring In Your Step we take a long and careful look at our life and learn to understand how we have got to where we are today - both individually and collectively – and why. We need to pause. Take a breath. Stop dwelling on dark negativity and turn our faces to the positive light. Actively choose to refrain from seeing only the ugly and painful and open our eyes to the beauty and wonder, the miraculous and tender which surrounds us… and also reflects our own potential.

'Spring In Your Step' seeks to gently guide you back into harmony with the rest of the world. To reawaken your knowledge of, and connection to the wonders of natural life around you – your world… your heritage… your birth-right. To do this all you have to do is simply reach out to what is closest to you and seek to evolve a more aware and compassionate way of living.

We will learn to cherish each day, both in the natural world and within our own humanly developed environment. We must learn to give way and re-integrate with what is around us. Through the medium of the spring season we begin by reaching out to what is next to us in our ordinary life. We learn to really see the grass, trees, flowers, weeds, birds and insects as they re-emerge at the end of winter. We need to make a new habit of acknowledging their existence, of observing them, of learning about them and then honouring them by actively supporting their mutual right to live and thrive, just as we expect and demand for ourselves.

We also need to look around and observe the weather in all its vagaries and nuances. Some people blossom in hot sunshine, others take nourishment from grey damp days, and some become excited by a storm, thunder and lightning, high winds or a heavy snowfall. We will learn to take a few moments and take joy in all the weather conditions, regardless of how unpleasant or inconvenient. When the weather conditions become too severe and make our lives uncomfortable, we learn respect.

All this is achieved by being encouraged to stop, look about you and really see what is there, and then participate in simple ways of interacting with and enjoying your world. A good way to do this is to make the very most of the ordinary and mundane and form the habit of being thankful for all the little things. Couple this to forming the habit of bringing lesser seasonal celebrations into your life and involving those around you in them also and you are well on your way to very fundamental change, because in the process, you will be reconnecting with the rhythms of the seasons and the earth – with the very essence of life itself.

Nor does it matter where you hale from geographically, or of what nationality, cultural background or religious persuasion you belong to. In our Twenty-first Century multi-cultural society this accessible and straightforward approach to life crosses all borders and boundaries and brings everyone into equal partnership in experiencing and celebrating life.

'Spring In Your Step' suggests lots of ways by which you can engage with one another and the natural world, from playing in the snow, and growing kitchen scraps on you windowsills, to making miniature gardens in dishes and designing a new ornamental but very practical garden feature. You will be encouraged to celebrate life in all its facets from simple days of note, such as World Radio Day and Earth Hour, to the full blown festival of Easter… and all the events, feasts and celebrations which come in between – and there are a huge selection to choose from!

To assist you in making each and every day more valued and special, there are seasonal recipes taken from my mother, Joan's manuscript cookery book – dishes which she cooked and goodies which she baked back in the 'fifties, 'sixties and early 'seventies. There are also a selection of her comments which I have found written in her cookery book or sparse journal entries and which give a fascinating window onto the life of a young post-World War Two housewife who chose to leave the centre of town and take on a form of the 'good life' as the 'Swinging Sixties' unfolded.

The poems by Agnes Gore Green were written by my grandmother in the 1930s. References made to 'Jim' and 'Ricky' in 'Comments from Joan' refer to my father and Joan's adopted brother respectively.

There are craft projects to furnish your seasonal calendar of mindful activities and jollity – how to plait a Brighid's Cross from rushes, how to dip wax tapers and form your own candles in earth or sand, how to set up a Valentine tree and make heart-warming Valentine garlands, how to draw sigils, decorate eggs, make Easter bonnets and decorate hats…

And there are memories of how my family and I used to live and work and celebrate sixty years ago when I was a child. I also include accounts of how we celebrate the turning of the seasons now in the hope that between the two you will feel inspired to try formulating your own authentic celebrations which accurately reflect your activities, interests and place in the world.

Life is frequently a challenge, painful, distressing and downright hard work. But it is also an endless adventure and opportunity for making lovely, enjoyable and memorable occasions, some of which we might appreciate alone or relish in the company of others. We can plan, plot and dream. Here we can begin to bring a new order into being, a new world into reality. What better time to do this than in the dark and drear months of winter? As the days lengthen, we can then begin to test out our ideas and put our plans into practice.

As you reach out in wonder and gratitude to the amazing world of nature and learn to embrace your fellow members of humanity in loving friendship, may you all discover the magical quality of perpetual spring in your hearts – an eternal optimism and youthfulness of outlook and appreciation, and always walk with a light and joyful spring in your step!

With my love,
Gillian

Snowdonia, North Wales, 2020

Chapter One

January - Winter still

'As days lengthen, the cold strengthens.'

'January brings the snow - make our toes and fingers glow', so the old children's rhyme declares…

Icy gales, freezing rain, iron-hard ground, brittle hoar frost, wickedly dagger-like icicles and those wonderous mornings when we awake to a bright, white world of snow – the deceptively soft chill layer which cloaks everything, deadens all sound, leaves our garden pots and containers looking like fantastic cupcakes and ice cream cones… and brings gleeful excitement and anticipation to every child's heart!

Youngsters don their rubber boots, thick jackets, woollen hats, scarves and mittens, oblivious to the wet and cold which will gradually soak even the most robust waterproofs. For snow loves us too and has an invariable habit of finding its way down our collars, into our hair, filling boots and soaking socks, seeping through trouser knees and dampening backsides and transforming mittens and gloves into ice-bobbled encumbrances.

Adult hearts may plunge at the prospect of closed schools, difficulties getting to work, shortages of fresh foods and frozen or burst pipes. But for children, (and those of us who remain young at heart), it is a time for unscheduled holiday and celebration, a chance to step out of the humdrum of everyday routine and do something completely different. The very nature of winter weather usually forces us indoors and keeps us prisoner there, but snow brings release and joyous activity. At the very least it brightens a dark world and provides enforced opportunity to stand back and marvel at the utter beauty of our amazing world.

If you can't get into work because of a snowfall – either because it has affected your transport, or you need to look after your children because their school has closed – don't be half hearted about it. Declare a family holiday! Make it fun. Get everyone out into the snow - including yourself – and really let yourself go. Build snow people, organise snowball fights, hurtle downhill on anything vaguely approaching a sledge and fling yourself down to make magnificent snow-angels. No matter how much work you might have piling up in office, home or elsewhere, forget it… just for one day. You have no choice, so you might as well get as much out of this opportunity as possible; it is what you would pay to go on holiday to do, so do it at home. The precious value in family bonding and of release and de-stressing will be incalculable.

Don't forget the little extras which can make it memorable, like jugs or flasks of hot cocoa or chocolate, or hot spiced fruit juice. Add a packet of biscuits or some chocolate and fruit (or homemade cake if you have time) and you have a snow picnic which will be remembered for ever more. Bear in mind that snowy conditions use up a lot of energy and everyone, especially children and teenagers, will appear to be permanently hungry.

Keep the special holiday feeling going even when you come indoors. Declare an amnesty from technology (even if you don't have a power cut) and light candles instead. Tell stories, play games or read aloud. Such opportunities do not often occur and are precious. Give thanks to the snowy, icy conditions which obliged you to make the most of this day.

Don't forget yourself in all of this. Later in the evening allow yourself a hot scented bath or a snuggle by the fire with your favourite person, pet or book. Mix yourself a strong hot toddy and sink into untroubled oblivion for the prefect night's rest – you will be so much the better for it the next day and in the weeks to come.

Ox Tail Braised

A wonderfully satisfying and sustaining dish to come home to in icy
weather when one has been out of doors for hours. Modern cooks
might wish to substitute shin beef, shanks or short ribs on the bone.

Ingredients

The larger joints of an ox tail
flour to coat
1 medium onion
1 lb (500 g) of carrots
small turnip or piece of swede
small stick of celery
Bunch of herbs
3 cloves

Method

- *Flour and pepper joints - or use a few pepper corns in the cooking
  – fry until brown.*
- *While the meat is frying, cut up the vegetables and roll in the flour.*
- *When the ox tail is brown, lift it out onto a plate.*
- *Fry the vegetables. When they are brown take them out and fry any
  flour left in the bowl.*
- *When the flour is brown, froth it up with stock or water to make a
  rich gravy.*
- *While the gravy is cooking, put the pieces of ox tail and vegetables in
  a fire proof casserole, pour the gravy over and bake close and covered
  until the vegetables are tender and the meat loose on the bone. It can be
  cooked either in the oven or (very slowly) on top of the stove in a pan.*
- *This is a very rich dish and is best made the day before so that the
  fat can be taken off before it is heated up and served. Serve with
  plain mashed potatoes and pickled beetroot. Any gravy left may
  have stock added and/or a glass of port or burgundy and can be
  served as a separate soup course.*

- *Can use ends (very thin) to make stock with. I was pleased to find these cut off before sale but the rest cost £1.22 (spring 1978) so was quite large enough.*

24th June, 1991: still eating beef, steak, etc. but have kept off ox tail – oh, how I long for it! - because of Mad Cow Disease. Feel somewhat uneasy about allowing Dafydd* to eat beef – anyway, he adores pork... now there is Blue Ear Disease from Holland among British pigs – but so far, I have not heard of it infecting humans.

HEATWAVE

January weather can assume many faces apart from the traditionally snowy one. For us now between the mountains and the sea it is frequently one long stretch of cloud-enshrouded, damp, dark and dismal days, occasionally interspersed by frosts or a winter gale. But there can also be days when the clouds clear away to reveal a summer-blue sky, the land relaxes under a warming sun, and the air becomes balmy and sweet.

These are the days to get out into one's garden – or go for a tramp with a picnic into the countryside. It is an amazing sensation to sit upon frosty grass and feel the real heat of the sun warming your back. Don't just sit and glare at the dead landscape through your unforgiving windows; put on some warm clothes and go and find out what it is really like out there. You may be pleasantly surprised.

Getting outside into the natural world of fresh air, diverse temperatures and activity is really the best thing that we can do

*Dafydd, Joan's grandson, only three years old at the time.

after our weeks – or even months – of being inured indoors and temporarily losing sight of the altogether bigger picture of life.

Late winter into early spring is also an excellent time to get all sorts of things done in and around your home. The natural world has temporarily retreated into hibernation; the leaves are off the trees and the herbage has died back below ground… one can now literally see the wood for the trees. Time to get out and clear, clean, sort, trim back… just be aware that if anything outside has been left standing since the autumn, some wildlife may have taken up shelter for the winter there. If possible, leave it a couple more months if you possibly can but if you really cannot wait, at least move it all, piece by piece, to a slightly different location so that anything asleep, hibernating or sheltering can safely get away. Also, just remember not to be too assiduous in your tidying – things like leaf litter shelter many tiny life forms and insulate the roots of plants from the frost.

If it stays dry it might even be possible to get some odd jobs done around the outside of the house too. Then when the weather becomes inclement once more – as it surely will – you can sit back and feel more comfortable about your enforced inactivity knowing that you have already achieved something practical and positive this new year.

So, get out there. Don't cringe – mentally, emotionally or physically – behind your front door. Get your body moving, your pulse racing, your heart pounding and your system moving. Even for a short time each day it will provide untold benefits for you and is just what you need after all the rich foods and indoor activity of Midwinter and Christmas.

I well remember when I was a small child that there were several years when we enjoyed what can only be described as a mini heatwave in mid-January, although, living where we did at the time in our own secluded little valley which had its own microclimate, perhaps we were the only ones to experience it. For a few days – maybe as long as a week - the sun would shine but cloud cover at night would provide a protective warming blanket to keep away the frost. As my mother wielded her fork, spade or bow saw and I followed suit with my miniature red metal and wood spade (originally bought the previous year for the construction of sandcastles on summer beaches) we would become progressively warmer and then hotter. Off would come the scarves and gloves to be quickly followed by coats or jackets which were all hung in neighbouring trees to keep them handy but off the ground, clean and dry. These were soon followed by cardigans and jumpers as we grew redder of face and perspiration began to flow. A couple of years my mother actually ended up wearing her sun-top as she dug over some vegetable beds.

These were the afternoons when we would end our labours by lighting a bonfire of all the dead, dry plants, grasses and brashy twigs we had accumulated as we tidied the land. Together we would finally come to rest on some convenient fallen log clutching large mugs of scalding hot tea or cocoa as the flames drove away the decreasing temperature and the light of the short winter's day faded into dusk. Here was the rich, fragrant scent of deep leaf-mould, the gritty feel of bark dust between our fingers, the knobbly discomfort of an unobliging branch beneath one's weary backside, the acrid sting of a drift of smoke, the contented tiredness of a day well spent in exhilarating physical activity made all the more precious from having been kept inside for weeks by inclement weather. Stiff but happy we would finally retreat into the warm shadowy stillness of the kitchen rich with the aroma of a casserole or 'tatie pie' for our evening meal bubbling away in the oven besides the glowing grate.

JANUARY BLUES

Every year we are told how difficult many of us find the month of January. Seasonal debt can cause some of us great hardship. There are many amongst us who have seasonal jobs or businesses and winter can be a very trying and worrying time. Then there is the weather to contend with; wall to wall grey rain and gales or frost, snow and fog. Not very encouraging, especially without the physical warmth, colour and emotional buoyancy which the anticipation of our Midwinter/Christmas celebrations can bring. Many of us suffer from depression and January is recognised as one of the most difficult times of the year for us to cope with.

I have thought long and hard about why this might be and I have come to the conclusion that, to a greater or lesser degree, no matter how much we might love Christmas and no matter how wonderful our celebrations might have been, we all suffer some degree of trauma around this time of the year as a direct result of celebrating Christmas.

Christmas is such an emotive time. Many people feel incredibly strongly about it. Some absolutely adore the festival and everything that appertains to it; others loath it with a passion. Some of us have suffered great heartbreak, grief and sorrow around the festival which brings recurring negative connotations each year – with all the family expectations and get-togethers it has an unfortunate tendency to be a prime time for disagreements and rows, family break-ups, separation and divorce. Others have to cope with Christmas without a particular loved one or with appalling loneliness. No wonder they enter January feeling hopelessly shell-shocked.

But what is wrong with those of us who have had a wonderful holiday, loved every minute of it... and feel as bad as the ones who didn't? I suspect that it might be something to do with that search for the 'perfect Christmas'. Many of us have memories of marvellous Christmases in our childhood or younger years which mature adult life can never quite manage to recapture. We yearn for it. We catch many tantalising glimpses. Even the act of fondly recalling can become heavily emotionally charged and ultimately wearing.

Love it or loath it, I think that Christmas is a total blitz on our memories, expectations and emotions and regardless of whether we have enjoyed it or not, we are all traumatised by the potent emotional vortex we annually take several weeks to create or revisit.

There is nothing terribly wrong with this, as long as we give ourselves a chance to recover. We need time to take stock, download and process all that we have recently felt and gone through. We need a period of relative calm and inactivity, a time when not very much is taking place; when (hopefully) not too much will be asked of us; when there are no extremes of activity or emotion to rock us while we re-establish our equilibrium… when, perhaps, the weather encourages us to wrap up warm and nurture ourselves, pay ourselves more attention, even if it is enforced through seasonal illness like 'flu… in fact, we *need* January.

LITTLE THINGS MEAN A LOT

It might help folk to enjoy the month of January more if they realised that many of the little things which everyone aspires to and loves about Christmas are not exclusive to Midwinter celebration but apply to all of winter and possibly most of spring too. Just because we have entered a new year… just because Twelfth Night has now passed and with it Christmas for another ten or eleven months, it doesn't mean to say that we also have to give up all the other lovely day to day pursuits as well.

Activities such as getting together with friends and family; simple, inexpensive but tasty and enjoyable meals with your loved ones; an indulgent and special sweet treat; roasting chestnuts (if there are any left) or enjoying winter fruits; going for walks, playing games, snuggling up under a thick rug to read, singing, playing or listening to music, simply taking time out… being kind to one another. None of these things need to come to an abrupt halt just because it is no longer December… unless you want them to.

There are also some 'special' days in January which can be made into simple celebrations: Distaff Day on the 4th January; Twelfth Night on the 5th or 6th January (depending on whether you count the Twelve Days of Christmas from Christmas Eve or Christmas Day); Plough Monday on the first Monday after Epiphany; Saint Dwynwen's Day and Burn's Night on the 25th January to name just some.*

Families with children have even more scope. When my son was little we would take time to play games with him for a little while

* More details of which can be found in my previous book *Merry Midwinter*.

after tea – simple things like 'Hunt the Thimble', or a few quick rounds of 'I Spy' while we prepared a winter supper — thick slices of homemade bread or spicy currant buns toasted until golden brown and served dripping with butter.

One of the nicest things to do with a child is to read aloud. As my son grew older, I found myself reading more and for longer to him, not less. He was home educated and eventually, this was how he received most of his education from me — there were many other and better sources, but this was my personal input! Some evenings we might spend between one and four hours up in his bedroom. Whatever books we read together would inevitably spark off conversations about their historical background (and all that that entailed), or politics, moral values, art, language, geography, the flora and fauna of the natural world or the sciences.

When I was a little girl my father would sometimes read aloud to me in the evenings by the glowing kitchen fire and I especially remember the winter nights when he read the book 'Heidi'. As we sat and read and talked, my mother would be quietly peeling sweet little clementines for us to eat, or my father would stop to roast chestnuts on the fire, or we might toast soft, sugary marshmallows instead... or slowly wade our way through bowls of nuts — hazels were my favourite while my mother loved brazils. The thread of the story was frequently interrupted while my father wielded the nutcrackers... and then personally elected to munch on 'monkey nuts' (peanuts) instead.

Perhaps instead of viewing January as a dull, boring month when nothing ever happens, we could all learn to look at it as a golden opportunity to try all sorts of different things which we might otherwise never have time for during the rest of our busy year.

The long dark evenings are a brilliant time to begin a new hobby or get stuck into some lovely craftwork. Take the opportunity to sew something. Or bite the bullet and begin to research one's family tree – I promise that once you start you won't want to stop! Or you might decide to try your hand at composing some poetry or sit down and begin that book you have always promised yourself to write.

Or catch up with your letter-writing (don't forget your 'thank you' letters after Christmas!). Or enjoy some time dreaming and planning a holiday or other activity for the lighter, warmer days ahead – let your imagination take flight.

You might simply wish to sleep – to retrench and recuperate and prepare yourself for the coming springtime when, like a perfect little seed or bulb, you will be able to burst forth into the personal beauty and activity and action.

I sometimes feel that this time of the year is like looking outside from within. A different kind of dreaming can be done armed with seed and gardening catalogues as you plan your next fruitful seasons in the garden. Or reorganise your garden altogether. My family and I recently visited the Winter Garden at Bodnant in the Conwy Valley. We were all captivated by its colour, beauty and vibrancy in the depths of the grey winter. Now we are seriously thinking of re-ordering our own front garden entirely and re-planting it as a medicinal winter garden… so far, only lots of tremendously exciting ideas floating around our heads, but that is surely half the fun!

One lovely activity is to make flowers from shells collected on the beach during a chilly winter's afternoon walk. Or to utilise the irresistible shells triumphantly carried home from holidays the previous summer.

Making Shell Flowers

This is an activity which really begins the previous summer. Collecting shells on the beach! So many of us do it — especially the youngsters. We gleefully bear our ocean trophies home… and then haven't a clue what to do with them! Making dainty flowers is just one suggestion. If aren't already in possession of a quantity of shells to begin with, you can always purchase bags of shells from craft shops or on the internet; If you are lucky enough to live within relatively easy travelling distance of the beach, so much the better. Make it a good reason to get out into the fresh air – no matter how cold – and go for a bracing walk on the strand to gather your shells!

To make shell flowers you need quite a lot of shells so that you can match them up in size and colourings. Also, be aware that the more delicate shells break easily so try to allow for natural wastage. On the other hand, don't be tempted to go mad and collect buckets full. Take about four or five times what you think you will need. Remember that there may be someone else who has just had the same idea – or read this book! – who might also be searching for shells. Those shells which aren't used can be saved for another project or be returned to the beach – it needn't be the same place – but please don't just dump them in a rubbish bin. Broken shells can always be smashed into smaller pieces and scattered in the garden or used to encircle plants to keep slugs and snails at bay.

When making up a shell flower you need to pierce the shell with the small point of a sharp pair of scissors or a strong darning needle. Or you might be able to borrow or buy a mini drill. Use a wooden board to work on and cover it with an old cloth to prevent the shells slipping or skidding. If children are attempting this project, it might be wiser to allow an adult to make the holes while youngsters assist or simply watch.

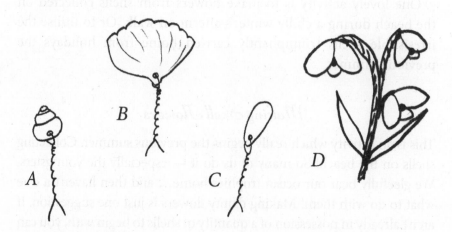

You will need

Shells, wooden board, some old material, small sharp scissors, mini drill or darning needle, thin wire, glue, green wool, cotton and felt.

To make

- Make one hole in small shells such as A and C and two holes in larger shells like B.
- Cut 30 cm of fine wire and poke it halfway through the hole(s) in the shell; gently bend it double and twist it to secure the shell.
- The long length of wire can then be wrapped round and covered in green embroidery thread, fine wool, cotton or strips of felt to form the stem.
- Cut out green paper or felt leaves and catch them in the stems as you wrap them.
- Multi petalled flowers (like a snowdrop, see D) can be formed by using three mother of pearl or white shells. Take a longer piece of wire and thread a small green bead onto it. Bend the wire in two, then wire three shell petals around the bead. Cut out long thin felt leaves and catch them into the stem near the bottom of it as you wrap it.
- Other flowers can be made in this way and a whole posy created. Experiment for yourself with a variety of shells, beads, synthetic stamens and ribbons.

COMMENT FROM JOAN: MID-JANUARY 1967

Had a very busy day. Chased Farmer Hough's cows out of the garden four times this morning. Jim couldn't get the Volkswagen van to start so Andrew and Brian were around trying to fix it until after 10:30 a.m. Wasn't expecting the Insurance man to call today – all dogs on lose and one of them nipped the fellow – faced with six lively young Alsatians it's a wonder they didn't tear him limb from limb!

Jill out with Wolf* later so I gathered a paper sack of wood; Jill says I look like a Tamil tea-picker – remembering the rags they wore I wonder what she means? Made steak pie, mince tarts and Chorley Cake and a large pork pie for Monday. Finished seed list for Dobies.

*Jill's dog

THE BEST LAID PLANS

Of course, sometimes the best laid plans have a way of getting out of hand. Like the time a few years ago when we joined forces with our neighbours to have a huge ash tree removed from the corner of our adjoining gardens. I hate having to fell any tree. I usually end up in tears, feeling sick with apprehension and almost physical pain... a ruthless murderer! But in this case the tree (which had consisted of several huge trunks) was over-shadowing and crowding everything else out.

My neighbours arranged for a team of men to come and fell it while we took the responsibility of clearing it all away. As our neighbours were not in good health at that time and we had wood burning stoves and open fires this was mutually very satisfactory. But even I, who had been used to felling and clearing away trees all my life, was amazed by the amount of wood that was then deposited in our back garden. In fact, it covered almost the whole surface of our land to a depth of approximately six feet. My son and husband with their bow saws and I with my trusty slashing hook soon got to work.

Never just shred everything into chips or mulch – see what else you can use it for as well. Don't simply pike off to the garden centre and buy something in kit form or ready done – use one of these cold grey January afternoons to knock up some trellising or an archway to grace your garden later in the season. Most of the satisfaction in doing anything is in doing it yourself. We sorted everything into piles for different uses: straight lengths for fencing poles and other construction work; other lengths to use as handles on garden spades and forks when they needed replacing; likely looking lengths went to be seasoned so that my son could use them on his lathe to turn into household items such as bowls and candlesticks. The rest were divided into piles to be cut... large logs to form the legs of rough, rustic benches or build the heart of a large hot fire; smaller logs (the term I use for them is 'loglets') to produce a sudden warming blaze and kindling to light it all in the first place or to quickly bring a pan or kettle to the boil. Some was used to simply leave in heaps as wildlife habitats. (Note that none was kept for use as garden stakes as many plants find the ash tree poisonous and will not even grow beneath its shade.)

Even so, there was still a quantity of wood which we could neither categorise, process or accommodate and which we finally fed onto a bonfire which lasted for many hours and towards the end of which produced the predictable flowering of foil-wrapped potatoes to roast in the glowing ashes, pints of scalding-hot tea, cobs of spiced fruit cake and jugs of mulled cider – the later perhaps not such a good idea when people are working with sharp tools, but at least no one lost any fingers or toes.

It was a full three day event which involved all of us, but we gained a huge amount of daylight – and wood to use and burn – and, of course, later that spring the base of the felled tree began to put out shoots again… it is still with us and prospers, even if only a third of its original height.

Recalling jobs getting totally out of hand, there was another occasion when I was very small – only three or four years old. Having only recently moved to the cottage which became their home for half a century, my parents decided to borrow a tractor from Mr Hough, the neighbouring farmer, and plough the large flat area of land which we commonly called the 'Square' and which my mother planned on turning into a huge vegetable garden.

My father, Jim, and my adopted uncle, Ricky, were organised to do the ploughing. It was one of those typically dry but cold, grey January days. It hadn't rained for a while so everything looked set fair to break the sods of grass and reveal the clay-grey soil beneath. What no one realised at the time was that there were a couple of water springs in one corner of the 'Square' and on about the third turn of the tractor it suddenly sank into much softer, wetter earth. No matter what the two struggling men did, the situation grew worse with the tractor now sunk to its axels in mire.

After some considerable effort, they conceded defeat and plodded off back to the farm to ask for help. Mr Hough, a dour man at the best of times and now in grumpy disapproval of pretentious amateurs, gloweringly arrived back with his second, larger, newer, more powerful tractor and began the job of coupling it up to the beleaguered machine. He would show these townies how it was done. But before he could drag it free, he also found himself sinking deeper into the churned ground and very soon he was in a similar state of sunken depression… in more ways than one. By this time, the light was failing so everyone agreed to call it a day and resume operations the next morning.

In the meantime, another neighbour, Farmer Jolly, was approached. He was a kindly man of sunny disposition; the father of a large and happy family who had patience in abundance. Early the following morning my father and uncle were out to await the arrival of the two farmers on Mr Jolly's spanking new machine, which was also larger and more powerful than either of the others. All the men got out spades and straw and began to semi dig out the two troubled tractors. I was allowed to watch from a distance, as long as I was careful not to get in the way and not to show the least sign of amusement, although by this time, the performance was deteriorating into something of a pantomime and my mother's lips kept twitching even as she proffered useful suggestions, moral support and endless mugs of tea and slabs of moist fruity Chorley Cake.

Finally, the men were ready to – hopefully – make a move. With engines roaring energetically, exhaust chimneys streaming blue fumes into the chilly air and shouts of encouragement and direction, Farmer Jolly's tractor got to work. It was a close thing and at one time they ran the risk of losing a third machine to the voracious land. However, Farmer Jolly became the hero of the day as he slowly but surely dragged first one and then the other tractor out of their muddy imprisonment. Cheers and handshakes all round and at last I could grin from ear to ear without running the risk of anyone taking offence!

Unsurprisingly, the ploughing of the 'Square' was never completed. The men had had enough. My father talked of getting a rotovator, but my mother was decidedly reticent – she had visions of it running away with him, and man and machine ending up crossing the orchard and going down the bank into the river. We returned to the old style of cultivation and my mother gradually dug the whole area by hand – an annual task I took over from her when I once reached my teens.

Old folk in Lancashire used to talk about good simple food which would 'stick to your ribs', meaning that it would be satisfying and keep you going for many hours. Steamed puddings are just such a dish and excellent at keeping the cold winter weather and coughs and sniffles at bay.

Steamed Pudding

Ingredients

6 oz (170 g) self raising flour (or plain flour with 1½ level teaspoons of
  baking powder
3 oz (85 g) white bread crumbs
4 oz (170 g) grated suet
4 oz (170 g) sugar (castor if possible)
1 egg
milk to mix
red jam – raspberry preferred

Method

- Mix flour, (baking powder if used), bread crumbs, sugar and suet in a bowl.
- Stir in lightly mixed egg and enough milk to make a dropping consistency.
- Place jam in well-greased pudding basin, spoon in mixture, cover and steam for 2 – 2½ hours.
- Serve with jug of hot custard - nothing like it to stick to one's ribs on a snowy winter's day.

WHEN EXACTLY *IS* SPRING?

As the end of January approaches, life can indeed seem very flat and drear. Christmas already feels like months ago and spring is hardly yet in sight. The land lies stark and colourless. The temperature drops below freezing.

In our house, the Winter Tree which graced our drawing room throughout the Midwinter/Christmas period with its gold, silver and scarlet finery now mimics the season outside our window – bereft of all the colourful decorations which were removed around the middle of the month, it has been left more sparsely dressed in frosted pale green moss and dozens of candles (electric in this instance so as not to present a fire hazard). It brings us light in the gloomy, short, dark days. It stands among us as an embodiment of the death-like reality of deep winter and yet is also an encouraging symbol of what is to come… the buds are already tightly formed on its twigs and it supports all its tiny lights in promise of the longer, lighter, warmer days soon to be with us.

When exactly does winter end and spring begin? The meteorological seasons begin on the 1st June – summer, the 1st September – autumn, the 1st December – winter (placing Midwinter just three weeks after the season has begun which I have always thought utterly nonsensical) and the 1st March for the beginning of spring. In this way the seasons are set to coincide with the Gregorian calendar making it easier to meteorologically forecast and observe the weather and for the comparison of monthly and seasonal statistics.

Astronomically speaking, the seasons are determined according to the 23.5 degree tilt of the earth's rotational axis in relation to its orbit around the sun. Yet despite the relative predictability of this, the actual performance of the weather – and therefore the starting and ending of spring and the growing season – can vary dramatically.

The solstices (21st June and 21st December) and the equinoxes (21st March and 21st September) are considered to be the astronomical transition points between the seasons. The astronomical definition of the spring season is between the spring equinox on the 21st March and the summer solstice on the 21st June.* If this is truly the case, then we had all better revise our ideas of springtime as it would therefore appear that our most popular and beloved spring garden flowers such as the snowdrop and crocus, and common early- spring wild flowers such as coltsfoot and celandine which all bloom from the end of January into March are not spring flowers at all but belong to the winter, as do our joyful golden narcissus and some varieties of daffodil.

In most people's minds the season of spring is defined as the transition from winter to summer, from cold to warm, from death to life, from no growth to full growth. In many cultures spring is celebrated with festivals connected to the importance of food production – the sowing or planting of crops. Many animals seasonally mate in late autumn or winter and bring forth their young some time during the spring… from late January onwards.

Many nations and traditions follow the beginning of spring as being in March. Germany welcomes spring at the vernal equinox around the 21st March as does the Persian culture with their festival of Nowruz which not only celebrates the beginning of spring but also of their new year. same day. In Japan, Hanami is celebrated where the centuries old tradition has been for people to welcome the springtime when the cherry blossoms begin to bloom – any time between late March and early May – and parties are hosted beneath the flower-laden trees.

In some traditions, the spring equinox is taken to fall in the middle of spring. In China, the spring season begins at Lichun on 3rd – 5th February. While in Bangladesh, the festival of Falgun marks the arrival of their spring around the 13th February.

The meteorologists and astronomers might flatly declare that a particular date marks the beginning of spring, but if there is still six

* In the Southern Hemisphere it is exactly the same for both the Meteorological and Astronomical calendars, except that everything is reversed. This means that Spring officially begins on the 1st or 21st September and ends on the 30th November or 21st December, and so forth.

inches of snow on the ground and all life remains furled tightly, still hidden beneath the earth, then spring is yet to happen. Conversely, if the weather is mild and leaves are unfurling and flowers are beginning to bloom in February, they can insist that it is still winter, but the natural world is bound by no human calendar and will please itself. but the natural world knows itself best and is living its own reality.

Perhaps more realistically ecological seasons base their definition on biological indications: for instance, the activities of animals, the activities/blossoming of plants, even the smell of the soil when it has reached the necessary temperature for micro flora to flourish. Again, these factors can all vary from area to area, district to district and in some places – like here in North Wales – from valley to valley depending on which direction the valley faces and the prevailing winds, or which side of the valley you are on if it doesn't get any sunlight in Midwinter.

One could argue that as the seasons integrate and unfold at their own speed, reacting to the variable weather and temperature and their own needs; the natural world is constantly being born, growing, coming to fruition and dying back again and that, actually, we only have two seasons, spring and autumn, in a never ending process of unfoldment. Some plants are still growing through the winter – snowdrops and crocus, for instance, while the sturdy dark green spears of my daffodils are always visible by the end of November or early December. Throughout late January, February and into March these delicate early flowers bloom in what we are told is our winter and at the end of our spring they reach their autumn and die back into the earth again, taking our summer as their winter and rest period.

Perhaps more realistically, there are six ecological seasons. Some South Asia calendars also employ a six-season calendar. The ecological seasons are prevernal - early or pre-spring denoted by tree buds; vernal – spring when the buds burst and become leaves; estivas – high summer when the trees are in full leaf; *serotinal* – late summer when the leaves begin to change colour; autumn – when the leaves drop; *hibernal* – when the trees are bare.

Around the world, seasons have locally been decided by the prevailing weather conditions, especially when they recur fairly predictably year after year; dry seasons; wet, rainy or monsoon seasons; the season of hurricanes or tornadoes. For others, the changing of the seasons depends on what is occurring in nature in that part of the world at a certain date. In Finland, Sweden and Iceland, the dates of the seasons are not based on the calendar at all but on the temperature. This means that the seasons within each country start and end on different dates depending on their regions and climates. In Iceland, for example, the first day of summer typically falls around the 18th April.

There are also seasonal winds, such as the French *mistral* which annually sweeps down from the northwest across the country and into the Gulf of Lion in the north Mediterranean. Interestingly this phenomenon occurs in winter and spring and is strongest at the transition between the two seasons. There are also the autumn winds which harry the city of Istanbul and its environs, leaving many of its inhabitants with accompanying seasonal headaches and migraines and the hot dry Loo winds which scorch their way across the plains of northern India, regularly sending people running for the cool of the hills.

PHENOLOGY

Not to be confused with Phrenology (which is something totally different concerning the relevance of the lumps and bumps on our skulls). Phenology is the study of periodic plant and animal life cycle events and how these are influenced by seasonal and interannual variations in climate as well as habitat factors.

The word was first coined by the Belgian botanist and horticulturist, Charles Morren in 1849 when he used it as a means of referring to the scientific discipline that studies the seasonal cycles of animals and plants; events such as the emergence of leaves and flowers, the first flight of butterflies, the first appearance of migratory birds and the dates of leaf colouring, leaf fall and egg-laying.

In the Nineteenth Century interest in the natural world grew dramatically and between 1891 and 1948 the Royal Meteorological Society organised a programme of up to six thousand volunteers to take phenological recordings across the British Isles. Unfortunately, just as evidence and the effects of global warming would have been becoming more easily apparent, recordings ended abruptly after fifty-eight years and the British were left without a national recording scheme for almost half a century.

The work was finally resumed by the UK Phenology Network which is now run by the Woodland Trust, the Centre of Ecology and Hydrology and the BBC Springwatch survey. Quite huge changes have been noted. For instance, the latest research shows that in spring the oak trees burst their buds more than eleven days earlier than they did back in the Nineteenth Century – possibly demonstrating the effects of climate change and an overall warming of the planet.

Admittedly, the scientists have a hard job on their hands. If the meteorologists define the seasons by temperature, I feel that we, here in Britain, might be in a pickle. If summer is defined as the three warmest months which are currently labelled as June, July and August, what about September which is often one of our warmest months and still with many hours of sunlight? Similarly, if winter is defined as our three coldest months and are currently noted as December, January and February, what about November and March which can both be equally as cold?

Which brings us back to the solar calendar which recognises the equinoxes and solstices as the midpoints of the season and not the start of them. Historically this was the recognised method for reckoning the seasons in mediaeval Europe and much longer ago than that in the Celtic lands where practically and spiritually very early spring still begins with celebration at the beginning of February.

The answer would appear to be that there is no answer. It is up to the individual to decide when their winter ends and their spring begins. Like all living things, there can never be a cut and dried time or date when everything suddenly does something... puts on a growth spurt, unfurl their leaves in unison, bloom at exactly the same time, or give birth all on the same day.

Instead, you must ask yourself when does it feel like spring to you? What criteria do you use? What constitutes spring for you? When do those signs first appear where you live? For me, it is a pulsing, wavering process of advance and retreat as the changeable weather and temperature plays cat and mouse with us all, but there does come a time when it is no longer unclear and we can all see, taste, smell and feel within our very bones that spring has well and truly arrived!

Chapter Two

The Birth of Spring

'If winter comes, can spring be far behind?'
Percy Bysshe Shelley

Wrapped in warm coats, gloves, scarves and hats and shod in sturdy boots, we trudge along the puddled path as a weak, shy sun peeps out from behind the billowing white cloud. All around us the Earth shows signs of stirring. It might only be the first day of February, but the fields are beginning to re-green and the golden gorse buds are swelling. Hazel catkins dance gaily mimicking the ecstatic wagging of the lamb's tails they are colloquially named after. The first of the new-born lambs stand in the lower pastures on spindly, wobbly legs looking around them in some curiosity and bewilderment. Birds are squabbling in the bushes, darting hither and thither in their frenzied pre-mating and all the while carolling in the new season as if their tiny chests would burst.

This is the afternoon of *Gwyl Ffraid* — as it is known here in Wales, but better known as *Imbolc* in Ireland, Scotland and other Celtic areas – and we are walking along beside our local river to a quiet, sheltered spot where we may be undisturbed and drink in this precious time of year. We find just the place above the riverbank on a spur of slate waste which, over the years since the quarrying ceased, has become thickly cloaked in cushions of springy moss and surrounded by willow and young oak trees.

Here we light our white candles and share the honey cake (still warm from my oven) with the land. We also drink deeply of the hot, spiced milk which we have carried with us in a large thermos flask – some modern conveniences definitely make life easier! – and we contemplate all that this wonderful new season might be bringing for us... what we are looking forward to... what we mean to instigate and how we propose to use the surging young energies of this time of year. Some of us may write our intentions on paper or last year's withered leaves and plant them in the ground to seed and develop with the rest of awakening nature. Others may whisper them into the air and allow the breeze to take them wherever they need to travel to.

For the Old Woman of Winter – the Crone or *Cailleach* – is dead and the young Maiden, *Brighid* (in Ireland) or *Ffraid* (in Wales) is born!

WHAT IS *IMBOLC* OR *GWYL FFRAID*?

The word *Imbolc* (pronounced *em-bowl/g* or *immol/g*) means *in the belly* and at this particular time of year we should all be experiencing a veritable fire in our bellies at this earliest manifestation of Spring. This celebration is also sometimes referred to as *Oimelc* (pronounced *oy-melk*) meaning *ewe's milk* and referring to the ewe's beginning to lactate for their newly-born lambs, for when the Celtic peoples weren't on the warpath, they were largely pastoral herders. This is the time of year when there is a quickening of life, a restless stirring of energy. The very earth is gestating, is in the early throes of pregnancy. This is a time of renewal, new life, new hope, fresh beginnings and an energy that reflects an insatiable appetite for growth and rebirth. We are filled with an undeniable energy and impetus that propels us to move forward, grow, acknowledge and begin to realise our hidden potential. Most of all it is calling us to celebrate the joy and promise that new life – in all its aspects – can bring.

The goddess most associated with *Imbolc* is *Brighid* who is the Irish goddess of light, fire, poetry, smithcraft, babies and children. She brings fertility to the land and her people. She is also the protector of the home and the hearth is her special sacred place. In Ireland a house was never considered home until *Brighid* had been duly honoured by placing a Brighid's Cross on the hearth or hung above the entrance. Brighid's Cross is the symbol of a fire wheel and it was believed that wherever it was placed or hung automatically came under the goddess's protection.

Back in the early 1960s when I was a small child, little was known at that time about such things outside Ireland itself. I well remember attending a family wedding in Tipperary and on the way back to Dublin, my mother insisting that we make a detour and stop in Kildare to enquire if a Brighid's Cross could be purchased there at all. We were given an address of an ordinary little house in an ordinary little street. My mother got out of the car and went to knock on the front door, returning a few minutes later, her face wreathed in smiles and bearing a daintily made Cross fashioned from rushes. It hung in my parent's cottage for decades. It was quite a relief when I also finally learned how to make one myself, but the original was still reverently retained.

In Scotland the women of the house would dress a sheaf of oats in woman's clothing and lay it in a decorated basket called 'Brighid's Bed', side by side with a phallic club. They would then call three times, 'Brid is come, Brid is welcome!' and leave candles burning by the bed all night. If the impression of the club was found in the ashes of the hearth the next morning, the year would be fruitful and prosperous. Similar practices were carried out in Ireland.

Back to the present and this particular afternoon we had chosen to spend time by the river because, although *Imbolc* is one of the great Celtic fire festivals – with the emphasis at this time of year on light rather than heat – Brighid is also a goddess of sacred springs, wells and water, all gifts of Life from deep within the belly of the Earth. One of the traditions on this day is to visit a sacred healing well – they are not uncommon if you do a little investigating and you might be lucky to find one not too far away from you. Many of these springs which were thought to cure various diseases were taken over by the local churches and buildings were erected over the head of the springs where the sick could take shelter while they drank the waters or bathed in them. Sometimes another shelter might also be built as somewhere where the very sick or travel-weary could spend the night.

On this occasion we had decided not to visit our nearest sacred well a few miles away but to keep it simple and walk from home along the river. This also gave me the opportunity of gathering some fresh rushes from along the banks with which to make my own Brighid's Crosses to protect our home for the coming year. Traditionally the crosses were made on the eve of *Imbolc*, as Celtic days – and therefore all Celtic festivals and celebrations – ran from dusk of the previous day to dusk twenty four hours later. But I had opted to construct ours by a warm fireside once we returned home and lit all our candles among the trailing fronds of ivy on our table.

The colour for this time of year is white, symbolising purity, but silver is also acceptable (possibly representing the heavy frosts still prevalent in early February) and various shades of green, bearing witness to the tender shoots pushing up through the soil and the swelling buds on some of the trees at this time. Snowdrops, as the first flowers to herald spring and also bearing pure white blossoms, are the flower of choice. The swan is the avian symbol of the goddess, Brighid, and is also white. The traditional drink, as already mentioned, is milk, although there are many ways in which to literally spice it up with cinnamon, cloves, ginger and other herbs and spices, or even by adding a tot of whisky to help drive the cold away.

Hot Drinks for Gwyl Ffraid

HOT SPICED MILK (enough for two): Measure out one pint (500 ml) of milk, two teaspoons honey, one teaspoon cinnamon and a grate of nutmeg into a pan and heat – do not allow to boil. Can be drunk straight away or will keep hot in a vacuum flask if you wish to take it outside.

FRUIT CORDIALS: Using homemade cordial from the previous summer and autumn (such as blackberry or elderberry) is best, but if you don't have any, shop bought bilberry, apple or currant fruit juice works just as well. You might wish to combine two fruit juices as this can give a richer flavour.

Measure one pint of diluted cordial or fruit juice into a pan. Add a dessertspoon of sugar or honey, a teaspoon cinnamon, half a teaspoon of ginger and a shake of mace. Bring to boil and simmer for a few minutes. Before serving, add some sliced or chopped apple to eat cup. (Also keeps well in a vacuum flask to take out – just remember to cut your apples pieces smaller so that they don't get jammed in the opening!)

GREETING THE NEW SEASON

By the beginning of February, the cold, inclement weather has certainly not finished with us, but at least we know that it cannot last much longer. The daylight is growing perceptibly longer – although the mornings might appear little different to midwinter. Green shoots and buds are making an appearance; surely this is a time to joyfully acknowledge and celebrate. How might this be done?

There is nothing on this Earth which does not respond well to love and gratitude but we can't appreciate something if we don't know that it is actually there, so the first thing to do is to open your eyes. Look about you. Watch out as changes in the natural world begin to occur. Many people look for the first emergence of the little green spears which herald the appearance of the dainty snowdrops and crocus. Also keep a look out for the mighty daffodil and his cousin the smaller narcissus – they can begin to peep out of their earthy beds as early as late November!

Don't just concentrate on the ground either. One of the greatest sources of springtime information is our trees. As the sap rises and the energy of a new season's growth begins to course through their branches once more, their twigs change colour. If you have a local park or some woodland nearby, watch it throughout the winter. What colour(s) predominates? Don't tell me that it is all grey or brown – how many *shades* of grey and brown can you see? Keep looking. When do they begin to change? Some trees, like the willow, will don an overall shade of pale yellow; others, like the birch, will turn a fiery red. Even if you can only find a single tree nearby to observe it is still well worth it.

There are many other changes which take place early in the season too. Birch, hazel and alder trees all develop catkins at the end of the previous autumn. They look like stiff little tails hanging down from the branches. Throughout spring, these develop into longer, supple tails which dance on the breeze, sending out puffs of golden pollen. These are the flowers of the tree. Hazel comes first in late January or early February, depending on how severe the winter weather has been; the others follow later. Don't forget to look out for the 'pussy willow' either; the tiny pads of softest silver-white which cover the upper branches of the willow trees and so called because they are reminiscent of soft kitten's paws.

I read a story recently about how the willow came to have its 'pussy' flowers: one day some very young kittens fell into a deep river and were swept away. They surely would have drowned had it not been for an old willow tree whose branches dipped low over the water. She spotted the dying animals and thrust her branches down into the river where the kittens became entangled in them and were able to cling on. Gently the willow raised her branches up above the current and there the kittens clung, soft, shinning little pads of silver fur, drying in the breeze, until their mother came bounding down the bank and carried them to safety. As a reward, each spring the willow has been allowed to bear the emblems of soft little furry pads in remembrance of the baby animals she so kindly saved.

While keeping an eye on what is happening in the trees, don't forget to watch the birds and their antics as they begin their courting rituals and nest-building. The traditional date for this to start was always Saint Valentine's Day on the 14*th* February, but I would suggest that our seasons are getting progressively earlier as global warming takes effect and, if the weather is reasonably mild, many birds now begin their procreative activities in January – I had starlings capering about at Midwinter in my garden.

The blackthorn blooms very early in drifts of tiny white flowers but many people do not realise that all trees have flowers; we just do not usually notice them, often because they are green in colour and blend in with their leafy foliage. Others, such as the oak and ash, appear before the leaves but are mistaken for precursors to the swelling leaf buds and not identified as flowers in their own right. Other trees, such as the elder, begin to send forth their leaves as early as January; the buds break and new green growth begins to emerge, then stops until later in the season when spring has more obviously arrived. I always look for the breaking elder leaves – they are my own first herald of spring.

There are also many shrubs which flower during the winter and or early spring; jasmine and witch hazel, viburnum, mahonia and heather among others. You may have some in your own garden, but if not (and without being intrusively nosey!) watch what is happening in other people's gardens and take pleasure from them. They might belong to someone else, but that doesn't mean that we can't feast our eyes on their fresh delicate beauty in the dark and dreary first months of the year, and if something brings you joy, spare a kind and appreciative thought for the gardener who has planted and tended it too.

Also, don't forget the wild flowers. Even at this early time of year you may look out for coltsfoot, butterbur, celandine, primroses... and just because they are common, do not ignore the humble dandelion and daisy – they are equally important harbingers of spring too.

Noticing these little but very significant changes is the first step. Actively acknowledging and giving thanks for them is the next. As you observe, give thanks for it by directing some loving gratitude towards the plant, bush, shrub or tree… imagine there is a beam shooting out of your chest where your heart is and direct it straight to what you are enjoying and thankful for. Or simply say 'thank you', either quietly in your head or even out loud. Your attention, kindness and gratitude towards the world around you will have a very positive effect on your own existence as like attracts like and the good feelings you bestow will bounce back and warmly colour your own day. Try it.

Taking all this further, and without denuding the plants and trees, carefully cut three or four twigs of little branchlets from whichever tree you have noticed flowering – and I say cut advisedly, take a sharp knife or secateurs – no breaking, pulling or ripping at a plant, please. Remember that these are living things… be careful not to damage, and also choose your tokens carefully so that their loss does not spoil the look of a tree or take too much from the wildlife – birds, insects, bees – which may be depending on such vital resources for food in the bleakest and sparsest time of the year. Always *think* about what you are doing and consider others.

Once you get your spring tokens home, honour them by arranging somewhere nice for them to be displayed. Use a beautiful vase or jug to stand them in. Position them where it is light – but not too warm - and where you will see them regularly throughout your day. This may be the centre of a table or on a little side table, a sideboard or even a part of a shelf. Windowsills are good but try to choose one out of direct sunlight, otherwise your wildflowers will just wither away as they bake in the increased sunlight magnified by the glass (greenhouse) effect – wild things generally don't prosper in extreme conditions. Avoid situations near radiators for the same reason. Also be careful that wherever you choose to put them, family pets or children cannot easily knock them over.

To this you may wish to add other tokens of the developing season as they appear and occur… early primroses in a tiny glass; coloured pebbles washed clean by winter rains; interestingly shaped twigs or pieces of wood broken in a storm representing the starkness of the passing season; skeletal leaves which have survived from last autumn. I am not suggesting you develop a whole nature table – although if you have children or grandchildren that is a lovely thing to do; it gives little ones somewhere to place their treasures gathered on walks… somewhere they can be seen easily but not get broken and spoilt. You might wish to place something in your special spot for only a day or two, and then return it to the natural world from where you found it, or in the case of twigs and flowers honour them by recycling them in the compost.

WHO WAS THE GODDESS, BRIGHID?

The goddess, Brighid, (pronounced '*breed*') is frequently confused with the saint, Brigit. They are remarkably similar in many ways and share a feast day. Shrouded in the mists of prehistory, it is thought that Brighid came to Ireland with the Tuatha de Danaan, a mythological people who reputedly came out of a cloud and later disappeared back into thin air. Modern investigation suggests that this belief may be based on the appearance of the Gaelic Celts who possibly emigrated from their home in Galatia (central Anatolia in modern-day Turkey). But we cannot be sure where she might have originated or just how old those origins might really be. Today there are many place names and girl's names which originate from Brighid/Brigit which suggests a widespread influence. Brigantia – meaning High One – was the name of the Celtic lands which included Northern England and parts of Spain and France.

Brighid's mother may have been the Irish goddess, *Boann*, (after whom the River Boyne is named), and possibly derived from the name for 'white cow' cognate with the Sanskrit *Govinda*.*

* Donncha, Dennis King quoted in 'Brigit, Bright Goddess of the Gael' in Imbas website.

As for her father, some legends describe her as the daughter of the Dagda, the Celtic 'Father Of All', a warrior and protector sometimes paired with the goddess Morrigan. The Dagda was a god of abundance who fed the world from his cauldron, *Undry*. He carried a huge club which required nine ordinary men to lift. With one end of it he could slay his foes but with the other end of it he could bring the dead back to life. This reflects the Celtic understanding that death and rebirth are a part of the same circle of existence. It also echoes Brighid's own persona as a goddess of fertility and birth, yet simultaneously being a warrior.

There are hints that Brighid may have had an older indigenous persona as The Lady of the Sea, daughter of *Lir*, the god of the oceans. Perhaps the Brighid we know was a merging of two distinct goddesses – and more to the point, two distinct peoples – the deity who arrived from the east with the Children of Danu blended with an indigenous ancestral sea goddess of the Formorians.*

Brighid was a fire goddess, linked especially to late winter, the growing light and the early promise of spring; spiritually and physically the return of the light but also new consciousness. She was the goddess of the hearth and as such she had much in common with the Greek goddess, Hestia, daughter of Zeus. Certainly as a goddess of liminal places, (thresholds), the hearth was the most important sacred place in either temple or home… an altar central to everyone and everyday life upon which the fire of transmutation burned bright, the smoke travelling through the gateway to the Other Worlds by way of the smoke hole or chimney.

However, Brighid's influence did not just reach as far as the alchemy of the domestic hearth; she also ruled the ancient art of metal working which, unsurprisingly, inspired great awe among early societies. To many, the craft of a smith was absolute magic, apparently transforming stone (ore) into tools and weapons of

* 'Candlemas' Amberk and Azreal Arynn K.

great power and beauty. Even in mediaeval times the secrets of the trade were closely guarded, taught by guilds and regarded almost in the same light as sacred religious mysteries. Perhaps this also illustrates another link with the Far East as it has also been suggested that the small dark Cymru originated from Taprobane (modern day Sri Lanka) and brought metalworking with them via India and Anatolia when they eventually settled in Wales.

With her fiery associations Brighid also brought the fire of inspiration to the arts – especially as a patron of poetry – but she was also a goddess of healing, associated with fertility, agriculture, the household arts (such as weaving and dying) and also of brewing beer. It is this very juxtaposition of fertility and childbirth with regal warriorhood and metal working which really marks Brighid as one of the great goddesses of life and death and as such she is similar in potency to Freya, Isis and Diana.

For Brighid is, first and foremost, a goddess of sovereignty; possibly a western equivalent of Epona, the white mare goddess, whom kings had to symbolically marry in order to govern in her name. The Welsh word for king is brenin, thought to mean *consort of Brigantia.* Bruide* the Pictish royal throne name was given to each pagan Pictish king who was viewed as the male manifestation of the spirit of the goddess. In her aspect as Brigantia, she has been depicted crowned and holding a globe and spear – we know her better by the name of Britannia and until recently she graced one side of our coins.

Was Brighid one goddess or possibly three distinct personas or sister goddesses; Sovereign Ruler/Bringer of Prosperity, Alchemist of the Arts of Blacksmithing, Healer and Midwife? Or, as Barbara Walker suggests, was she an amalgamation of an umbrella title for three separate goddesses? According to Walker, these triple deities were called the 'Three Blessed Ladies of Britain' or the 'Three Mothers' and were identified with the moon.**

* Shrine website.
** *'Women's Encyclopaedia of Myths and Secrets'* Barbara Walker.
A possible connection to the Welsh 'Blessings of the Mothers' on Christmas Eve.
I wonder? See my previous book *Merry Midwinter*, p. 231.

How to make a Brighid's Cross

You will need

16 long green rushes, (straws or pipe cleaners may also be used), 4 small rubber bands or 4 lengths of coloured wool, kitchen scissors.

To make

1) Hold one of the rushes horizontally. Fold a second rush in half. See Fig. 1.

2) Place the first horizontal rush in the centre of the folded second rush. See Fig. 2.

3) Draw the rushes firmly together and hold the centre overlap tight with your finger and thumb, as in Fig. 3.

4) Turn the two rushes held together clockwise by 90 degrees so that the open ends of the second rush are pointing horizontally to the left as in Fig. 4.

5) Fold a third rush in half over both lengths of the second rush so that they lie vertically against the first rush as in Fig. 5 and Fig. 6.

6) Always hold firmly to the rush you have just added – it will keep the rest in place. You can always push the rushes closer together as you work so that the structure and pattern being created remains even.

7) Fold a new rush in half horizontally across the first and third rush, as in Fig. 7 and Fig. 8.

8) Repeat the process by rotating all the rushes 90 degrees clockwise and adding a new folded rush each time – as in Fig. 9 - until all the rushes have been used up.

9) Secure arms of the cross with elastic bands. Alternatively, wrap and tie with coloured wool. The advantage to using elastic is that it will hold the cross more firmly as the rushes dry out and shrink; however, coloured wool is more decorative.

10) Trim off the ends of the rushes on all four arms of the cross with the kitchen scissors to make them all the same length. Your Brighid's cross is now ready to hang on the wall.

NOTE: You may use more than 16 rushes if you wish. You can also use two rushes at a time to make a fatter, chunkier cross.

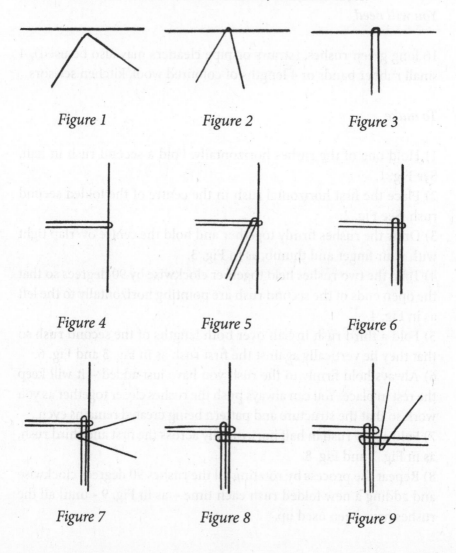

Figure 1	*Figure 2*	*Figure 3*

Figure 4	*Figure 5*	*Figure 6*

Figure 7	*Figure 8*	*Figure 9*

ENTER FFRAID

Ffraid, (pronounced *'fried'*) is the Welsh version of Brighid. Both names originate from the Indo-European family of languages and have evolved from b*rig-o/brigh* meaning exulted one, fire goddess, power, strength, vigour and virtue.

Legend has it that Ffraid travelled across the sea from Ireland in the company of another woman, Modweena. They floated across on a tiny island – a lump of turf which had broken away from Ireland – and which then finally washed up on the shores of North West Wales, becoming attached to the headland at Deganwy, (between Llandudno and Conwy). Ffraid carried on up the River Conwy to found a church in the Conwy valley.

There actually is a church of Llansanffraid at Glan Conwy in the diocese of Saint Asaph which was originally founded in the Fifth Century by Maelgwyn of Gwynedd. Ffraid is also the patron saint of another church a few miles away at Treaddur Bay on the Isle of Anglesey. Here the local church history explains that Sant Ffraid was born in 450 AD in Faughart in Ireland – same date as Saint Brigit and one of the places which Brigit's druid benefactor might have taken her pregnant mother to – and that her feast day is the 3rd February. There are more churches dedicated to Saint Ffraid in the southern half of Wales which was always more greatly influenced by Irish incomers bringing their traditions of Brighid and Brigit.

The fact remains that Ffraid is yet another manifestation of the spirit of the early spring season; the epitome of the promise of returning life, increasing light and warmth, and the precious conviction that the community will survive another year.

MAIDEN FFRAID

She pulses through the slumbering Earth,
Emerging young and free and wild;
And soft awakens all the land for
the Maiden, hardly more than child.

All edged with catkin-dancing fringe
Her dress is of a pale, fresh green,
With snowdrop-petalled cap and muff,
And mantle of white frosty sheen.
Yellow coltsfoot button her boots,
Golden celandine adorn her dress,
While butterbur soft collars form
And greening buds caress.
Her hair is lamb's wool, damp with showers,
Soft cream her fair complexion;
Her eyes kaleidoscopes of flowers,
Her smile of deep affection.
Dark winter's death gives way to life,
And this herald of new life dawning;
While hope springs afresh where e'er she treads
In the springtime's early morning.

SO, WHO WAS SAINT BRIGIT?

There are various theories about Brigit's origins but a popular one is that she was the illegitimate daughter of an Irish chieftain, Dubthach, (pronounced '*Duffac*' and meaning the Dark One) of the family of *Etech* from Leinster. He fell in love with a slave at his court, a young woman by the name of *Brocca* or *Broicsech* (pronounced '*Brocksheh*', meaning Baby Badger) and got her with child. When *Dubthach's* wife found out, she was furious and he had to send the pregnant girl away.

In the *Book of Lismore* it was written that a wizard prophesied that Brocca would bear a daughter 'conspicuous, radiant, who will shine like the sun among the stars of heaven'. However, *Brocca* was sold to a magician (possibly a druid) who took her to one of several possible destinations: Iona, then known as the Druid's Isle; the village of Faughart near Dundalk; Uinmeras near Kildare; Offally, or somewhere in Connacht. Apparently, *Brocca* gave birth to Brigit as she stepped over the threshold of her new home – a very suspect thing to do as thresholds had great spiritual and magical significance to the early Celts. If this wasn't enough, a pillar of light or fire shot from the baby's head (similar to Saint David – see Chapter Seven).

As a child, Brigit was generous but pious. As she grew up she received many offers of marriage but she refused them all. When it looked like she was going to be forced to accept one of them, Brigit poked out her own eye so that, disfigured, she would be undesirable. Her family relented, whereupon she popped her eye back in and it instantly healed so that she could see through both of her eyes once more.

Unsurprisingly she found herself headed for a religious life and became the first nun of Ireland. Saint Mel of Armagh is believed to have conferred abbatial authority on her, meaning that she was made an archbishop in her own right with the authority to appoint bishops and ordain priests. We are encouraged to view Brigit's beginnings as humble in the extreme, but there is another way of interpreting them: daughter of royalty (when illegitimacy did not carry the same stigma as in more modern times), she was sent away with a druid, a member of one of the most learned fraternities in Europe at that time, who might well have educated her as Celtic society then did not distinguish between the sexes. She soon hurtled to a position of highest religious authority.

More, she began by building herself a little cell under an oak tree (most sacred tree of the druids) and gathered companions about her. Their tiny enclave grew to be a great nunnery and monastery – a famous centre for learning and around it grew a cathedral city. Today it is still known as Kildare, the 'cell of the oak', a very particular tree which Brigit loved and blessed every day.

Many daughter convents sprang from the mother house in Kildare. It is also believed that Brigit was a close friend of Saint Patrick: "…there was so great a friendship of charity that they had one heart and one mind. Through him and through her, Christ performed many miracles."*

Book of Armagh – 8th century document

Ancient history is full of many anomalies and disparities and one wonders how realistic this belief might be when set against the reputed dates of the two saint's lives; Patrick supposedly being born in 387 AD, and dying in 493 AD – which would have made him 106 years old at the time of his passing – and Brigit being born between 439 – 452 AD and dying between 518 – 525 AD. It is possible that the younger woman could have known the older man, but Patrick would have been pretty elderly.

Less easy to equate with reality is the claim that Brigit was present at the birth of Jesus and acted as midwife to Mary in the stable. This seems to resonate more with the belief that the Goddess Brighid was patron of midwives. Another legend tells of how when Jesus and Mary were escaping from the wrath of Herod, some of the king's soldiers caught up with them and Brigit saved them, distracting the men by placing a crown of candles upon her head and dancing across the sand dunes and luring them away. The image this creates is more in keeping with that of (Saint) Lucy who wears a crown of candles on her head and embodies the spirit of Midwinter and the cornucopia-carrying grain goddess on the old Solstice date of 13th December in Scandinavia and some other European countries. Either claim is complicated by the problem of supposedly having taken place a good four hundred years before Brigit's birth. The fact that the Irish exalted Brigit as the foster mother of Jesus is very significant as in ancient Celtic society, where sons (and daughters) were usually sent to be brought up in the households of influential neighbours, this role was supreme. More, that in the language of the Celts, the religious implication is that Brigit, in the role of foster mother, conferred sovereignty on Jesus.

Brigit died on the 1st February at a good old age – somewhere between 74 and 88, depending on which dates you choose to believe – and was buried in a jewelled casket at her own monastery of Kildare. But three and a half centuries later, Viking raiders made Kildare a dangerous place and somewhere around the year 878 AD. Brigit's bones were taken to Downpatrick where they were placed in the shared tomb of Saint Patrick and Saint Columba. However, in 1185 Brigit was on the move once more, this time just as far as Downpatrick

Cathedral. Unfortunately, during the reign of the English king, Henry VIII and the dissolution of the monasteries, the monument of the three saints was destroyed.

Saint Brigit became known as the patron saint of Irish nuns, and also of New Zealand, meditation, peace-making, travellers, poets, scribes and calligraphers, dairy maids and cattle, blacksmiths, healers and midwives… and fugitives. Interestingly, much on this list mirrors those aspects of daily life also under the special protection of the goddess, Brighid.

Unfortunately, gods and goddesses tend to be rather remote, awesome and inaccessible – although Brighid was relatively approachable through her many aspects of protection. Christianity was attempting to make their deities infinitely more approachable and familiar: Jesus was a god who became a human, Mary a woman caught up in divine events, Magdalene elevated from prostitution to close companion of Jesus… all bridges between this physical world and that of the divine. But whereas the goddess, Brighid, was an exulted bestower of sovereignty, the goddess of the sun, the power within the current of mighty rivers, a warrior, healer, alchemist/smith, and inspirer of the arts, Brigit was a farm girl who tended sheep, got drenched by rain and splattered with mud and gave away food to the poor people… who grew up to found a great abbey. A warm and compassionate person who had an iron will and a quick temper, who argued with kings, and loved art, and liked her beer. Brigit the woman could be a big sister, a beloved aunt, a heroine… a friend*. Two sides of the same coin perhaps?

WALKING IN THE WILD

If you would really like to experience this time of year, go for a walk. In the countryside or through a park is best, but even around the streets of your town. Walking is one of the best ways to exercise healthily and an activity that all ages are capable of enjoying together. There is no better way of coming into contact with your environment than to leave the car behind.

* '*Candlemas*' Amber K and Azrael Arryn K

47

Even if the weather is wet and windy, wrap up warmly and step out briskly, swinging your arms as you go; the blood will soon be pumping around your body and I can guarantee that you will rapidly feel toasty warm! It gets the body working – so much of our life is sedentary now, even for small children – and helps to flush out all the toxic deposits which naturally occur and can so easily accumulate.

When I was a child, I had no such problems. Living outside town in the countryside meant that I was always out in the garden or woods and every day after school, once I got off the bus, I still had another mile and a half to walk down the private lane to our cottage.

Sometimes this was great fun; splashing or wading through the larger puddles or stopping to breach the edge of the bigger bodies of water with the heel of my boot and watch it all drain slowly away. Walking the brimming ditches was even more of an adventure. This time of year used to be known as 'February fill-dyke' and when I was young it certainly did fill the ditches to their tops.

If the weather was bad, I did not always particularly enjoy this last leg of my homeward journey, muffling myself up and bracing myself against the onslaught of wind, rain or snow – and sometimes all three at once! But if something has to be done, it is always better to get on with it and get it over, there was no other way I was going to reach home, so I would step out bravely, even against the prevailing wind which roared across the open fields and constantly flung stinging pellets of rain full in my face. The wind alone could bring one's cheeks out in a frost burn... being a naturally pale child it was the *only* time I ever sported rosy cheeks.

Sometimes Farmer Hough would be driving home and occasionally take pity on me and give me a lift. But if I heard jolly whistling and turned to see Bill Fishwick approaching from behind me, I was often tempted to dive into a field and hide. Mr. Fishwick was older with deeply set piercing blue eyes in a deeply lined and weathered face, greying hair sticking out untidily from beneath a greasy old tweed cap and the most fearsome bushy eyebrows I have ever beheld. But he was kindness itself and always stopped to have a chat. He never failed to ask me what I had learned at school that day. He can't have had a very good opinion of my expensive private education because, being totally in awe of his eyebrows, my mind would go completely blank and I could never think of anything to report to him so invariably replied "Nothing".

Bill lived in a little cottage further up the valley from us, but his route home shared a lot of the way with ours and he would invariably offer me a lift. All well and good, but he didn't own a motor vehicle at that time; he rode a bicycle, so I would be scooped up and dumped unceremoniously on his crossbar while he sat back on the saddle and peddled industriously. Swooping between the larger puddles and gaily sailing through the smaller ones, sending spray and liquid mud flying in all directions while I was bounced and jolted until my teeth positively rattled in my head. We soon arrived at the parting of our ways which was also the spot my mother walked to each afternoon to meet me. On Bill Fishwick days I usually arrived before her and, thanking Mr. Fishwick politely I would make my hasty descent from his bone-shaker and be off down Rocky Hill as fast as my legs would carry me.

Bill did eventually buy a small van but by that time I was at secondary school and our home times rarely coincided. I suspect that he would have kept to his bike, but Bill told my father one day that he had got himself a housekeeper and so he had to have better transport for her sake. He was obviously quite in awe of the woman: "Aye," he proudly informed my bemused father, "And na she's cum we even 'ave cerpits and sit-darn cheers" which translates as "Now she has come we have carpets and easy (sit-down) chairs". Goodness knows how he lived before then – I never saw inside his cottage – but his comment was a revelation.

It was quite a while before we actually met the lady in question and learned her name, and until that time we fell into the habit of referring to her a "Cerpits". Eventually we discovered that the lady's name was Alice. She was a lovely little dumpling of a woman, in later middle age, with extremely curly hair and the thickest-lensed spectacles imaginable which also served to magnify her twinkly bright eyes behind them. She loved to chat and would keep my mother and I rooted to the spot in the lane for a good gossip whenever our ways crossed. Even so, Bill was obviously not always available with his old van to ferry her up and down – she didn't drive herself – and many is the time we have come across her walking down the lane clutching several bulging string bags of groceries after the Tuesday or Friday market and stopped to give her a lift home.

Here is a wonderfully warming and comforting pudding to pop in the oven while you put your shopping away – the fragrant tang of the lemon, sweet memory of summer sunshine in the fruit and light-as-a-feather meringue make this simple and old fashioned nursery dessert a gourmet's delight.

Queen of Puddings

Ingredients

½ pint (500 ml) of milk
½ pint (500 ml) of breadcrumbs
grated rind of 1 lemon
1 oz (25 g) butter
2oz (50 g) sugar
2 egg yolks
2 tablespoons of raspberry or other jam

For the meringue:
2 egg whites
2 oz (50 g) sugar

Method

- Heat the milk and stir in the sugar and butter to dissolve. Add the lemon rind and breadcrumbs and leave to one side for half an hour to give the breadcrumbs time to swell.

- *Beat in the egg yolks and pour mixture into a greased pie dish.*
- *Bake at 350°F/175°C for about half an hour, until set.*
- *Remove from oven and spread a thick layer of jam on the top, heating jam if necessary so that it will spread easily.*
- *Whisk egg whites very stiffly then fold in 1½ tablespoons of sugar.*
- *Pile on top of pudding and dredge with rest of sugar.*
- *Return to oven (300°F/150°C for 20 – 30 minutes until meringue is lightly coloured and crisp to the touch.*

COMMENT FROM JOAN: FEBRUARY 1968

Yesterday went to town shopping. Tried meat from new butcher's called Melia's in Chapel Street. Bought brisket, 4lbs at 3/6 (17½p.) a pound. Noticed mince was only 2/6 (12½p.) a pound - I pay 4/9 (24p.). Talking to Mrs Hough on the market – she says that they have had a baby girl since last November; hope to adopt her March/April; even with her five small boys she has always wanted a daughter. We all went to Mother's for tea.

Today I persuaded Jim not to go to church. We are all overtired. Gave them boiled beef and carrots for lunch, cold beef and huge salad at tea – brisket excellent, no wonder there was a queue. Tidied primrose bank and replaced bridge over stream.

Jim wants me to go with him to Chesterfield* tomorrow when he goes to collect a load of potato pie dishes.** He told me that last time they had a great display of earthenware casseroles and bread mugs.

---

* My father worked at that time as the manager of a fancy-goods warehouse and sometimes he was lucky enough to get out for a run to collect or deliver goods if a driver was off sick or there was extra work to do.

** Lancashire potato pie is not the same as Lancashire hot pot and traditional potato pie dishes came in various sizes and were straight-sided without a lid – or even a lip for a lid – so that a pastry crust could be laid across the top and cooked before serving. I haven't seen a potato pie dish for many years, except for the one on my top kitchen shelf which belonged to my great grandmother and must be well over a hundred years old.

Chapter Three

Candlemas

"If Candlemas be fair and bright, Winter will have another bite;
But if Candlemas be dull and rain, Winter will not come again."

The beginning of February is also known for another celebration – on the second day of the month there is Candlemas when the Church blessed special candles. But this explanation in itself might not be as straightforward as it seems. The suffix *mas* possibly doesn't refer to the church 'mass' but the Anglo-Saxon word *meast* meaning feast (literally food mixture).

Difficult to distinguish between Gwyl Ffraid/Imbolc/Saint Brigit's Day on the 1st February, there are many significant associations attached to the date of Candlemas. In Scotland, this time of year marked the official end of forty days of Yule celebrations; whereas in the Isle of Man, Candlemas was regarded as the middle of winter when – hopefully – half the stores of fodder, food and fuel laid down against the lean winter months should still remain.

In other Celtic countries traditions lent themselves more to actual candles. In Ireland, people donated candles to their local churches and took their own to be blessed and then kept symbolically alight in their own homes. In Wales, blessed candles were placed in a window as a sign that this was the last day when it would be needed to work by. I feel that this is pushing economy to the extreme as the days are still very short at this time of year, but having said that, candles were very expensive to buy – even their poorer cousins the tapers and rush lights could be relatively expensive and certainly time consuming to make. In Brittany, candles blessed at this time of year were kept in each house and lit for protection whenever there was a thunderstorm or illness.

Long ago in Ancient Rome, this was the time of year when the festival of Juno Februata, the virgin mother of the god, Mars, was celebrated. Candles in her honour were carried through the streets and women observed rites of purification in connection with fertility. As representative of the early Catholic Church, Pope Sergius was horrified by these pagan practices and changed the focus of the celebration to the 'Feast of the Purification of the Virgin' as it coincided with the fortieth day after Christmas – the time span required in Jewish law for a woman to be considered cleansed after the birth of a son. (I have also read that the length of time was doubled for purification after the birth of a daughter to eighty days, but I am not entirely sure of the truth of this.) Candlemas was certainly deemed the day that Mary took the baby Jesus to the temple where it was prophesied that he would be a 'Light to the World'.

THE CHURCHING OF WOMEN

I remember my mother telling me about the practice of 'churching' women after they had given birth. I thought little of it then, but times have changed and we are all surely better educated and informed? Women had to remain at home for the four – six weeks after the birth of their child. Many considered that childbirth made a woman unclean (or unholy) because it resulted from sexual activity... sexual abstinence and virginity being equated with 'holiness'. Without the moral overtones, the act of childbirth was still regarded as unclean due to the amount of blood and other bodily fluids which are present at this time.

Perhaps it can be argued that there are some valid, practical reasons for taking such a stance and not expecting a new mother to re-join the busyness of her local society so soon after giving birth. It was also possibly a way of discouraging the medically unhealthy sexual attentions of the husband, conversely encouraging friends and family to rally to the mother's support. Hence until the latter half of the Twentieth Century, Christian women still needed to be 'churched' after the birth of a baby before they could be allowed back into the religious and even social fold. But segregation works both ways and what protects and supports can also reject and marginalise. Reports from the middle of the Twentieth Century speak of women feeling ostracised and 'unclean'. In Ireland women were often not allowed to even pick up a knife for food preparation for fear that they would somehow taint it.

The ceremony and practice of 'churching' women still continues in eastern Christianity – the rite was dropped by the Catholic Church after the Second Vatican Council of 1967. Now the Catholic Encyclopaedia states that a blessing is given by the Church to new mothers after recovery from childbirth and the Church of England says very much the same. Personally I would feel much better about the whole thing if the woman in question wasn't still met at the church door and led or 'allowed' into the church by a male priest, or the fact that only married mothers are afforded this privilege – presumably the rule still stands that if you give birth to an illegitimate child you are ever after denied entry to the church. I think that it would resonate much more appropriately with modern woman if she had some form of rite of passage where a single female or group of women supported and nurtured her and made her official re-entry back into everyday life one of joyful triumph.

After all, this time of year is all about the feminine principle and the regeneration and birth of life – it is the very essence of what springtime revolves around and is as beautiful and miraculous as it is necessary. Whether we enjoy all the glorious spring flowers, love to hear the incredible bird song or feel energised by the gentle showers or mild spring sunshine; if we chuckle at the sudden antics of new-born lambs, excitedly anticipate Valentine's day or gorge on chocolate eggs, we are marking one single and vital activity... that of the Mother giving birth to Life.

Let us not forget the masculine role in all this and gender – of all persuasions – weaves a much-needed supportive web of teamwork to facilitate and nourish our community as a whole. There are those who bring forth new life and there are those who provide support and care... emotionally and spiritually as well as physically. One alone could not do without the others. Let us get this thorny topic in perspective. We are *all* vital to the overall enrichment and wonderful diversity and success of our society today. Springtime celebrates this too.

YOUR OWN LITTLE LIGHT

A lovely activity for this season of newly emerging light and growth is to make your own candles. It is not difficult to do and is something that we sometimes do as a group with the grove, (Druid gathering), or simply individually at home.

The first artificial light humanity used was firelight, from the time of primitive man sitting in his sheltering cave with a blaze of logs to keep both cold and animal savagery at bay until the end of the Nineteenth Century. Fire was needed to cook with and heat the home, therefore it was always there. It was good to sit beside at the end of a work-wearying day while tired fingers would still nimbly spin, knit or stitch by touch more than sight. Families talked together, invited their neighbours in, shared a jug of some convivial beverage and told stories and sang songs. The light of a blazing fire was more than enough to do all these things by – what need had they of anything extra? Candles were very expensive and tapers and rush lights time-consuming to make and messy and smelly to burn. Why incur an extra expense when one already had the light of the fire?

The Ancient Egyptians dipped papyrus wicks in melted animal fat. Similarly, the Chinese emperor of the Qin Dynasty made lights from melted fat over two thousand years ago and the Alaskans at some point discovered how to make candles from fish oil. Beeswax candles first became popular in mediaeval Europe – they did not smell and smoke – and finally, along came the candle made from products of the petroleum industry.

There are lots of wonderful places which supply candle-making equipment, but it really isn't necessary. To make your own dipped tapers, all you need is some natural (cotton) string, a quantity of wax (you may melt down the bottoms of all your old candles if you wish), two deep pans, or a tall metal jug and a pan (one inside the other), and somewhere to hang them to dry - this can be over the handle of a wooden spoon or rolling pin or even the stele of a sweeping brush, depending on how many you plan to make! Just bear in mind that it needs to be high enough for the taper to hang without touching anything, and broad enough so that if you make them in pairs they don't stick to each other while they are drying.

How to make a wax taper

- Put some water in the larger pan and place the smaller pan or jug containing the wax to be melted inside it with a folded cloth between the two pans so that the top pan does not overheat. Place over a heat and melt gently. (Remember that you aren't cooking the wax, simply allowing it to become liquid.)
- For two six-inch-long tapers, cut eighteen inches of string; hold the sting in the middle keeping the two lengths at least an inch apart and lower into the melted wax, hold for a few seconds and then gently lift it out again.
- Hold it for a few seconds allowing the wax to dry on the strings. Keep repeating this process and you will be surprised at how quickly the wax thickens into cylindrical candles. You can make your tapers as thin or thick as you like – the thinner they are the faster they will burn.
- When you have got them to the required thickness, hang the pair over your wooden handle to set and harden. Lay a paper beneath them to catch any stray drips.

- When completely cold, cut the string joining the tapers and trim to about ¼ inch in length to form the top of the wick. The bottom of the tapers might have accumulated a blob of wax without any wick running through it – simply cut this off with a sharp knife and return the discarded wax to the pan to be re-used.

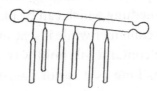

How to make an earth candle

- Melt your wax in the same way.
- Fill a plant pot with finely sifted soil and make a large rounded hole in it. Poke your finger further into the soil three times – these will form 'legs' for your candle once it is made – see illustration.
- Cut a length of string – at least four inches longer than the depth of the hole. Weight one end at the bottom of the hole with a pebble and tie the other end to a piece of twig (or a pencil, knitting needle or piece of dowelling will do) and rest it across the hole so that the string is pulled straight.
- Gently pour a little wax into the hole, slowly covering the sides first where the wax will solidify almost immediately on contact. When all the sides are coated, the middle can be filled in with melted wax being careful to leave about a quarter inch of room at the top.
- Allow to go completely cold and harden, then cut the wick free to about ¼ inch in length and carefully pull the candle out of the earth. A thick layer of soil will have stuck to the outside of the candle decorating it in a truly 'earthy' way and just right for this earth-conscious season.

Earthcandle

Eggshell candle

Damp sand can also be used to form different shapes; the wax may be coloured with food dyes and/or scented with essential oils. Just remember to dip the string wick in melted wax before you start, weight the bottom of it with something to prevent it floating and tie the top end to something which can be placed across the top of the container while it sets and hardness.

You can also use any container to hold wax with a wick running through the centre, as long as it is not flammable and is low/flat enough to see the flame or see-though – try glass jars and wine or drinking glasses, little pottery dishes, eggshells or seashells.

Here is my mother's recipe for making your own fresh, natural yoghurt. Drained to form cottage cheese, it makes a deliciously creamy fresh spread for sandwiches or crackers. If you wish to use it to make cheesecake (as in the recipe in the next chapter) you will need to make two or three lots, so begin making your yoghurt two or three days before you wish to bake - or before you read the next chapter!

Yoghurt
(dated around 1967)

Ingredients

1 ¼ pint (125 ml) milk
1 tablespoon instant milk powder
1 tablespoon plain yoghurt – Bulgarian bacillus

Method

- *Stir dried milk into milk, bring it to the boil and let it cool to 100° F/37°C., just above blood heat. Pour into a glass jar (with screw top) and add starter yoghurt, stir, replace lid and leave by Rayburn (warm stove) overnight or until nicely set. Do not leave too long or it will be rather sharp.*

- *I drain this yoghurt, make cottage cheese (this amount makes just about ½ lb (250 g) – use it mixed with chopped tomato and cucumber as savoury spread on crackers or for cheese cake – use the whey to mix in soda bread or savoury scones.*

In 1993, my mother inserted a note into the top of this recipe which adds that she found she no longer needed to add the dried milk powder, but lately I have found my yoghurt so thin that I think I will try adding it again.

To begin with, Joan used to scald a square of cheesecloth and, doubling the material, would pour the yoghurt into it, gather all the corners and tie a similarly scalded string around it, using it to also hang the yoghurt to drain over- night over a bowl. Then she bought a French pottery cheese jug which had a wide neck and matching drainer which fitted into the top – made draining the yoghurt much easier!)

CANDLELIT BEDTIMES

When I was a child, we often didn't have electricity at the cottage. Sometimes we generated our own, but in my earlier years the generator was old and the twenty-four-volt light it produced was feeble to the point of being not much use at all. We didn't actually have much need for electricity; our cooker was the fire oven and hobs over the open flames, our fridge and dining room light ran on bottled gas and our radio was one of the new early-sixties transistors run off a battery – television didn't even feature in our lives then… we had no interest in it. My mother preferred candlelight, finding it far more soothing and relaxing, so that is what we used out of preference.

On my little bedside table, I had a candle in a blue and white pottery candlestick, a little pale blue kelly oil lamp with a white, opaque shade and a box of matches. These were my only lights and as I grew up I became adept at balancing candle or lamp, (which, minus its shade, gave a better light), so that I could read my books, often long into the night when I should have been fast asleep, but I have always been addicted to a good tale well told!

My problem was that even the light of a single candle was easily discernible through the crack beneath my bedroom door. If I heard my parents approaching up the stairs, I would hastily blow my candle out. But that presented another problem as both candles and paraffin lamps leave a temporary odour in the air for a few minutes after extinguishing. If either of my parents decided to open my bedroom door and peek in to see if I was asleep, they could always tell that I most certainly wasn't, because they could instantly smell the fact that I had only just put my candle out.

As I grew a little older – six or seven years old – I was given my own torch, a super shiny silver metal affair that changed from a white light to red or green by turning the top. It wasn't bright enough for reading by though. When I later got ordinary torches I did try a few times to use them to read in the privacy beneath my bedcovers but the batteries never lasted long enough – and my parents were far too savvy not to know why I was using so many batteries – so I gave up and went back to using my candle.

In the many years I used this mode of lighting I only ever had one accident with it, and that was long after I had grown out of childhood. I used to lie down with my book in my hand and balance my candle next to me on my pillow. I had been deeply engrossed in a novel — probably a Mary Stewart, Jean Plaidy or Victoria Holt as history was my favourite reading matter then – when I suddenly looked up from my book to discover that unbeknownst to me, my candle had tipped backwards and was busily melting the white padded headboard! Fortunately, it didn't actually catch fire. I was so embarrassed by my carelessness that for some time after that I devised artistic ways of arranging my pillows so that the results of my dangerous folly wouldn't be noticed.

Of course, my mother eventually spotted it one evening when she popped in to say goodnight. "What on earth happened there?" she enquired mildly. When I explained, she merely raised her eyebrows and said, "Damned lucky!" That was all. She was well aware that she had taught me all she could about safety with flames and fire and there was absolutely nothing more that she could add to it.

Despite the fact that my bedroom was above the living room and that the chimney breast beside my bed used to get lovely and warm heated as it was by the living room fire beneath, sometimes it would still get freezing cold in winter. The effects of this have remained with me all my life. I still much prefer a cool or cold bedroom, even in winter, and cannot sleep properly in a warm room. I loved to wake on a winter's morning and find that Jack Frost had decorated the insides of my window panes with the most delicate ferns and leaves of ice!

During the long, harsh winter of 1962 – 63 my mother allowed me to have a little Tilly Pressure Heater in my bedroom. It was put in my room some time before I was due to go to bed so that the chill would already have been taken off the air. I well remember the loud hissing sound that it made, the lovely red glow that it cast around the room, and my father or Uncle Ricky coming in to energetically pump more air into it so that it could be left longer until after I had gone to sleep.

On less freezing nights I would delight in snuggling down in my cosy bed, warmed by hot water bottles and heaped with woollen blankets and feather eiderdowns, listening to the winter and early spring storms raging around the chimney stack. The rain would drum thunderously upon the slate roof above me while up on the hill in Farmer Hough's field the huge old oak, birch and sycamore trees would thrash and sough in the onslaught from the March gales. I knew that we were relatively sheltered in our little valley and I took gleeful satisfaction in enjoying the unbridled ferocity of storms, knowing that nothing could possibly hurt me.

When I was seven years old, my mother's ward, Lynne, came from Trinidad to stay with us for a year and then my post bedtime activities became far more varied and daring. We would snuggle down beneath the bedclothes together and talk and talk for hours, as little girls do, freely sharing our dreams and quirky observations of our day which frequently led to hilarious outbursts of uncontrollable giggles and laughter.

"…Are you two not asleep yet?" my mother would call up gently. Only after several such enquiries would my father open the bedroom door, poke his head around it and quietly say, "Come on now…" and we knew that this was the final warning and we dare not push our luck any further that night.

It was Lynne who first thought of dribbling scalding hot wax onto the palms of our hands and then, as it set but was still malleable, mould it into all manner of shapes, including doll's house cups, saucers and plates. Thick and discoloured the results were hardly beautiful or artistic but to our young eyes they were immensely satisfying.

Our bedtimes were not always noisy, chatty or active though. Sometimes we would lie quietly among the flickering shadows that our candles cast from each side of the bed and play at shadow puppets across the expanse of the chimney breast. At other times we would take it in turns to write words or messages on each other's back and have to guess what they were. This was particularly useful when our candles had been determinedly extinguished by frazzled parents and we had been left in the dark.

Lynne and I also discovered that gently running our fingers up and down each other's backs was very soothing and would very soon send one or other of us off to sleep as also sometimes unintentionally happened in the middle of a game of 'messages', much to the disgust of the one left awake!

Both Lynne and I kept diaries which we conscientiously wrote entries in every night. Even at a very young age I felt compelled to record what was happening around me in my life. Lynne began keeping her journal because she had the most atrocious memory and it was a way of recording her activities so that she could later recount her news to her parents when she wrote her weekly letter to them. It was a habit which I have never lost. Sometimes in my busy young adult life I would go for several months at a time without writing anything but even to this day I regularly record in my journal. These entries now are not merely descriptions of what I have done or even thought and felt but include descriptions of what my friends and family around me have been getting up to, along with letters and cards received from further afield, photographs, newspaper cuttings, and even shopping lists, to-do lists, menus and supermarket till receipts.

Lynne and I also loved to sing together. We took it in turns to play my guitar which had belonged to my mother but which she had passed on to me in my early teens. A lovely light and delicate instrument made from sycamore and other gorgeously polished woods it had been made in Rome by Antonio Petroni in 1879. I adored it, even if its metal strings (apparently more authentic for its age and type) did play havoc with my finger ends.

By the time Lynne retuned to Britain from the West Indies to begin boarding school at Chislehurst in Kent when she was fourteen – and I was nearly twelve – we were well into all the latest singable pop songs, current musical film songs and folk ballads. I would source and collect the words and Lynne would learn the guitar chords at school and then come home in the holidays and teach them to me. Even better was when she joined the school choir and learned how to harmonise. And where did we refine these brilliant performances? You guessed it… sitting up in bed with a candle balanced on each knee!

One might also say that this is where my writing career also truly began to emerge. My mother had unhappy childhood memories of her own mother sitting composing poetry while the fire died in the grate and the family came home for a meal to find no housework done and nothing to eat, which made my grandfather – not a patient man at the best of times — extremely cross and often led to raised voices and rows. So, when I began to show more than a small child's passing interest in authorship, my mother tried to discourage me and made it plain that she didn't approve.

Instead, I simply went underground, writing complicated historical stories in my lunch break at school or at night – by the light of the ubiquitous candle – after I had officially gone to bed. My favourite scribblings were begun after Lynne had finished teacher training college and begun her probationary year of teaching in a sterile 'new town' built in the late 1960s. It was a lampoon of old and new colliding which I would save and read aloud to my old childhood companion whenever she came home to visit us. Again, even though we were now both young women, we still shared a bedroom and we would dissolve into gales of laughter at the absurd scenarios I dreamed up... and yes, this hysterical entertainment was usually shared – you guessed it – after we had gone to bed.

COMMENT FROM JOAN: 2nd FEBRUARY 1967

Gas went this morning and didn't want to take the other cylinder off the fridge so used candles in the dining room. Kept Jill off school so that we could walk up to town this afternoon to be early enough for show at the Grand Theatre in Blackpool – Julia Lockwood and Ron Moody in 'Peter Pan'. Met Ricky in lane at 3:25 p.m. so arrived on time. Excellent performance, then supper and home.

Muffins
From an 1826 recipe, but written into
Joan's manuscript cookery book around 1978

However, you might wish to celebrate this wonderfully invigorating but chilly time of year, there is nothing nicer than a muffin, toasted crisply on the outside and soft and buttery on the inside.

Ingredients

2½ lbs (1.1 kg) strong white bread flour
½ pint (250 ml) milk and 1 pint (500 ml) of water (totalling 1½ pints
*   plus more water if necessary to make a softer dough than bread)*
½ teaspoon salt
¼ oz (6 g) sugar
1 oz (25 g) yeast

Time

2 hours to rise and prove. To bake, 8 – 10 minutes.

Method

- *Mix flour and salt together.*
- *Cream yeast with the sugar.*
- *Mix milk and water and heat to a lukewarm temperature.*
- *Mix all ingredients to a very soft dough and knead well.*
- *Cover with cloth and put in a warm place for 1 hour to rise; then another half hour if needed.*
- *Roll out about ¾ inch thick and cut into rounds with a cutter, place on greased trays and allow to rise again for another ½ hour.*
- *Bake in medium/hot oven for about ten minutes, but keep them white and a little like underdone dinner rolls.*
- *Alternatively, cook them on a moderately warm greased girdle (a thick-bottomed frying pan will do) putting the side that was on top during proving on the girdle first.*
- *When the first side is cooked, turn the muffin and cook the other side. (When cooked they should be 3 inches across and 2 inches thick.*

Never split and toast muffins, it makes 'em dry. When required, toast both sides then tear (I do not cut them) both sides apart, spread with melted butter, replacing both sides together. After a minute or two turn the muffin upside- down to distribute butter evenly throughout.

We particularly like grilled ham or bacon on them, sandwich fashion and with a nice home-made tomato soup served first it can make quite a substantial meal instead of a snack. Especially as on our once-per-month visit to Blackburn Market I sometimes manage to buy ham or bacon pieces for 4/- (20p) per pound at my ham stall – and with bacon at lowest 12/3 (56p) per pound this is excellent value, the pieces being merely too thin or half rashers etc.. When I think of our regular 1/10 (9p) per pound streaky rashers of five years ago my heart breaks. Who would think of today's prices then?

JACKIE MAKES A NEW FRIEND
(A story to share with children)

Each day for a week it had snowed. Jackie had been out there, rolling big snowballs in the field, tobogganing down the little slope to the stream, making snow angels on the lawn and building a snowman which was almost as big as himself. His dad had to help him lift the huge head onto its icy shoulders. Carefully the little boy had formed the snowman's features –large dark stones from the flower border for his eyes, a long orange carrot for an impressive nose and broken bits of twig which his mum had helped Jackie to form into a great friendly grin.

Jackie was an only child – no brothers or sisters to have snowball fights with or to help build a whole family of snow people. He worked with care and kept adding details to his jolly, chubby snowman whom he took to calling 'Mr Chubbs'. He pulled lengths of glossy green ivy leaves off the garden wall and lovingly wound them like a scarf around his snowy companion's neck. Down by the stream he found thicker twiggy sticks with which to make skeletal hands and his mum gave him fat balls to hang on them for the birds to feed on. Other stones were used to push into the front of its body for coat buttons. Sprigs of shiny, dark green holly were cut with great care – the leaves were very prickly – and stuck into the top of Mr Chubbs' head for hair and an empty terracotta plant pot was brought out of his dad's shed and placed upside down on the snowman's head at a jaunty angle to form a stylish hat.

Jackie had got into the habit of running out first thing in the morning before school and checking on his icy friend; charging out into the back garden again as soon as he returned home in the afternoon to tell his new friend all about his day; sitting on an upturned bucket besides him to drink his steaming hot mug of cocoa. And every night, just before he got into bed, Jackie would peep through his bedroom curtains and wave goodnight to Mr Chubbs standing out on the back lawn below him.

Now Jackie stared in dismay. As usual he had rushed out to greet his frozen friend before breakfast but what had happened to Mr Chubbs? All around was the sound of dripping water from roof, trees and bushes. Great patches of green grass showed through the blanketing white and where the snowman had stood the night before there was nothing more than a pile of dirty slush and a tangle of twigs, stones and holly and ivy leaves topped by a bruised and lonely carrot. The little boy let out a wail of despair and two fat tears crept out from his eyes and began to roll slowly down his cheeks.

"Whatever is the matter?" asked a gentle young voice and with a start, Jackie spun round to find that he was not alone in the garden. An older teenage girl was standing a few feet away, smiling at him.

"Who are you?" asked the little boy, so surprised that his tears began to dry at once.

"My name is Freida. I'm a neighbour of yours; I live close by, but I have only just arrived." The girl replied. Jackie wasn't quite convinced. She was dressed rather oddly in a long grey-green dress with a deep border of frilly yellow around the hem, she carried soft furry grey mittens and a bunch of white snowdrops and purple crocus was stuck in her hair which corkscrewed in a wild mass of pale golden little curls which bounced and swayed all over her head when she moved it. But she had a lovely smile and her eyes sparkled with good humour. The problem was, older people often didn't take Jackie seriously and would tell him not to be silly. Would this girl think that he was silly too? The little boy decided to risk it.

"Mr Chubbs was my friend." Jackie pointed sadly at the pile of rapidly melting snow. "And now he's gone!" the child hickuped.

"Oh, is that all?" the girl chuckled.

"But I didn't want him to go." Jackie protested, "I want Mr Chubbs to come back."

"I am sure that Mr Chubbs and all his family across the land have enjoyed the icy cold and spending time with all you children," Freida's voice became more gentle and her smile tender as she moved closer to the boy. "But the land is getting warmer again, spring is coming and, you know, Mr Chubbs would feel very uncomfortable if he tried to stay longer. Everything in its right time and season." Jackie didn't look at all convinced. "But Mr Chubbs will be back again next winter when it snows." the girl encouraged. Jackie still looked doubtful.

The girl laughed. "Look, I'll show you. Take my hand and come with me." Without further ado, Freida impulsively grabbed Jackie's hand and tugged him towards the hedge and suddenly they were on the bank of the stream. "Spring is here!" she declared airily, waving her other hand high in the air around her.

"No, it isn't," Jackie persisted, "It's still winter. It's only the beginning of February and everything is bare and dead."

"Are you sure?" Freida chuckled. "Look again… more closely." The girl turned and began to walk along the side of the stream, through the trees towards the field. "Look!" She pointed to the sheltered land beneath the trees at the water's edge. Jackie gave a little gasp as he spotted fresh green leaves and bright golden daisy-like flowers growing in little cushions and carpets all along the bank. Where had they come from? "They are celandine, my dear. And look there!" Freida pointed upwards to where a young hazel was dancing with lamb's tail catkins. On other branches buds were swelling and some of the branches had changed colour, from dark grey to pale yellow and deep red. "They are not dead at all they have all just been sleeping but now it is time for everything to wake up again."

Out into the field, Jackie spotted some sheep quietly grazing and standing next to one of them on incredibly thin, wobbly legs was a tiny new-born lamb. Delighted, Jackie made as if to run towards it but Freida held his hand tightly and pulled him back. "It is only a few hours old, Jackie, and its mother wouldn't want humans interfering at this stage – only the shepherd is welcome just now. Wait a couple of weeks until it is stronger and there are more lambs in the field, and then you can come and sit at the edge of the pasture and see if they will come up to you. For now, just quietly watch from the other side of the hedge."

As they walked on, Jackie looked around him. Up on the hill he noticed spears of a deeper gold among the bushes where the first of the gorse was coming into flower.

They had reached the stony, sandy ditch which ran along the lane and here Jackie spotted more yellow flowers standing on whiskery stalks. "Coltsfoot. Good for coughs. Do you like coltsfoot rock?"

Freida breezed on. "And over there on the grass verge is Butterbur – it's called that because the farm women used to wrap their butter in its leaves to take to market." Jackie could well understand how you could easily wrap up a pack of butter as he gazed at the plate-sized leaves with their oddly-shaped lollypop blooms made up from many tiny pale flowers growing around the stalk.

They walked a little further along the lane back towards their house. Jackie knew full well that he wasn't supposed to be out on the road without one of his parents but as he wasn't alone he felt that it would be alright... Freida must be almost grown up. "Look over there, Jackie," the girl swept her free hand in the direction of their neighbour's garden and he could just see little drifts of pale snowdrops coming into pointed bud above the fast melting snow... and nearer to the front door were some clumps of gold and purple crocus, also in bud. When did all this happen? Jackie wondered. He hadn't noticed any of it before, but then everything had been covered in a thick blanket of ice for some time, so he supposed that he couldn't have seen it – all this time these brave little flowers must have been growing away under the snow!

"And then, just think what comes with the springtime," Freida whispered excitedly and Jackie closed his eyes as he suddenly thought of all the other lovely flowers which would fill the garden and the fields which would be lush with grass again; Easter with chocolate eggs to hunt and sticky spicy fruity hot cross buns to eat... and beyond that, on into summer with its tree climbing and picnics, ice cream, outdoor games and trips to the seaside and the long holidays from school. A great grin of pleasurable anticipation spread across the little boy's face.

"If ever you are lonely, you can always come and find me." Jackie's eyes popped open again. Freida was smiling broadly at him, her eyes sparkling with mischief. "Where?" the little boy demanded. "Oh, I shall be here and there around the woods and fields – I like to spend a lot of time outside, you know, but I shall often be on the bank of the stream near the bottom of your garden. It's a favourite spot. You'll always find me there."

"Jackie Wilmott! What are you doing out on that road alone? What have I told you?" Suddenly his mother's voice broke into his reverie and Jackie spun round to see her striding through their front garden gate towards him looking very cross indeed.

"Yes, I... er... I know, but I thought that as I was with Freida and sh... she is almost grown up that it would b... be alright." Jackie stammered and then felt a wave of relief as his mother reached him and bent down to give him a hug.

"Oh, Jackie, you and your imaginary friends! There's no one here – you're all alone... and out on this dangerous road too." Jackie struggled out of his mother's embrace and span around, but of Freida there wasn't a sign.

"But she was here!" the little boy insisted. "She's our new neighbour and she told me that she has just arrived." Jackie's mum just gave a lopsided grin and shook her head. "Freida told me that I could always find her out in the fields or woods, and she would wait for me down by the stream. Come on, I'll show you. Let's go and find her now!" With that, Jackie pulled his protesting mother back in through their gate and round to the back of the house and down over the lawn, past the even smaller heap of melting snow that had been Mr Chubbs, and through the gate at the end of the garden onto the path besides the stream.

In vain, the little boy looked up and down and all around him but it would seem that Freida was not there. All he could see was a little bush, not much taller than himself... two young trees intertwined – one covered in soft, downy, grey 'mittens' of 'pussy willow', topped by a hazel tree just poking up through the top branches of the smaller willow and covered in gayly dancing yellow lamb's tail catkins, while all around the little trees grew a carpet of golden celandine and a single clump of white snowdrops and purple crocus.

"Goodness!" exclaimed Jackie's mother, "I've never noticed that growing there before – how pretty!"

Jackie just smiled quietly to himself. He didn't realise then that he had misheard Freida's name which was really Ffraid but somehow he understood that he had found her and she would always be there.

Chapter Four

Valentine

"Frost-locked all the winter – seeds, and roots, and stones of fruits,
What shall make their sap ascend that they may put forth shoots?"
                                                    Christina Rosetti

I have always felt that there is something very special about the time around Saint Valentine's Day – one of those curious times which belongs nowhere and everywhere – it is neither winter nor spring but can be celebrated as either or neither. Most importantly, it gives us all an opportunity to celebrate 'love' in all its many forms. People tend to think of it as an occasion just for romance and lovers, but it can also be seen as a time to celebrate friendship, comradeship and blood ties too; an occasion when we can briefly step out of the busy round of modern life and simply glory in our gentler, finer feelings and honour those around us who make us happy and whom we truly love, care about and are thankful for.

SAINT VALENTINE'S DAY

For the origins of who Saint Valentine was and how he came to be celebrated on the 14th February we have to travel back in time to Ancient Rome. The Romans regarded February as a month of cleansing and purification – something we still act out today in the annual spring cleaning of our homes. For the Romans it was also a time to celebrate fertility and love. The festival of Lupercalia was celebrated on the 15th February. It was named after Lupercal, the grotto cave where the infants, Romulus and Remus came ashore after floating down the Tiber River in a basket and were suckled and raised by a great she-wolf. They later grew up to found the city and nation of Rome. February is the beginning of the mating season for wolves; animals which mate for life and whose union was historically seen as a sign of the coming spring and the eternal union between the Earth Goddess and the Sun God.

The festival of Lupercalia also honoured Facinus, also known as Lupercus, a goat-footed god of gardens, crops, flocks, animals and music – closely related to the god Pan, Satan and the Wild Man of the woods at Midwinter.* Goats were sacrificed to Lupercus at this time and the Luperci (priests) carried goatskin thongs around the towns and cities with which to hit everyone they met. This token scourging was welcomed as ritual purification but for women it was also seen as a symbol of increasing or renewing their fertility. Younger people celebrated by putting names of willing girls into a jar from which the young men would draw names to discover who were to be their partners for the festivities.

At the end of the Fifth Century A.D. Pope Gelasius (the leader of the Roman Church at that time) became utterly horrified by such a 'cheerfully scandalous festival' and promptly banned it. There resulted such a terrific outcry that in the year 496 A.D. Gelasius had to apologise to the people.** However, the festival wasn't reinstated in its original form. It was moved to the previous day and changed to the feast of Saint Valentine on the 14th February when it was decreed that various saints' names were to be placed in a receptacle for people to draw out and discover which saint was to be their personal focus of prayers and devotion for the celebration. We can only speculate how popular this alternative celebration might have been, but it is interesting to note that Gelasius, who had only been pope for four years, left the position very soon afterwards that same year.

* See Chapter 9 of my previous book 'Merry Midwinter - How to Rediscover the Magic of the Christmas Season'
** Farrar, 'Eight Sabbats', p. 65

Like so many others, the details of Saint Valentine's life are confused and there is some debate as to whether there may have been two saints with the same name. Some accounts tell of Saint Valentine who was born in Teri, Italy, in 226 A.D. and became a priest and physician and who suffered martyrdom during the persecution of the Christians by Emperor Claudius II in 269 A.D.. Other narratives identify him as the bishop of Teri who was martyred in Rome and whose relics were later returned to Teri for burial. Although the Roman Catholic Church continue to recognise him as a saint of the church, saint Valentine was removed from the General Roman Calendar in 1969 because of the lack of reliable information about him. He is the patron saint of lovers, epileptics and beekeepers.

The more likely reason for Valentine's execution was the fact that he reportedly disobeyed the emperor's decree which made it illegal for soldiers of the Roman army to marry. It was thought that men who had wives and children waiting for them at home would be more timid in battle and reticent to lose their lives. It is said that Saint Valentine was happy to marry willing couples in secret and joined many people in marriage for which he paid the ultimate price – hence him later being made the patron saint of lovers.

As with all these ancient customs which originally came about as people lived in rhythm with the natural world and life in general, the practice of choosing a partner and celebrating love and procreation was impossible to eradicate and continued in one form or another across the Roman Empire and in other places around the world. Until quite recently in Scotland, the Saint Valentine's Day ballot – similar to the Roman practice - remained very popular, as was the sending of a home-made card or gift to the girl whose name was drawn. It was also popularly believed that the first single person of the opposite sex, outside the family, that you met on that day would be your future spouse. In other Celtic countries boys would sometimes wear Valentine slips on their sleeves and court and treat the girls whose names were written on them – presumably after choosing them randomly from a selection vessel on Valentine's Eve. In Wales, young men spent the long dark winter evenings carving beautifully intricate wooden Love

Spoons to give to the girl they most admired as a sign of their feelings and future hopes.

The time around the middle of the month of February has long been widely celebrated in many forms. In our more northerly lands there was the Feast of Vali who was the son of the god, Woden. Celebrated on the 14th February it was a solar festival marking the growing strength of the Sun, the end of Winter, the survival of the community and also loyalty and kinship.

From the feminine aspect there was also the Honour of Vara, a lunar festival which bore witness to the vows of lovers. The goddess Vara was similar to the Greek goddess, Athena and the Egyptian goddess, Ma'at, representing truth and responsibility and was a close companion of Freya, the Norse queen of the gods.

I LOVE YOU!

Here in Britain we have gradually relaxed over the last few decades into a more accepting and demonstrative society but it is still not enough. One cannot simply assume that our nearest and dearest know how much we care about them. The practical ways we have of demonstrating our feelings can so easily be misconstrued and while I am a firm believer in 'practicing what I preach' I am also a staunch advocate of leaving nothing to chance and actually telling my loved ones in words of one syllable exactly how much I care.

Those three little words which are often thought of and heard like some magical spell do not just belong to romantic couples; they belong to all of us – children and parents, siblings, relatives, friends, work colleagues. Use wherever they will be most appreciated.

Otherwise, try some alternatives which might not come across as so startling: "I deeply appreciate your time and company", "Your friendship means a great deal to me" or "I care deeply about you". Admittedly, in this day and age of blurred gender definitions we need to be careful not to do or say something which might be misconstrued, but if that is your concern then say so… straight out; "I'm not implying anything else…" or "No ulterior motive here, but

I really would like to say…" accompanied by a firm handshake, or holding someone's hand or, best of all, giving someone a great big bearhug. And look into their eyes, engage them, give them a great big smile. Be open and wholehearted… wear your feelings in your body language and across your facial features. We tend to forget that we communicate just as much by our attitude as we do by physical actions and more, our intentions actually precede us so that others have probably already got the drift of what we are about to do and say before we even get there.

Surely what we are all aiming for is to feel, experience and give out *unconditional love* which does what it says, loves without prejudice, judgement or conditions… loves us for all that we are; not just the obviously good or nice bits but all the rest as well. This goes far beyond romantic love which is usually subjective, transient, very conditional and frequently self-centred to some degree. To experience the feeling of unconditional love, try thinking about how you feel when you look at a puppy or kitten… or a sleeping baby or young child… that explosive gush of limitless emotion which asks for nothing but simply surges out from you while you bask in a perfect moment.

There are all sorts of ways that you can bring some love and smiles into the lives of those you care about. Make your own Valentine cards to send to friends, (there are some suggestions for simple cards later in this chapter), but in this case, make sure that you sign them so that the recipient knows who cares! Or drop someone a note – written by hand on a real piece of paper as the personal touch conveys so much more than just what the eyes pick up.

Get your family, friends or neighbours together for a little (or large!) celebration of your interconnectedness. This may focus on the coming spring with flowers, seeds, salady foods and light fruit drinks, or hearts and chocolate, or cosy activities and comfort foods surrounded by candlelight and warmth. It may feature family from one's background or people from your local community. If some of the people attending are from different cultural backgrounds, ask everyone to bring a favourite national dish to form a potluck supper and celebrate our amazing diversity and individuality.

THE LOVELINESS THAT IS YOU

The loveliness that is you
Is shown in many ways;
The way you laugh at your children's games
And join them while they play.
The way your face lights when you smile,
The music of your voice,
The grace of movement that is yours,
And, if I had my choice,
I'd spend my days contented
Knowing I could share my life with you,
And I'd tell you much, much more about
The loveliness that is you.

Jim Bradshaw

VALENTINE TREES AND GARLANDS

In my own home, we have by this time removed all the Christmas decorations from our floor-to-ceiling Winter Tree in the drawing room and it has been standing quite stark and bare for some time – except for all the little candle lights which we still light up every day. As Valentine's Day approaches, I sometimes hang coloured hearts on our Tree instead. In this case I have three or four dozen heart-shaped baubles – some with flowers on and a few are bright red but they are mostly in soft, pale shades of blue, pink and ivory. They have been collected over the past thirty-five years but are becoming more common.

However, you needn't go to much expense. If you have a Winter Tree or simply decide to stand a smaller branch in a pot of soil or sand on a table to make a Valentine Tree, you can then cut out coloured card or paper hearts (in one or more colours). Encourage youngsters to do this for you. Ask older children to find appropriate quotations to write on the hearts before they are hung so that you have a heart-warming focus of wonderfully uplifting and inspiring thoughts or use this as a celebratory activity and ask everyone to write something nice on each heart as you decorate your Tree together. You might wish to ask everyone to also decorate the hearts with patterns or attach material or lace – use your imagination and begin a new family tradition with something which could in time become an heirloom.

Whatever approach you choose make sure that you have some activities planned which you can all join in with – quizzes, games like charades or forfeits or, if you are going to be a smaller group, card or board games. It doesn't really matter what you choose to do; it is just a vehicle to bring everyone together. On a more personal level you might ask everyone to bring a poem to read, or a piece of music to listen to – or a musical instrument to play or song to sing if you have friends and family who are talented in that way.

With the theme of appreciation and love in mind, you could always play what we at Quaker children's gatherings used to call 'cosy-glows'. A large piece of paper is given to everyone which you write your name at the top of and then pass round for other people to write you a nice message.

For instance, this might be one of the reasons they like/appreciate/love you, or they might share a happy/funny memory of you together.

If you wish to make the messages more private you can cut out enough paper hearts for everyone present to give one each to everyone else. They needn't necessarily be red; they can be plain white paper. If there are too many for you to cut out yourself, make up some card templates of heart shapes and provide a bundle of pencils or pens and scissors for folk to cut their own. Once the messages are all written they can then be given to each recipient to take home and read privately. Another lovely thing to do is when you have read them, thread your hearts on a piece of cotton, wool or string and hang them up somewhere you will see them often throughout your day – a wonderful reminder of how much you are loved and appreciated.

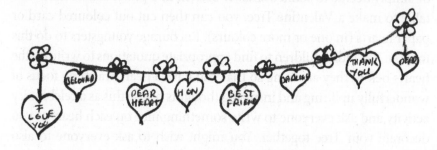

COMMENT FROM JOAN: 14ᵗʰ FEBRUARY 1967

My modern Greek Lingaphone course arrived. Jill and I still neither lost nor won – kept Jill off school as both of us feel as if we are starting with flu. Jim arrived home tonight with Valentine gifts - chocolates for Jill and I and a Dick Hames record for me – oh, and a box of squashy cakes!

Making Valentine Cards

It isn't necessary to spend pounds and pounds buying cards to send to your loved ones, especially if you plan on sending tokens of your loving regard to several of your friends and family – it is the essence of the thoughtful and lovingly hand written message that is really the point.

COLOURED CARD is available either in A4 size which can simply be folded in half or larger sheets which will need to be cut, as are envelopes which can also be purchased in bright colours.

GLITZ: Find a heart-shaped biscuit cutter or heart shapes of various sizes and make yourself some templates in thick card. Your greetings card can be decorated with hearts of varying sizes cut from red or other colours of card and embellished with glitter, wisps of lace or tiny jewels bought in reasonably priced packs from book, craft or haberdashery shops – keep an eye out in shops like The Works for all manner of seasonal accessories at pocket money prices. Using a large heart as a template to draw around you might prefer to make heart-shaped cards, gluing narrow – or not-so-narrow! – lace around the edge and writing your message in the middle. The possibilities are limitless with all the availability of scraps, pictures, braids, motifs, beads, etc. Paper doylies are also extremely effective; they come in many sizes and designs, in white, gold or silver and a portion or whole doyly can look gorgeous laid against a coloured background and finished with a single red heart or flower.

FREEHAND: If you are at all artistically inclined or accomplished, you might like to draw something of your own using some of the vast array of marvellous gel, paint and felt pens which are now available. Yes, these can involve an initial outlay of money but if you purchase a decent set they will last longer – I have a couple of sets of pens which I bought several years ago and have used extensively but which are still going strong.

USING PRESSED FLOWERS: You may prefer to keep it very natural and seasonal and press spring flowers like early primroses, crocus or narcissi (snowdrops being white tend to discolour as they dry) and carefully glue a little Valentine bouquet as illustration on your card which becomes a real gift of your time, love, effort and garden and also includes the relevance of the season. Pressing flowers is quite simple: cut best blooms when dry. Carefully arrange between two pieces of white tissue paper placed in a large book or between two books – or a pile of books. Smaller, less thick flowers can dry out in a week if kept in a warm room. Just be careful how you handle them, they can be very fragile.

POETRY: While there are lots of beautifully eloquent poems for us to find and copy into our cards, many of us are able to compose some kind of verse – even if it is only basic rhyming doggerel... but if we have written it ourselves it is our own personal and unique doggerel. It is also easier to encapsulate feelings, emotions, memories and observances succinctly in rhyme than straight prose – have a go and see what you come up with.

CHILDREN AND YOUNGSTERS: Don't forget to encourage the younger generations to get involved, whether it is a three-year-old making an enthusiastic collage of a card for grandparents, a ten-year-old making jokily kind cards for classmates or a lovelorn teenager manifesting their deepest feelings. With younger children you might suggest exchanging cards between siblings and parents as a family activity – baking or buying a special cake or making a nice little meal to all share whilst ceremoniously opening your cards together – lots of ooohs, aaaahs, laughter, blushes and cuddles! It is an easier, less embarrassing way for shy or less articulate family members (of any age!) to share their true feelings for those closest to them. Establish the activity when children are young and it will grow into a revealing and welcome habit which helps them to express themselves as they grow older and more inhibited with the perceived constraints of maturity.

FUN ON THE ICE

When I was a child back in the late 1950s and '60s we often didn't see any snow at all – much to my utter disgust. The rest of the country – especially the eastern side – was usually deeply cloaked in the stuff at least once each winter but we hardly saw a single snowflake. What we did experience was frost and living in our little valley which had its own microclimate it was often much warmer in the summer but very much colder in the winter. Sometimes the hoar frost was so thick that it looked like it had snowed but the white and brittle world it created was iron hard and completely unforgiving. Temperatures at night would frequently drop to -5°C or -10°C and once the thermometer in my mother's herb garden recorded a night time temperature of -23°C.

Living at the bottom of a steep hill with only an ancient sunken lane for access it was easy for us to become snowed in and cut off from the rest of the world but we more frequently became iced in. Starkly clear nights of spectacular but cruelly clear starlight and moonshine gave way in the daytime to wide blue skies and blazing – if short lived – sunshine which would melt the surface of the ice only to be refrozen again by the plummeting temperatures the next night.

The result was a hillside lane with a slick and smoothly frozen surface up which no vehicle could gain enough traction to make it to the top. My father would spend weekday mornings playing the game of revving the engine and then setting off along our flat driveway with his foot as close to the floor as he dare get it. The object was to go as fast as possible in the hopes that the momentum would take us up the steepest bit to where the land began to even out and he could carry on the rest of the way. One of the main problems to this plan was that there was a relatively sharp bend to the right directly outside our gateway so that no matter what speed he picked up along the driveway he had to slow down to some extent and even then, he would run the risk of starting to slide from side to side all up the track so that whichever vehicle he was driving looked more like it was dancing the 'twist' than seriously travelling forward.

I was usually called on to assist in these often futile efforts… walking back down the hill to retrieve spades, sacks, buckets of ashes or bags of salt and sometimes even planks of wood. On occasion I was also used as ballast and dumped in the back of a van with sacks of provender or coal to help weight the back wheels so that the tyres gripped the surface of the lane more efficiently. Clinging on tightly to anything solid as we hurtled over the roughly potholed surface was exhilarating but exhausting. Sometimes the strategy worked and we would career wildly up the lane, tyres spinning and grinding, belching clouds of exhaust fumes and the stink of hot rubber, wildly careering and not daring to slow down or lose momentum. One and a half miles later we would shoot out onto the tarmacadamed and completely frost-free road on the edge of town like an angry metal cork from a picturesque white bottle.

There were times when our attempts were in vain and we would regroup back at the cottage to fortify ourselves with large mugs of steaming tea and cocoa and slabs of sticky parkin or flaky, thickly buttered squares of Chorley Cake oozing syrupy black currants. My father would usually have to change his clothes having fallen on the treacherous lane more than once and then he would stoically walk the three miles into town to where he worked.

I was far luckier and got to stay at home. Apart from having to also walk the three miles into town I would then have missed my connecting buses to school meaning that it would be lunchtime before I could finally arrive there. My parents didn't like to think of a six- or seven-year-old child wandering around on her own catching buses and walking around quiet streets unaccompanied. Gleefully I would race back upstairs to my bedroom and tear off my detested bottle- green school uniform. My morning would then be free to help my mother with her baking in the warm and steamy kitchen or curl up by the range to read a book or play with my beloved doll's house or model railway. Later in the afternoon my mother and I would sit beside a blazing fire and out would come books and maps and we would read together or discuss history, literature and philosophy and the faraway places where many of our friends lived and all the different customs they practiced and foods that they ate. So, my education would continue in a different form and it is little wonder that, once back at school, I found the maths, spelling and comprehension of a formal classroom so limiting and boring.

Now I do not live down in a valley but up a hill, so it is possible to have similar problems in reverse – we can easily get out but not in again. At least the hill is short, even if it is steep, and the surface of the road tarmacked. However, it does sometimes freeze and produce the familiar sheet of ice and my husband has been known to take a wheelbarrow down the hill for an extra sack of coal from the merchant at the bottom, or further up the hill to distribute fresh milk and bread and home baked treats to elderly neighbours.

Always be aware of others around you who may be finding extremes of weather a strain on both their physical, emotional and financial resources. This doesn't just apply to the elderly either – even in our centrally heated and electrically lit homes it can affect people of any age and disposition. Mothers at home with young children instantly spring to mind, or fulltime carers. Yes, to a degree we are all shy and don't wish to appear interfering but better end up with a metaphorical flea in your ear or a red face rather than have someone close by suffering in loneliness and desperation.

Extremes of weather (and not just in winter) give us a good excuse to knock on a neighbours door or speak to them in the street; enquire if there is anything they need getting when you next go to the local shops or into town, or would they like to share the journey and come with you? Take them some hot homemade lemon cordial or biscuits. Or invite them round for a hot drink or meal with you. It doesn't matter if it is only baked beans on toast – sitting in someone else's warm house with someone to talk to for a while can provide a much-needed break and be a real life saver. You may need a similar act of friendship in return yourself one day. Admittedly most people will smile and gently refuse, but at least they know that the offer is there and that there is someone close by who has noticed that they exist and care.

If you do get the opportunity to get to know your neighbours better, exchange phone numbers so that you mutually always have someone you can turn to. If someone lives alone, especially if they are not steady on their feet, get them to give you three rings on the phone every night once they are safely inside their house – it doesn't cost anything except a little thought. And no, I am not being overly dramatic. I well remember soon after we first moved to this part of Wales there was a case reported in the local newspaper of a forty-year-old woman living in a village a few miles away who had been going home one winter teatime. She was walking up her garden path and slipped and fell and broke her leg. On the edge of the village no one heard her cries. It was bitterly cold that night. The milkman found her the next morning. Unfortunately, due to shock and hypothermia she hadn't made it through the night and had died before help could reach her.

No, we are not our brother or sister's keeper. Of course not. But we do all live in a community and have a joint moral responsibility for one another. It is not enough to simply pass by on the other side of the road. Ultimately the buck stops here… with YOU. However, you will also benefit. Taking responsibility and involving ourselves in our surroundings also increases our sense of personal empowerment and gives us greater feelings of self-worth, adequacy and position, not to mention friendship and company. Thinking of Valentine's Day, as I mentioned previously, love can show itself in many different guises – so be an ambassador for unconditional care and love… start today.

FLOCKS IN THE WILDERNESS

As a child I well remember that in icy times such as these, even the paths through the leafless and unprotected woods would be frozen and treacherous and the fields could become skating rinks so that there was no possibility of walking safely anywhere which meant that I was effectively stuck indoors. I loved to watch the birds especially at this time of year – the blue tits having conversations and sparring with themselves in the wing mirrors of the vehicles; the robins who would sit singing in the damson tree by the back door and the little tree creepers – pale brown shadows fleetingly glimpsed moving up and down the ridged trunks of the hawthorn outside the living room window. Then there were the clouds of birds which descended three times a day on our driveway where my mother put out rolled barley (which came in hundredweight sacks) and other grains, bread, apples and peelings for them: sparrows, wrens, tits, bullfinches, starlings, woodpeckers, blackbirds, thrushes, woodpigeons, jays and magpies and even the waterhens from the river. My father would grunt that we were the only cottage to have birds too heavy to get off the ground and fly and that we might as well be keeping poultry and getting something back for all our efforts. He had a point. We once counted twenty-four waterhens feeding and sometimes in the worst of the weather we would even have ducks and heron drop by. Despite our numerous cats, the bird population prospered.

Unfortunately, times have changed and here in our village in North Wales the birds are not nearly so numerous or varied. We have lots of fluttery little house sparrows who descend in a small cloud for the mixed seeds I put out for them. We also have blackbirds and the occasional robin or tit and sometimes magpies and a nesting pair of collared doves; but we have lots of starlings and jackdaws – even a seagull or two if the weather has been stormy enough to drive them the three miles inland. Unfortunately the little birds seem intimidated by the larger ones. I have tried various feeders and bird tables over the years but the smallest birds prefer their seeds scattered amongst the canes in the raspberry patch where they can feast in the sunshine without fear of feline or avian predator; the starlings and blackbirds love the flat top of the wall outside my kitchen widow, the latter often disdaining the seed I put there, giving me Paddington 'hard stares' until I relent and throw them some of their much-preferred bread.

The jackdaws will eat just about anything and are very noisy and bossy but great company and I love to sit with my morning cup of tea and watch their courting relationships develop. One couple of jackdaws have their territory in our old fir tree and there I see them perched together like the old couple they are, sat hunched side by side, one periodically turning to look at the other as if they are passing comments on the state of the world that morning. Every so often one or the other with utch up closer to the other. The partner will often return such approaches with a sudden look or respond by sidling further away along the straight expanse of branch. Sometimes this carries on until the end of the branch is reached and suddenly the pursued partner will suddenly take off into harassed flight, landing on another branch further down the tree, only for the whole process to begin all over again.

In these days of loss of habitat and food sources and threat from pollution and chemical poisoning our once prolific and prosperous wildlife needs all the support it can get. Man is not an island and having stolen or destroyed the natural resources belonging to our local wildlife it is our responsibility to give something back to them – not because it is something we enjoy but because we ALL owe it the living creatures we have so cruelly and thoughtlessly deprived. It doesn't matter how little it might be, as long as it is consistent through the harsh winter months and even on into the spring as birds work themselves to a frazzle to feed and bring up their young when some easier but appropriate food source is usually extremely welcome. So have a think about what you can do to assist our feathered friends. All of us can hang at least one feeder outside a window. Bird nuts and seeds are usually cheaper if bought in larger amounts. You may even wish to make your own fat balls. And yes, please do wholeheartedly enjoy the entertaining and beautiful spectacle which you will invite into your garden or windowsill in the process. We are back to Saint Valentine and our message of love for all – let's spread some around our natural world too.

FEED THE BIRDS

It doesn't necessarily have to cost a lot to provide some provender for our little feathered friends. These days we are often told how much human food we waste and some – although not all – is good for birds too. So, before you hurry down to your local pet shop, look at what you have in your own larder of fridge first.

Bread of any sort is traditionally fed to birds of all kinds and this is fine as long as it is a part of a more varied diet. It has little nutritional value to birds but acts as a good filler so long as they have other sources of protein. In parts of the country it has recently been discovered that populations of ducks and swans who have been deprived of their bread rations by a newly aware and concerned public have been suffering from malnutrition and some have even died of starvation, so please don't stop altogether, just be aware that they need other types of food too.

Garden birds are unable to metabolise salt and it is toxic to them, but bacon rinds finely chopped or ground (and as long as they aren't too salty) are fine to give the tits. Baked, roast or mashed potatoes (but not chips) are also welcome. Apples, pears or other fruit, including bruised or part rotten ones cut up are very popular with thrushes, tits and starlings. Pastry, cooked or raw, and if it is made with real fats, is excellent. Cooked rice – white or brown and without additional salt – is readily accepted by all species during severe winter weather conditions. Uncooked porridge oats are also welcomed by some. Dog and cat food can be an acceptable substitute for earth worms, but dry biscuit may be too hard or cause choking so always soak well first before putting out.

Polyunsaturated margarines and vegetable oils are unsuitable for birds as are fats which have already been used in the frying pans and roasting tins when cooking. It is a breeding ground for bacteria and also has negative implications with the salt which has been added to the cooking food. However, it can be very satisfying to make your own fat cakes or balls and something which children might like to become involved with or even take over as one of their personal responsibilities. To make your own, use about 1/3rd fat to 2/3rds ingredients. Melt beef suet or lard and add a mixture of things such as sunflower or nyjer seeds, nuts, dried fruit which has first been soaked, pinhead oatmeal, cheese or cake. Add your chosen ingredients to the melted fat and mix well. Fill containers of your choice – empty coconut shells, plastic cups or tit bells make ideal bird feeders – and allow to set hard. Alternatively, you can leave the whole mixture to set in its bowl and then turn out onto your bird table or cut up into chunks and fill your feeders that way.

If you are filling your bird feeders you may like to consider who really needs what; black sunflower seed, sunflower heads and nyjer seeds are particularly attractive to goldfinches, siskins, greenfinches, tits, house sparrows, nuthatches and great spotted woodpeckers.

PLEASE NOTE: Birds die because of bacteria carrying salmonella and other harmful illnesses from filthy feeders and bird tables, so please keep a separate scrubbing brush and give all your feeders a good scrub in hot water once a week – finish off by pouring a kettle of boiling water over them to help sterilise. Don't use any soap or detergent as it may contain ingredients harmful to wildlife.

Grated cheese and grated or crushed peanuts (but *never* salted or dry roasted) attract robins, dunnocks and wrens. Peanuts can be high in aflatoxin, a natural toxin which can kill birds, so buy good quality nuts from a reputable dealer. Robins, blue tits and other insect-eating birds such as pied wagtails will greatly appreciate fresh meal worms.

Similarly, some domestic foods which are fine for birds are harmful to dogs and cats so make sure that other animals can't eat your bird food by mistake. Also be aware of where you are putting your bird food and the fact that it may attract vermin such as mice and rats.

Water! Birds, just like any other living thing, need a supply of clean, fresh water all the year round. People might become aware of water shortages in fine, warm, sunny weather but rarely realise that water shortages in freezing temperatures can also become desperate. Birds and animals do not consume anything that is too hot or too cold, which includes frost and snow. So please, try and supply water all year round – a large dish or an upturned dustbin lid will do just fine – unless you have the space and inclination to build a pond in your garden which would be even better. Again, keep your container(s) cleaned regularly and fill with fresh water. In icy cold conditions a fresh container may need putting out once or twice each day while the frozen one is brought inside to thaw! Also remember that birds need water to bath and clean themselves, although in hot dry conditions they will use dust baths instead.

Lastly, while you may be planning what you are going to grow in your gardens during the coming summer, again, please bear our avian population in mind. Berry-bearing trees and shrubs such as hawthorn, rowan, holly, honeysuckle and ivy will not only provide fruit for birds to feed on but will also give them somewhere to shelter from both the weather and predators, offer good nesting sites and attract insects for them to eat. Cultivated and wild flowering plants such as sunflowers, evening primrose, fennel, teasel and shepherd's purse provide both seeds to eat and attract insects. Leave the stems long through the winter and only cut down in early spring. In summer allow your lawn to grow slightly longer and, if possible, leave areas of grass at different heights to optimise food potential for the birds and in winter try to leave a patch of long grass in which they might shelter.

HALFTERM HOLIDAYS

Regardless of the lack of the white stuff when I was a small child, by the time I reached my early teens the weather fell into the pattern of providing a few cold, snowy days around early to mid-February to bring a final climax to winter before spring truly arrived. This cold snap could last from two or three days up to a fortnight and was particularly well-timed as it usually coincided with school half term holidays. My foster sister would also travel home from her boarding school in Kent for her half term break. Lynne might have been two and a half years older than me and, in her mid-teens, seemingly far more sophisticated and grown up, but when it came to playing out in the snow, all that was completely forgotten.

Long days were spent in the neighbouring fields with our toboggans, where we carefully constructed icy runs to avoid the frozen tussocks of grass which lurked beneath the innocent white mantle of snow. Struck at speed they could so easily send a toboggan and rider flying into the air. One of my school friends, Laura , and her younger brother and sister would walk down across the fields from the neighbouring village and come and join us. From just after breakfast until the daylight had completely faded, we made the very most of the weather conditions. Feet would become numb with cold as snow found its way down inside wellington boots… hands like scarlet blocks of ice as woollen mittens became sodden with melted snow. No matter how carefully dressed, powdery white crystals would inveigle themselves up sleeves, under scarves, inside hats and hoods and down collars, especially if a toboggan went too fast and was unable to stop before hitting the fallen willow tree at the bottom of the field which would then send the hapless rider sprawling deep into snowy drifts.

Sometimes we would pause to build a snowman- a seasonal stranger to greet other walkers taking that path. Laura's little brother, Ralph, would inevitably begin to bombard it with snowballs and soon we would all be drawn into a chaotic battle with no allies and no quarter given while icy missiles were wildly flung in all directions. The valley would echo with our shrill cries of outraged delight.

Several times throughout the day, we would all troop back through the wood along the path by the river to our cottage to be restored by my endlessly patient and hospitable mother. Multiple layers of wet outdoor clothing were peeled away and set to dry by the fire while dry socks and gloves were found for everyone. Mugs of hot cocoa were thrust into nerveless hands and huge platers of hot, homemade burgers or hot dogs were set down among us to be fallen upon ravenously and devoured within minutes. There is nothing so sharp set as an appetite created by playing in the snow for several hours.

However, our very favourite sustenance were the huge deep and creamy yellow cheesecakes which my mother loved to make. These were baked following an old recipe which she had received from a family of Austrian Jews who had been friends and business associates of my grandfather. It was in the days before cheesecake became a popular and common dessert in our supermarket chiller cabinets. These confections were giants compared to the puny, mass-produced treats and had a half inch crunchy base with a solid creamy layer two and a half inches thick above that. My mother used to top all this off with mounds of tinned pineapple and strawberries and dollops of freshly whipped cream. A hefty wedge so adorned was a full meal in itself and used to fortify us for the rest of the afternoon until well after dark.

How can one possibly remember such exhaustion and discomfort with such fondness and glee? Yet those joyful, carefree days remain entrenched in my memory as times of pure freedom and bliss. Lynne obviously felt that way too. She regularly manufactured reasons not to return from her spring half-term holiday on time – sometimes a whole week late! The first time the reason was legitimate due to very bad weather conditions, but after the third consecutive year of excuses and late appearance, Lynne's headmistress – a Lancashire woman herself – informed her errant pupil that if it happened again, she needn't return at all. The following spring the weather assisted Wynne's punctuality and saved her from possible disgrace by not providing any snow at all!

Cheesecake Yahni

Ingredients

1 ½ lb (550 g) cream cheese (cottage cheese will do)
6 oz (170 g) sugar
1 ½ tablespoons flour
¾ teaspoon each of grated lemon and orange rind
¼ teaspoon vanilla essence
3 eggs (6 if small)
1 egg yolk
2 tablespoons double cream

Cookie Crust:

¼ lb (110 g) flour
2 oz (50 g) sugar
teaspoon grated lemon rind
A few scrapings from a vanilla bean
8 oz (225 g) butter
1 egg yolk

Method

Cookie crust:

- Mix all cookie crust ingredients together with wooden spoon and pat or spread into bottom and sides of a nine-inch springform pan.
- Bake in pre-heated oven (hot, 400°F/200°C.) for ten minutes or until lightly browned.

Filling:

- Have cheese and eggs at room temperature. Cream the cheese until softened.
- Beat in the sugar, flour, grated orange and lemon rind and vanilla essence altogether.

- *Add the eggs and one egg yolk, one at a time, beating well after adding each, (I whip the eggs first as well).*
- *Stir in the cream and pour into the baked crust.*
- *Bake in preheated, very slow oven (250°F/120°C.) for one hour or until firm.*
- *Cool. Either top with strawberry glaze or crushed pineapple and whipped double cream.*

Jill didn't used to be fond of cheesecake but now she adores it – Jim says the name 'cheesecake' is off-putting, so we are thinking of a new one – Ricky just groans, points to his tummy and talks of slimming!

Note: Cookie crust costs 1/4d (7p) if made with Stork margarine. Filling 7/6d (38 ½ p). It will easily cut into 12 portions so is very reasonable. (Prices from 1968, when my mother listed them in her manuscript cookery book as 3d (1p) for the sugar, 4/9d (24p) for the cream cheese and 1/2d (6p) for six small eggs.)

Chapter Five

Carnival, Shrovetide and Lent

'Work with your virtues, rather than against your faults'
Anonymous

Each year I am saddened when radio stations cease to play Christmas music after Boxing Day, decorations are all put away after the 1st January and all celebration is banished. Little wonder that so many people become depressed! Traders hurry to set up displays of Valentine and Easter goods before the end of the first week in January... even before the 6th January, the date of the traditional ending of the Twelve Days of Christmas. Here in the Celtic lands, historically the celebration of Christmas only drew to a close with the end of the month of January, the coming of very early spring and the celebration of Gwyl Ffraid / Imbolc / Candlemas.

In other words, the celebration of Christmas was, in reality, the celebration of Winter, a time when the exigencies of bad weather forced the agrarian population to spend most of their time indoors. What better way to while away one's snow- and frost-bound days than by catching up on all the domestic spinning, knitting and mending and all the smaller agricultural tasks of repairing and making while stories were told, music played, contests and games entered into, and copious amounts of food and drink consumed? Folk didn't have a few days of Christmas cheer and then shuffle off into their dark, sparse and cheerless little houses to sit huddled against the elements alone. They gathered together in each other's houses and drew together in each other's warmth and company until the worst of the weather and darkness had passed.

It also appears to have been so for other communities around the Northern Hemisphere. In Hungary they celebrate Farsang, meaning carnival, which begins on the 6th January as Christmas finishes and the Christmas Trees are taken down and put out. It is a period marked by the eating of rich foods and the enjoyment of many colourful and loud celebrations, masquerades and balls. It was also traditionally a time for weddings. This season has always been quiet for agricultural workers when little could be done outside on the land and time could be spared to prepare for (often hundreds) of guests to take part in and enjoy the whole celebration.

Farsang lasts between one and two months, depending on the date which Easter falls and Lent begins, (there is an explanation of this later in the chapter). The high point of the whole period comes with Farsang Farka, 'the tail of Farsang', which is celebrated during the last three days before Lent begins on Ash Wednesday. It is an almost manic last burst of merriment and fun culminating on Shrove Tuesday with the construction and burning of scarecrow-type figures. As we shall see later in the chapter, this burning (or in some cases, drowning) of effigies to signify the death of Winter and the onset of spring is quite common across Northern Europe.

FIRST THINGS FIRST... CARNIVAL TIME!

Many of us are familiar with the celebration of 'Carnival' some time in February, which is more generally thought of as the last big glitzy bash before gobbling up all our pancakes. After that we enter Lent, the six or so weeks which precede Easter when we might giggle and joke about 'giving something up' – especially chocolate.

This gross simplification of a whole chunk of our annual calendar does it a grave mis-service. In the Twenty-First Century we like to think of ourselves as liberated and fun-loving party animals, but in the past there were a remarkable number of occasions when society openly and actively encouraged and supported its members in casting off the tight restraints of 'good behaviour' and throwing morals and manners to the four winds in total rip-roaring celebration. Traditionally these were times when everyone was not only allowed to act out of character, eat and drink to excess, face and destroy their fears, and put their lords and employers in positions of ridicule and subjugation but openly expected to actively take part in doing so. Many scores could be settled, grudges served, and resentments played out relatively harmlessly in a spirit of celebratory exuberance watched over and condoned by the great and the good. A seasonal opportunity to 'let off steam'.

Generally speaking, Carnival is seen as the western Christian and Greek Orthodox festive season which occurs before the liturgical season of Lent, some time in February or early March. It typically involves public celebrations such as parades and street parties with an element of circus about them. Traditionally there is also the use of elaborate costumes and masks allowing people to set aside everyday individuality and engender social unity. Again, it also provides the opportunity for anonymous satire of the authorities, overturning everyday normal values. In modern times, carnival is widely celebrated in Portuguese, Spanish and Italian speaking countries, as well as other areas of Europe, the name deriving from the mediaeval Latin *carnelevamen* which means the 'putting away of the flesh', one aspect of Lent being to abstain from eating meat. The most famous of these extravaganzas is the Brazilian Carnival in Rio de Janeiro.

In some places, these amazing sensory spectacles of music, rhythm and colour are known by the French name of *Mardi Gras*, meaning 'Fat Tuesday' which doesn't sound nearly as exotic but, again, demonstrates this as a time to eat up all the remaining fats in the household before the coming of Lent.

Holi is a Hindu festival of Nepal and India which celebrates the end of Winter and the beginning of spring. It begins on the day of the last full moon of the Hindu luni-solar calendar month, and, as with so many events, the date varies with the lunar cycle and typically occurs in March but can also take place in early February. Holi celebrates that the dark , bitter days of Winter are at an end and good has once more triumphed over evil so it becomes a time of new beginnings, a good time to forgive and forget, to attend to one's relationships… to put a period to past errors, end conflicts and enter into forgiveness of past wrongs, in oneself and others… to rid oneself of accumulated past emotional impurities… to finally pay one's debts but to also forgive the debts of others… to wipe the slate clean and begin again. All colours of the rainbow are thrown indiscriminately in the streets and it is a time of singing and dancing, of laughter, jest… of visiting friends and extending hospitality… of treats… of bonfires… love and the sheer joy of just being alive.

Another interesting example of carnival takes place in Slovenia with Kurentovanje, a celebration which lasts for several days up to the beginning of Lent and which consists of parades, masked balls, concerts, children's events, and licentious behaviour. The central figure is Kurent, a big shaggy creature with a long red tongue, horns, snout, whiskers and two red-ringed eyes. He represents an ancient fun-loving Slavonic pagan god of hedonism – a Slovenian Bacchus – whose role is to scare off Winter. His costume is made of stinking sheep hide from which five heavy cowbells are hung. On the Sunday before Ash Wednesday, there is a big parade with men cracking bullwhips, ploughmen to 'waken the soil', giant hens to lay fertile eggs for Easter and horses representing lively healthy livestock. An old woman carries an old man signifying carrying the memories of departed Ancestors. Oranges are tossed to the crowd as a sign of the bounty of the warmer weather which is soon to come.

Germany approaches things slightly differently with processions on Shrove Monday – especially popular and famous in Cologne, Dusseldorf and Mainz – which features a court fool or jester type character. He carries an owl on his shoulder, symbolising his wisdom, and in his hand he carries a looking glass with which to show the people who they really are. He plays lots of pranks and tricks, openly flouting authority and making fun of well-known figures. In Erfurt, a large mediaeval city in the centre of Germany, there is a ceremony on the Saturday before Shrovetide begins in which the jester is presented with the key to the town hall, but it is definitely back in the councils possession again by the dawning of Ash Wednesday!

It strikes me as very typically British that, instead of some colourful occasion full of song and dance, we should traditionally choose to play football. Yes, it is true. But these was not the sedate games of our modern times but mass or mob football which involved an unlimited number of players and very few rules, the general idea being to score goals at opposite ends of the town or village or wherever the game was being held.

Mass football had been popular in mediaeval and early modern Europe since the Thirteenth Century. But the game was often undisciplined and violent, causing damage to property and injury to participants and spectators alike. It was regarded as an unsavoury waste of time and energy, distracting the working man away from more useful and profitable occupation. All these factors contributed to the many attempts to get the game banned in both Britain and France.

With the Enclosure Acts of the Eighteenth Century and the resultant social unrest which this contributed to, the call for mass football to be played was now used as a cover for violent protest, a pretext for organised riot with 'teams' of five hundred men or more causing thousands of pounds worth of damage. In 1835, the British Highway Act finally banned the playing of football on public highways and gave a maximum penalty of forty shillings to anyone who 'shall play at football or any other game on any part of the said Highways, to the annoyance of any passengers.' Who amongst us realised that when we were playing out as kids, kicking a football around in the road or street, we were actually breaking the law!

As with many things, people manage to get around the various difficulties and restrictions imposed upon them and some of these community Shrovetide matches still continue to this day. In the town of Ashbourne in Derbyshire, a 'Royal Shrovetide Football Match' is still played on Shrove Tuesday and Ash Wednesday. A similar event takes place in Atherstone, Warwickshire and

Sedgefield, County Durham. In Saint Columb Major in Cornwall they 'Hurl the Silver Ball' while in Alnwick, Northumberland, they play 'Scoring the Hales'.

Pancakes
Spring 1964

There are many forms of pancakes - large, small, thick, thin, sweet, savoury – made with a variety of flours. Originally, the pancake was peasant fare; something very basic, quick, and easy to fill hungry stomachs in the middle of a busy working day, when there was only an open fire to cook on.

Now all manner of 'wraps' and tortillas are immensely popular but let us not forget our own heritage with oat cakes, Scotch pancakes, drop scones, and Yorkshire pudding (to name just some) being related to our humble pancake. A plain pancake with the traditional sugar and lemon (followed by a piece of raw fruit) is a balanced breakfast, lunch or supper dish. Your kids and loved ones might think that they are getting an indulgent treat, but they are just another way of serving up a cooked egg with a slice of toast and jam.

So, get out your thick-bottomed frying pan, your planc, griddle or skillet, and get beating the eggs!

Ingredients

4 oz / 110 g self raising flour
2 eggs
¼ pint / 150 ml of liquid (milk, water, or milk and water mixed)
Pinch of salt if making for savoury fillings

Method

- *Mix ingredients together in a bowl – a good brisk whisk with a balloon whisk will do the trick – to make a batter. (How thin or thick you want your pancakes to be is entirely up to you and depends on how much liquid you add.)*
- *Heat your lightly oiled or buttered pan over a moderate to hot heat – it should almost be smoking and sizzle if you let a few drops of batter fall on the surface.*
- *Ladle some batter into the pan. How large or thick you want your pancake to be depends on how much batter you use for each pancake. I generally use a soup scoop full for each one, but you can measure the batter in tablespoons if you like – three or four.*
- *Cook for a minute or two until golden with the edges beginning to lift up and curl back from the pan. The pancake is now ready to turn over. Slip a fish slice (these days you might use a palette knife or something similar) under the pancake and quickly lift it and flip it over onto the other side. Make sure that the pancake is lying flat against the surface of the pan with no folds or wrinkles.*
- *Cook for another minute, then turn out onto a warm plate.*
- *Continue to cook the rest of the batter, serving them as you cook or stacking them on a plate in a warm oven.*

Fillings

Have whatever you are going to fill your pancakes with ready assembled before you begin to cook them so that you can quickly fill each one while the next one is cooking.

SAVOURY FILLINGS can be absolutely anything but chopped cooked meats, grated cheeses or mixed salads are quick, easy and simple. There are many recipes you can look up for more complex cooked fillings. Gooey gruyere and smoked ham make a special treat or as a rich starter to a celebratory dinner. Using up the ends of cheeses from the cheese board is another option, with a few strips of smoked

salmon and a sprig of watercress to top it off. Or why not set out bowls of hot or cold cooked veg, salad, chopped fresh herbs or spices and let everyone fill their own pancake as they come hot off the griddle?
NOTE: If you run out of bread, you can always run out a batch of slightly thicker, smaller pancakes and serve with bacon and scrambled eggs, or with jam instead of toast – delicious!

SWEET FILLINGS can, again, be made up from just about anything you can think of but you simply cannot go wrong with any combination of fresh or cooked fruit matched with chopped nuts and any flavour of ice cream or natural Greek yoghurt and/or thick whipped cream. And there is always the traditional favourite of a hefty sprinkle of sugar and a good squeeze of fresh lemon juice… or thick maple syrup.

SHROVETIDE

The word shrove, as in Shrovetide or Shrove Tuesday, derives from the word 'shrive' which means to be forgiven. Christians traditionally used this time to visit their confessor to be shriven (forgiven) their sins, to do penance and be ritually purified – and to be released from any guilt or pain they may have caused. Some Christians use Shrove Tuesday as a time of self-examination, of considering what wrongs they need to repent and what amendments of their life or areas of spiritual growth they especially need to ask God's assistance in dealing with.

In Britain, Shrovetide is the name given to the last few days before the beginning of Lent – a period of several weeks when, historically, practicing Christians were obliged to fast and deny themselves many types of food including meat, fish, fats, eggs and dairy produce. Families would feast before Lent began to use up all the foods which would not keep until the end of the forty-day Lenten period.

I do wonder just what most people *did* eat during this time of late winter and early spring. Before modern farming techniques and the year-round production of fruit, salad and vegetables, foods grown and harvested the previous summer and autumn would, by this time, be getting scarce. Thankfully, bread was still allowed and this, along with thin soups and gruels, was probably the staple diet of many people at this time of year anyway. Perhaps the observation of Lent provided a good reason (apart from dire necessity) to exist on very little and gave people spiritual fortitude to get them through annually lean and trying times.

Shrovetide developed into several days of prescribed feasting and celebration, beginning with Egg Saturday. Followed by Quinquagesima Sunday, the fiftieth day before Easter, depending on which way you are counting and which calendar you are using – more of this anon. Then there was Collop Monday, when collops of bacon were traditionally served with eggs for breakfast and the fat rendered from these would be used in the cooking of the pancakes the following day. In Cornwall, this was sometimes referred to as Peasen or Paisen Monday after the custom of eating peas porridge or pea soup on that day. The celebration ended with Shrove or Pancake Tuesday.

Shrovetide was generally celebrated with games, dancing, sports and revelries of all kinds. Games of football remained popular and continued to be played in the streets. In Cornwall 'Nickannan Night' was celebrated on the evening of Shrove Monday when boys would run riot through the towns and villages, hiding gates, taking door knockers and generally causing chaos and mayhem – reminiscent of the liminaly themed mischief of the 'Trick or Treaters' of Calan Gaeaf / Hallowe'en.

It has been suggested that the custom of eating pancakes the day before Lent begins can be dated back at least to the Sixteenth Century. This is hard to verify. Batter cooking, which also includes dishes like Yorkshire Pudding, Toad In The Hole, drop scones and oat cakes (the large soft pancakey ones), is an ancient form of cooking which is quick, simple and (originally) did not require the use of an oven.

In Newfoundland and Cape Breton Island, small tokens are frequently cooked into the pancakes – similar to the British tradition of including charms in the Christmas Pudding. It is easy to imagine the delight children take in discovering the objects which are divinatory by nature. For example, the person who receives a coin will be wealthy, a nail indicates that they will become or marry a carpenter, and so on.

Not only do we eat pancakes on Shrove Tuesday, but we also run pancake races. One can only speculate as to how this slightly bizarre tradition might have begun. How might all the good people have been enticed to begin running through the streets brandishing griddles and heartily tossing the contents as they went?

There is a charming little story about this. Shrove Tuesday was once a half-day holiday which began at 11 a.m. with the ringing of the church bell. It is said that in the year 1445, a housewife from Olney in Buckinghamshire was so busy making her pancakes that she forgot the time until she heard the church bell ringing, calling the congregation to prayer. The harassed woman dashed out of her house to the church whilst still carrying her griddle, tossing the pancake upon it all the way to prevent it from burning. Hummm…

The reason why Shrovetide and the beginning of Lent fall on different dates each year is that they measure out the last few weeks before Easter. The date for Easter varies from year to year because the time it is celebrated is calculated by the moon. Easter Sunday is decided by the first Sunday after the first full (paschal) moon after the Spring (Vernal) Equinox, which occurs on the 21st or 22nd March. Using the Gregorian Calendar – which is our regular, everyday calendar in the west – the very earliest Easter Sunday can fall is the 22nd March and the very latest date it can fall is the 25th April, which gives over a whole month of possible variance for all the other attendant celebrations to fit into our yearly and seasonal calendar.

To give an idea of when Shrovetide might most often occur, in the Twenty-first Century Pancake Tuesday takes place in February sixty one times – so well over half Shrovetides fall in that month. The earliest Shrove Tuesday can possibly be is the 3rd February and the latest it can occur is the 9th March.

COMMENT FROM JOAN: 2nd MARCH 1967

Began work on the terrace at the back of the cottage – found some old pavement about a foot down. Felt too fagged to do anything much so later had bonfire of storm wood in the glade. Man came about roto-cultivating ground – a trout fisherman who likes Alsatians* – reminded me of Daddy, He is coming to do garden next Saturday, or first fine day. First daffodil is out… my crocus are beautiful, rich purple. Need to order more cress and fertilizer. Letter from Monica this morning; just think it was only posted in Columbo on Tuesday, 28th.** Johnny Morris on Home Service 7 p.m.

LENT

The meaning of the word Lent comes from the old English word to 'lengthen', referring to springtime when the days begin to get noticeably longer.

In the Christian church, Lent is a period of preparation for Easter when the soul is cleansed through penitence and abstinence and giving things up. It is unclear but Lent has likely been observed since apostolic times, though the practice was not formalised until the First Council of Nicaea in 325 A.D. Certainly, by the end of the Fourth Century a forty-day period of preparation known as Lent existed with prayer and fasting being its primary spiritual exercises.

In western churches it begins on Ash Wednesday, six and a half weeks before Easter, and provides for a forty day fast (Sundays excluded) in imitation of Jesus Christ's experience of fasting and temptation in the wilderness before he began his public ministry. In eastern churches, Lent begins on the Monday of the seventh week before Easter and ends on the Friday that is nine days before Easter

---

* German shepherd dogs
** Monica Gunaratna– 'Aunty Monica' as I called her – was one of my mother's dearest friends whom she had met and spent time with when we were out in Ceylon/Sri Lanka. Some years later, Monica and her daughter, Srini, came to stay with us at Drybones.

and is known as Great Lent which includes both Saturdays and Sundays as relaxed fast days.

Ash Wednesday is the day after Shrove Tuesday. During a special church service, the priest draws a cross on the forehead of each member of the congregation with ash. This ash is prepared by burning palm branches which had been blessed and handed to the congregation the previous year on Palm Sunday, the last Sunday before Easter. (Palm Sunday celebrates Jesus' triumphal entry into Jerusalem when on-lookers spread palm branches in his path.) The ash symbolises the 'dust' – or earth – from which our physical bodies are composed. It is also a symbol of repentance with the focus also on victory over sin and death.

The order of the Sundays in Lent leading up to Easter was memorized in the following doggerel which can be traced back to '*A Dictionary of Englyshe and Welshe*' published by William Salesbury in 1547:

> "*Shrove Sunday, another Sunday, Sunday which comes,*
> *Sunday at hand, the Sunday of Sons, (Mothering Sunday)*
> *Peas' Sunday, (also known as Carling* Sunday) Flowering Sunday,*
> *Easter and its days.*"

Parched Peas
(also known as maple, carling or pigeon peas)

Ingredients

Quantity as desired of (dried) peas, steeped overnight in boiling water.

Method

- *Bring peas in pan of water to boiling point and simmer gently until tender but not mushy. I like to add a little salt to the cooking water but as salt is generally sprinkled over peas when served, it is a matter of taste. These peas can be eaten hot or cold, served as a vegetable but usually handed out on little saucers to eat with the fingers standing around winter bonfires or talking around the hearth.*

- *I remember when I was very small an old, old man (or so he seemed) used to stand at the end of Cumberland Terrace selling ½ d* worth from a large market basket covered with a snowy cloth, and sometimes I was actually permitted to buy some myself. He only came on Friday.*

It is strange to think that when my mother is referring to her young childhood she is talking about a time which is almost ninety years ago – another world altogether!

MAKING THE MOST OF IT ALL

Today, many of us in Britain – as with other parts of the world – do not represent any one particular religion, creed, race or cultural background. Yet these religious activities and celebrations are woven into the Twenty-first Century society in which we live. Christmas and Easter are the two main events of the year which are celebrated by millions of people around the globe while millions more at least know about them – and frequently pay them some form of lip service, if it is only to observe that trading will be slow or non-existent while they are taking place.

Many religious observances are based on much older celebrations which reflect the cycle of the seasons and our historic, long standing role within the natural world. This is easy to see when reading about all the carnival activities of a whole variety of countries and cultures – the death, execution or driving away of old Winter, however that is personified and played out, and the celebration of

* In today's decimal money this would be a fraction – about 1/6th of 1p.

the coming of Spring. People are people and remain very much attached to the ancient beliefs and activities which originated back in the dim mists of time.

I would like to encourage everyone to take some of these ideas and use them for their own personal seasonal celebrations. Think up ways in which you and your friends and family can celebrate the turning of the seasons. Is there a carnival which you can visit? Would you like to try and organise a 'carnival party', with dressing up or masks, fireworks and delicious foods? Or how about instigating one or two little customs of your own around the time of Shrovetide? Cook a meal with other dishes which feature eggs, such as omelettes or Anglesey Eggs – it doesn't have to be expensive or difficult. Organise games – it doesn't have to be outside, it could even be of some board game. Organise a treasure hunt around the house. Join in with a pancake race or organise one of your own. Have a competition for who can come up with the most tasty pancake fillings.

It is the little things which sometimes happen almost accidentally which can turn an ordinary drab day into something enjoyable and memorable.

WHAT MAKES A DAY SPECIAL?

When are your special days? A birthday or anniversary, perhaps? The start of your holidays? What is it that actually makes it special for you? Some unusual activity – going out for a sumptuous meal, perhaps, or doing something different... diving with sharks or sky diving, camping out in the wilds, climbing a mountain, attending a summer ball? But what about the special days, (like birthdays), on which you still have to work and attend to all the usual mundane chores... what makes them so special despite your lack of celebratory activity?

Remember when you were a child and the days which were simply magical because you had friends coming to play with you for the afternoon, or you were being taken for a special treat that evening... but the whole day was coloured by your anticipation and excitement and everything about it – even the boring and most ordinary – suddenly took on an extra sparkle? Why was that? The bed you had to make was just the same bed; the pots you had to help wash after breakfast were still the same pots; the homework you had to finish was just as dull or difficult. So, what was – or is – different about 'special days'?

I would suggest that what is different about certain times and occasions is you yourself. The sky is no bluer, the grass no greener, food no tastier, silly jokes no funnier, but everything appears better and larger than ordinary life *because* that is the way you are choosing to see it, because you know that it is a special day. Making the choice to approach and see everything differently makes it special. Nor do you have to have a valid reason to view it as special. Every day can be seen as special. Suppose you suddenly discovered that you only had one day left to live? That would make the most bland, rainy, annoying day incredibly special and precious... wouldn't it?

Every day is a blessing – an amazing gift of exciting potential and opportunity... to do something interesting, to try something new, to tenderly enjoy old and precious memories, to show people you care, to marvel at the sensations of joy and love, to enjoy the affection of your pet, to appreciate the beauty and wonder of the natural world all around us, to revel in a downpour of rain, to derive huge satisfaction from even the smallest task well done.

We all have problems and difficulties in our lives... concerns about our work, business, financial status; physical handicaps, illness or health scares, (for ourselves and loved ones), worries over our children, our animals, our local communities... Can you actually do anything about them *today*? If you can, that is wonderful! Go and do it and today will automatically become a special day in a different way because you became empowered and took charge of your life and made a positive difference.

More often than not, we are powerless to change or improve whatever it is that is bothering us. Very often it actually concerns someone else and it is neither possible nor appropriate for us to even attempt to effect change. So, if you can't alter your life for the better, ask yourself if this particular concern is going to directly impact your day *today*? If not, then do the little exercise I have mentioned before; imagine a great carved wooden chest, or a beautifully decorated box with a silken lining; see your worries as physical items in front of you and imagine literally picking them up or firmly ordering them into the box. Imagine slamming the lid shut and turning the key in the lock and then take the key and imagine putting it into your pocket. You now have control over your fears and worries because you have contained them and put them out of the way where, at least temporarily, they cannot hurt you. Nor can they get out to harass you unless you allow them to because you hold the key.

Now your concerns are out of the way, you have a whole day – *this day* – in which to achieve something… to enjoy… to *live*. It is your very own day, which makes it incredibly special. What are you going to do with it?

I fondly remember when I was a young single mother. Occasionally, my mother would arrive with a couple of my favourite cakes which were sold at the village grocer's – very large pale pink fondants with the softest, lightest sponge beneath the sticky sweet icing. She would put the kettle on and while it came to the boil, she would organise my little son to play at something quietly, then we would enjoy half an hour of peaceful talk over our cup of tea and cake. It brought a ray of pure gold into my otherwise exhausting and sometimes fraught day. Or she would pop out to the village shop and return with some succulent lamb chops which she would lightly fry for our evening meal and serve with dainty slices of soft buttered bread. As I relaxed, the conversation would flow, laughter would be heard and the whole atmosphere would lighten and lift and my harassing day would end as a bright and happy memory.

As a young and single mother, I experienced some dark and lonely days, just like anyone else. But in choosing to nurture my little son's day, I usually discovered my own comfort and salvation. After walking back from the shops in the pouring rain, I would decide to finish my work early and set out a tea tray with crumpets to toast, or thick slices of bread. I'd get the room all nice and warm and possibly light a candle or switch on the side lamps to make the dull room jolly; ask my son to choose a story book and then spend a cosy hour toasting by the fire while we read and talked – invaluable quality time spent with my little one on the back of an unpleasant or tiring day. Or I would decide to purposefully wrap us both up and go for a glorious tramp through the rain and wind, purposely jumping in every muddy puddle and revelling in getting thoroughly wet… or spend the morning busily baking in the kitchen with the (dubious) assistance of my three year old. He learned that time spent helping me to make cakes in the kitchen earned him tea and stories by the fire and even now that he is in his early thirties, we both still love to come together for a blessed hour of 'time out' when we cut into soft eggy sponge cake and pour amber streams of liquid into china cups as we chew over the day's activities and news.

Do not forget to nurture yourself and give yourself time and treats. Even if it is only a fifteen-minute break in a hectic day, plan it and carry it out. Be honest with yourself. Say to yourself – and everyone else – this next fifteen minutes is mine, and don't feel guilty about it either. Have a favourite beverage to drink or snack to nibble on. Listen to some of your favourite music, close your eyes and put your feet up – literally! – placing your feet higher than your head is good for your body in lots of ways. Indulge. You will be all the more ready and efficient afterwards. Invest in yourself.

Yes, you choose to see your day in a certain way but sometimes we are up too close or too weighed down to make the effort. Do you know someone who might appreciate you changing the tenor of their day, as my mother did for me? Sometimes, when we cannot find the energy or impulse to do this for ourselves, we can still manage to do it for someone else – and miraculously, when we weave this simple magic formula for others, we find that it has also worked its spell on us too.

A Natural Spring Decoration

Just because Christmas is long gone and Easter is almost as far into the future, there is no reason not to have some form of decoration in our homes, something which represents the time of year and, again, brings the outside in.

Find a log of wood. You might do this by taking a walk somewhere out in the country where there are trees. But beware! Do not move wood which has lain for some time and disturb all the insects which will have made it their home since it came to rest on the ground. Nor should you take too much. You are looking for a piece around 12" - 14" (30 – 35 cm) long. You might be able to beg or buy a log from someone who supplies firewood. Any way round, you are after a nice smooth clean log, or one that has an interesting, irregular shape, perhaps with a junction of another branch coming off it. Even better if it has ivy already growing around it, but if not, you might like to carefully cut a length of ivy from a wall, the ground in the park or a churchyard. Always be careful to take very little, only as much as you need, never to damage the rest of the plant and never to leave a mess where you have harvested from.

Take your log home and brush it off and dry it out by leaving it somewhere warm for a couple of days. Cover a metal tea tray or a chopping board with silver kitchen foil. It must be large enough to accommodate the log and this will provide a safe and fireproof stand for it. (Also, you might also wish to cover your stand in green fabric, like velvet – to mimic soft green grass – or some other colourful material, but that might constitute more of a fire hazard, so you didn't read it here.)

Using the log as a stand and backdrop, you can now decorate over and around the log with mosses, sprigs of catkins, twigs sporting large and obvious buds like the coal black ash or sycamore, candles, tealights, little pots of spring bulbs or tiny vases of cut flowers – snowdrops, celandine, primroses and early primulas, coltsfoot and crocus look especially nice. If you know someone – or yourself – who has a very broad drill bit, you can make holes in your log to securely hold tea lights or candles. Otherwise, stand them around the log – at a safe distance so that there is no danger of it catching fire – firmly fixed into proper candle holders. You might wish to make a couple of spring fir cone gnomes (see Chapter Twelve), or some little snowdrop and crocus figures as found in the book '*All Year Round - A Calendar Of Celebrations*' by Druitt, Fynes-Clinton and Rowling.

Make sure that you position your log decoration somewhere not in direct heat and also not in a draft while its candles are lit. Such decorations can be left for days or even weeks if it is in a cool place, just don't forget to water any rooted plants and check water levels in containers of cut flowers.

This type of decoration makes a lovely centre piece for a spring dinner party, or a display on a windowsill, bookcase or table; or as a decoration for a birthday tea, perhaps with fairies or unicorns around it. Look at the natural world and see what it gives you at this time of the year. Yes, there are lovely fresh things to be seen and used. It isn't only for Midwinter festivities that we can turn to the natural world for seasonal decorations or for signs that the long winter is coming to an end which must surely gladden our hearts and bring us joy.

IDEAS TO HANG YOUR HAT ON

Admittedly, it is probably easier to have a specific idea, a framework, to focus your special day(s) on, and, at least to begin with, not attempt to do too much, too often. Perhaps you might think about having a little celebration for some reason every other week or so - remember that any outlook or activity can be habit-forming, so make them happy and repeatable.

There are many occasions throughout the entire year for you to choose from. Springtime is no exception. The month of March alone is positively bristling with celebratory dates.

On the 1st March there are three possible reasons to celebrate. In Lanark, Scotland there is Whuppity Scoorie when children run around the town bell near dusk swinging balls made from crumpled paper around their heads. They only stop when the bell rings at 6 p.m. after six months of silence during the desolate, dark winter days. Town officials believe it originated to chase away evil spirits before the start of spring. There is also Matronalia, the Roman feast of mothers and the renewal and reawakening of nature. Husbands were expected to give gifts to their wives.

For us here in Wales, it gives us a chance to wholeheartedly rejoice in our Celtic Welshness, for this is Saint David's Day, the patron saint of Wales. Daffodils are already blooming in many gardens and are brought in to decorate the home. They are also worn on lapels and in hats, for it is said that if Dewi Sant sees your daffodil on his special day, he will grant you a wish. Children dress up in national costume. Wales being known as a land of song, singing and concerts, (especially of choirs, Welsh hymns and traditional folk songs), and music, (particularly the harp and the Welsh triple harp) are definitely the order of the day. There are lots of traditional foods to choose from too; savoury dishes like cawl, Glamorgan sausages, Anglesey Eggs and sweet favourites such as bara brith and Welsh Cakes.

You can take your pick of saint's days during this month as there is also Saint Non's Day on the 3rd March. Non was the mother of Saint David and particularly special to me as I carry her name, Nonita, which is the Latin version of Non. Non actually means 'nun' and it was a joke amongst the family at home that I could be a 'nun' and a 'monk' at the same time! Our spiritual retreat on the Llyn peninsula is called Cae Non, which means Non's field and was so named by my son in honour of me finding it. But I digress!

Non was the daughter of Cynyr Ceinfarfog, lord of Dyfed. She was born in Pembrokeshire in the late Fifth Century AD. Unfortunately she was seduced or raped by Prince Sandde of Ceredigion and became pregnant. She gave birth to Dewi (David) at Caer Fai on the coast just south of Mynyw (where Saint David's is situated today). For some unknown reason, she was out in the middle of a raging thunderstorm. The tale is told of how Non, in the extreme agony of the birth, pressed her fingers into a nearby bolder so hard that she left their impression in the rock. When the babe was born, a brilliant white light surrounded him, the bolder was split in two by a dramatic lightning strike, and a spring of water gushed forth out of the ground. This sweet water became known as Saint Non's well and reputedly has the power to heal those who are mentally ill. Non brought Dewi up at Henfynyw near Aberaeron and later, together, they founded a nunnery at nearby Llanon. Later in life, Non moved to Cornwall and founded another nunnery at Alternon, ending her life in Brittany where she founded a third nunnery at Dirinon in Finistere.

There are several instances in early Celtic Christianity where young girls were violated or murdered by thwarted suitors and then mysteriously brought back to life to become saints and holy women. The archetypal significance of the storm, the light, the rock and the spring are also intriguing, as is the suggestion that Non's father, Cynyr Ceinfarfog, was the guardian to whom the infant King Arthur (he of the Knights of the Round Table) was entrusted, to be brought up at Caer Gynyr (later known as Caer Cai) near Bala in North Wales. When one also considers that Merlin first came to attention as a boy when he diagnosed the problem of the two warring dragons at Dinas Emrys just outside Beddgelert one might begin to think that there is far more to this than merely some pregnant lass giving birth in a storm. I feel that the numerous stories of the early Celtic saints of the Fourth, Fifth and Sixth Centuries are often amalgamations of much older tales and beliefs. They encapsulate something which resonates deeply within our cultural psyche and which has little to do with any modern religion, except that it was usually the monks within the confines of their monastic scriptoriums who first wrote these stories down.

Within the same month there is also Saint Piran's Day, (Cornwall), on the 5th March and Saint Patrick's Day, (Ireland), on the 17th March but there are many other equally lovely occasions to celebrate during the months of spring. In February, for the environmentally minded, there is World Wetland Day on the 2nd February. On the 13th February there is also World Radio Day for those who wish to celebrate this amazing invention which has brought not just joy and entertainment to billions of people around the world but also learning and connection too. Or if you prefer some more exotic and oriental, there is the Chinese lantern Festival on the 8th of the same month. Back into March there is the Japanese Doll Festival on the 3rd March, International Women's day on the 8th, the Tibetan Butter Lamp Festival on the 9th and World Contact Day on the 15th. Teenagers might appreciate celebrating World Sleep day on the 20th March. Nature lovers might be drawn to mark the International Day of Forests on the 21st March, or World Water Day on the 22nd, or even World Meteorological Day on the 23rd. But I feel that all of us can identify with occasions such as World Happiness Day which also takes place on the 20th, or Commonwealth Day which happens earlier in the month on the 9th.

However, there are two very special days which I consider supremely relevant to us all, wherever we might live in the world and wherever our ancestors might have originated from.

The first is Mother Language Day which takes place on the 21st February. It is to promote linguistic and cultural diversity and multilingualism. It was originally created by UNESCO, (The United Nations Education, Science and Cultural Organisation), to promote a fuller awareness of one's mother tongue, the linguistic and cultural traditions throughout the world and to inspire solidarity based on understanding, tolerance and dialogue.

The second is Harmony Day on the 21st March, which is also usually when the Spring Equinox occurs, and we have astrological balance and equality around the entire globe. Harmony Day began in Australia in 1999 in a call for a day of cultural respect for everyone who calls Australia home. Orange is the colour associated with this event. Interestingly, one of the traditions which has sprung up around it is the remembering and honouring of personal ancestors, who they were and where they originally came from.

There are so very many 'special days' to join in with in springtime if you wish – a selection are listed at the back of this book – or you may just wish to connect to all the marvellous reawakening and new growth which is going on around us in the natural world… even if we can't see it. But if there is one thing which I feel ALL of us should celebrate, it is Harmony Day. To misquote the words of a song from the old 1960s musical *Oliver*, 'If I ruled the world…' I would have everyone joyfully celebrate this day!

Chapter Six

Bringing the outside in

"The earth still holds her breath. - But oh! Soon, soon she will let out that slow; Great exhalation in whose flow all leaves and buds and blossoms blow."

Horace

I find that one main aspect of late winter and early spring is the exhilarating feeling of fresh beginnings… of time and space to plan and do new things – or perhaps return to old favourite pastimes which have been neglected. Finally, all seasonal decorations have been removed and carefully stored away – and the house looks rather empty and stark. Life itself can feel somewhat bare, a bit drab and aimless.

The outdoor world looks no less vacant, washed and swept clean and almost colourless by the winter rains and gales. To me it resembles a wonderful blank canvas on which to paint a whole new picture of the year. On the frequent days when it is either too cold or wet to get out, the days are still short and the dark evenings long and dark, what better time to cosily sit and plan and dream?

DREAM TIME

Now is the perfect time to formulate new activities so that as soon as there is more daylight, the weather begins to improve and we feel more energised and motivated, we are ready to burst into action!

If you fancy a new activity and are seeking inspiration, why not pick up a local newspaper, visit your local library or college and find out what clubs, classes, workshops and sports activities are taking place in your area. You might not find what you want, but at the very least you will know what there is.

The very best way of choosing what to do next is to ask yourself what makes your heart sing? What do you regard and look forward to without any reservations? What makes you smile – no, positively grin – to think about? What do you feel constantly drawn to? *This* should be your priority... your new goal for the year. So, what if it seems far-fetched or impractical? Nothing is absolutely impossible. At least begin your journey towards it and see where it takes you. Emulate the wonderfully wise aboriginal people of Australia and dream it into being. Thoughts have an energy of their own and can be made tangible and real.

In this day and age of so much information being literally at our fingertips via our electronic devices, colourful sales catalogues can still wield an enticing charm all of their own. Travel brochures can bring a touch of the exotic and a spirit of freedom and adventure to the dullest winter's evening, and children still enjoy cutting out pictures from them and pasting them into scrapbooks later! Dream about where you might wish to travel. Do some research online. Find books or programmes about your chosen destinations and immerse yourself... lose yourself in beautiful new places among fascinatingly different peoples and cultures. In this way you have already begun to expand your mind and travel without having even stepped outside your front door.

Seed and plant catalogues are also excellent sources of inspiration and information for gardeners. Even if you only have a very tiny pocket handkerchief of ground, or a back yard, balcony or large windowsill, you can still enjoy growing something. People with gardens might wish to completely redesign their land. Don't be too hasty to rush outside with a spade! Find a pad of paper and a pencil first and begin doodling with ideas of what you might like. Nor do you have to be an artist to produce a rough diagram or sketch.

You might think up ten completely different themes for your garden before you choose one – or none of them – but at least you will have had great fun and satisfaction in the process; you will have stretched your imagination and begun your dreaming process, and that in itself can be very satisfying and cathartic.

COMMENT FROM JOAN: 7th MARCH 1970

This *Comment From Joan* is much longer than usual, but I feel that, in its entirety, it gives a snapshot of a woman shopping, processing and planning her meals for the next few days, although my mother's love of cooking and way of utilising ingredients was by no means standard for 1970 and probably had more in common with culinary practices decades earlier when the pig had just been killed. She used to describe to me how, as a small child in the 1930s, she would watch her father, shirt sleeves tightly rolled up, rubbing and rubbing salt into joints of pork to preserve them. It is enlightening as to how one can cook things together when 'making from scratch', but she had the advantage of a fire oven which was always hot and cost no extra to run than the heating of the room. The difference in prices between now and fifty years ago is positively mind boggling.

Prices rise constantly, and not by small amounts, as yesterday at Booth's supermarket, the usual bottle, (2 pints, 40 fluid oz), of Sunflower oil had risen from 4/11d (25p) to 5/11d (30p) – I hadn't bought one for about a month. Since 'the experts' say that animal fats may not cause large deposits of cholesterol in the body I have gone back to deep frying in lard – now 1/6d (7 ½ p) per lb instead of 1s (5p) this time last year. We are told that prices will rise steeply if we join the Common Market. Butter (Lurpak Danish best) is 3/8d (18p) per lb with others as low as 3/- (15p).

Ham pestles are now 1/10d (9p) each instead of 1/- (5p) as last year – and smaller – only about 6 oz of ham on now, but they are still a good buy, with stock for soup, jelly for pies etc. and cooked ham selling at 2/8d (14p) per ¼ lb. Fat and skin do for dogs, but only Rowen and Prince eat it – faddy Alsatians!

As there is marvellous quality British steak to be bought at Marsden's Pork Butcher for 5/10d (29p) per lb, other 'made up' dishes seem hardly worth the money, but one needs variety.

Yesterday I bought:
1 Pork Shank, 3/- (15p)
1 Boiling Fowl (2lb 12 oz), 5/1d (26p)
2 Ham Pestles, 3/8d ((18p)
2 Shoulders of New Zealand Lamb 2/6d (12 ½ p) per lb
2 ½ lb Top Leg of Pork (for pies and sausage), 7/6d (37 ½ p)
(They let me have it cheaper because they didn't have my usual belly-pork at 3/- (15p) per lb.)

I put the pork shank and chicken, plus leeks and carrots, in my one-gallon marmite*1 and left it barely simmering in the oven for hours. I cooked the two pestles in another earthenware casserole at the same time. This morning I trimmed the fat and skin and bone off the pestles and put the boiled ham in the fridge ready to make ham croquettes, potted ham or just plain sandwiches. Stock I boiled down and put in fridge ready for pea or lentil soup or pie jelly.

The meat was falling off the pork shank and fowl. I got a good bumping pound** of pork (which tasted like chicken) and about 1 ½ lbs chicken – these pieces I have placed in a dish ready to bake into a pie.

GARDENING INDOORS

If you don't have any outside space, the weather is too bad or you don't feel up to it, why not grow some plants indoors? If you have windowsills, or a table-top next to a window– or floor space near patio/balcony doors – you

---

* In this instance, a marmite is a French earthenware cooking pot with straight sides and lid, a bit like an earthenware bucket.

** A bumping pound is an expression used in our family to describe when our scales (the old fashioned kind you had to manually balance) didn't just balance equally but bumped down on the heavy side, which meant that it was one – two ounces heavier than the required weight; in other words, a generous measure.

can fill small or large pots or window boxes with soil and plant all kinds of things. The only constraint here is if your pots are indoors, make sure that you have water proof dishes for them to stand in so that you can keep your crops watered. Salad things are particularly appealing at this time of the year. Lettuce, tomatoes, cucumbers and lots of green salad plants where the tender shoots or leaves are harvested when the plants are only a few inches/centimetres tall are all possible. Some plants, like tomatoes, require more of an investment in space and time as they will take several months to come to fruition. Here is one good reason to do a little research as there are so many dwarf fruit and veg bred specifically for patio tubs and hanging baskets – if this is the way you choose to go then have a good look around. Herbs such as basil, thyme, sage, oregano and chives grow easily and are then to hand while you are busily preparing a meal.

You might also wish to visit one or two local garden centres… you needn't even buy anything, (at least, not straight away), simply go for ideas and inspiration… a good cup of coffee and perhaps a chat with a friend. Make it an outing and then bring your ideas home and think about what you have seen and discovered. Write lists and draw more plans. When you feel relatively confident that you know what you want, make your purchases. If this spring's choices don't work out as well as you had hoped, well, you have learned something and can always try something different next year. Life is a lottery… a bit of a gamble… but it is this very uncertainty which also adds spice and interest.

You might like to involve your children or grandchildren in growing a hyacinth bulb in a special glass propagator so that they can watch the roots and shoots developing. Or you could introduce broad beans suspended in water in a glass jar and watch the same processes of growth take place.

SOMETHING FROM NOTHING

Many of us remember growing carrot tops on our mum's kitchen windowsill or little trays of mustard and cress which we could then proudly harvest to be shared in salads and sandwiches. But how about helping your child to create a whole miniature garden of their own?

Recycling kitchen scraps can bring immense satisfaction and rewards. It is also a lovely activity to share with children in these days and weeks when it might be difficult to get outside or they might be poorly. While you are preparing a meal, show them what you are doing and what is left – for example, the bottom of a cabbage stalk or tops cut off carrots. Later get them to help you place them in containers of water or fill small pots with soil and plant them. Help them to keep them watered at the right times and encourage them to keep a look out for signs of growth. When new plants have grown and are ready to be harvested, how proud they will be to add their own living ingredients to the family meal!

SUGGESTIONS FOR RE-GROWING KITCHEN SCRAPS

Basil, bok choy, cabbage, carrots, celery, corriander garlic, pineapple and lemon grass can all be re-rooted by suspending or placing the stubby stalk bottoms or tops, or (as in the case of basil, a length of stalk with a few leaves still attached to the top), in water and then, when roots have formed, planting them out into pots of soil.
Green onions, leeks and scallions; place the bottom and base of green shoot in water and will happily grow there.

The roots or bottom of the heart of romaine lettuce can be planted directly into soil, as can the bottom cut from an onion or a chunk of raw potato which contains at least one 'eye'. Break off a piece of root ginger from the main rhizome and place it in a pot of soil with the smallest buds facing down and keep in direct sunshine. It will grow roots and shoots. When ready to harvest, pull up the whole plant and use the root, breaking off a small piece to replant in fresh soil and so begin the whole cycle all over again. Seeds from tomatoes, pumpkins, hot peppers, etc. can be gently washed and dried before being replanted directly into soil. Stalks from mushrooms can be stuck in soil leaving only the very top exposed... and you might get another top growing on it!

All the water propagated plants will need to have their water changed every other day or few days. Some plants, like the pineapple, require more specialist handling and can take up to two years to produce another fruit. Unfortunately I haven't the space to offer full growing instructions here, so before you tackle any veg, fruit or salad scrap growing, do a bit of simple investigation online first and find out exactly what each needs to make it a success. It really isn't difficult and your initial care will be well rewarded.

THE WATER GARDEN

This is a particularly lovely project for children. All you need is a fairly flat waterproof tray. A glass bowl or pyrex-type baking dish with as large a flat base as possible might be best for this project. Even better would be if you can find something with a hole and rubber bung in the bottom so that it is possible to drain and change the water regularly. (Otherwise it may become stale and smelly and the plants begin to rot instead of grow.) Carrot tops may be placed flat-side down, singly or in groups, interspersed with pretty stones or pebbles collected from garden, park, road side or beach. (Be sure to wash and disinfect/sterilise them before placing them in your little garden. Your child may wish to use their little model boats or other waterproof toys to furnish their garden or scene. Allow their imaginations to take flight as one day it might be a mango swamp and another day it might be the seaside. Of course, to begin with, all that will be visible are several – or lots – of little round orange humps with slightly green tops, but they will soon begin to grow into shrubs, trees and forests – whatever your child imagines them to be! Just keep the water fresh and topped up.

Lentil Soup
Late 1950s

Excellent for keeping out the cold: thick, comforting and delicious

Ingredients

1lb (500 g) lentils (red or brown may be used but if brown lentils, they will need to be soaked for 24 hours previously)
3 pints (1500 ml) of water or stock
1 carrot, peeled and sliced finely
1 onion, peeled and chopped
2 sticks celery, finely chopped (or ¼ teaspoon of celery seed may be used instead)
1 oz (25 g) butter or dripping
2 or 3 bay leaves, depending on size
Bouquet-garni of sage, thyme, parsley
Seasoning

Method

- *Melt fat in pan and steam-fry chopped onion*
- *Sort lentils and then add along to onion in pan along with rest of ingredients*
- *Put lid on pan and bring to boil, and then simmer for an hour.*
- *Remove bay leaves and sieve. (Much easier these days to liquidise but do remember to remove the bay leaves first!)*
  Serve with crusty home-made bread thickly spread with best butter.

I hope that this all makes sense? In the original version in my mother's handwritten manuscript cookery book she had crossed a few words out, commenting that it wasn't a good idea to listen to the 'Goon Show' on the radio while trying to write at the same time!

MINIATURE GARDENS

If you mention miniature gardens in the U.K. it refers to living gardens on a small or tiny scale. These are not to be confused with 'fairy gardens' which tend to feature manmade accessories and 'fairies' – more toys than anything – and where plants are of secondary importance or interest. In Canada and the United States, there isn't such an obvious distinction between the two.

It is great fun to help a youngster to create and plant up a miniature garden. Please also bear in mind that this might also provide an interesting project for someone recovering from a physical or mental illness, or who is suffering from a disability, or an elderly person who no longer has the strength, agility or opportunity to work outside in a full-sized garden. Again, discussion, research, books, magazines, drawings, designs and trips out to your local garden centre all add to the anticipation and fun.

A good container for a miniature garden might be something like a (clean, new) plastic cat litter tray or washing-up bowl, but, in fact just about anything can be used – bowls, boxes, plastic veg containers, lamps, old shoes, jam jars, wine glasses – anything and everything can be utilised. The only consideration is drainage. If your tiny garden container has a hole or holes in the bottom, so much the better. If it hasn't and is made from wood, holes can be drilled… with plastic, drainage holes can be melted into the bottom by heating something thin (like a metal skewer) and then gently melting the plastic as you poke the implement through, otherwise it is all too easy to crack plastic and spoil it. Just remember to wear a glove or wrap some protective material around the handle of whatever it is you are heating so that you don't burn yourself. Also bear in mind that you will need some kind of dish or saucer under your container to catch any liquid which might seep out after watering, (unless you are able to carry it outside each time for watering), and something good, thick and waterproof to stand it on to protect your furniture or flooring.

Use organic potting soil with no added fertilisers or water-retaining polymers. Just remember that some types of unadulterated proprietary brand compost can dry out quickly, so make sure it is kept moist. A layer of sand or gravel in the bottom before the soil is added will aid drainage and help prevent containers getting waterlogged and roots rotting off – this is especially important where gardens are being grown in glass or china receptacles.

You may wish to keep the garden all on one level, or heap some of the soil up to make a 'hill' or little 'hills' but remember that as you water your garden, before your plants take a real hold, the soil might gradually wash away and flatten out. If you are using the kitchen scrap method, a selection of plants can be grown on in water or soil on your windowsill before planting them out in their final positions in your 'garden'. Remember that whatever you plant, it might only be small to begin with, but as it develops, it will probably get considerably larger as it begins to grow so allow space for it. Similarly, don't try and grow a plant which it too large for your miniature garden, like a tomato plant! You might like to experiment with water features in your garden. Make a shallow hole in the soil, line it with a plastic bag, edge it with small stones heavy enough to anchor all the edges of plastic and then fill with water. Toys may be incorporated into the garden but I would use these sparingly. Instead, encourage your child(ren) to make accessories for themselves and see how ingenious they can be. Wooden ice lolly sticks can be made into fences or benches; jam jar or bottle lids can be painted with a drop of left over gloss paint (or left plain if they are already a suitable colour and design) and planted with mustard or cress to simulate pots and planters. (Note bigger lids may need drainage holes melting or punching into their bases.) Garden furniture can be fashioned using spent corks from wine bottles and some small tacks or nails. Look around you with fresh eyes and perspective and see just how much can be made from other things, especially if it involves recycling. This helps all of us – not just the young ones – to look anew and become more creative. Like most things, it also becomes a habit.

There are many different types of miniature garden to make – all fascinating and absorbing in their own way and which will enthral and enchant both youngster and adult alike. More permanent and long-term gardens can be assembled around a particular theme such as small cacti, gardens containing succulents or a selection of alpine flowers and miniature rock gardens. Sand gardens can be constructed by using prettily coloured stones and shells and drawing patterns in the (damp) sand like a mini meditation garden.

PLANTS FOR YOUR GARDEN: Miniature and dwarf trees (or plants pruned and kept small to look like little trees and shrubs) should be paired with small-leaved perennials and ground cover plants. Then make sure that there is at least one manmade item in the garden to convey the small scale to the viewer and place it all in context – something like a bench or a chair, a garden tool or model of a bird or cat, for instance. Also bear in mind that it has to look right. Small 'trees' add height and mimic the real outdoors. Shorter plants and shrubs act as 'bedding plants'.

Below is a short list of suggestions for tiny and small plants which will hopefully give you some idea of the sort of thing you are looking for. Really, there are no 'miniature plants', just life-sized plants which are very, very small. One of the best ways of sourcing suitable plants is to find a garden centre with a good alpine, succulent, house leek or cacti section and trawl through it checking the dimensions each one will finally grow to but at least this way you can actually see for yourself how small the leaves, (and possibly flowers), actually are. You might be wise to keep to plants which enjoy full sun or only grow plants which flourish in semi-shade or prefer dry, moist, warm or cooler conditions as, unlike a real garden, you can only offer the same growing conditions to everything in your miniature environment.

- Thyme (*Thymus vulgaris*): kept trimmed will resemble little bushes and trees
- Miniature Curry Plant (*Helichrysm Italicum*)
- Microphyllums: has very fine needle-like leaves
- *Rhodohypoxis baurii*: native to South Africa and resembles a tiny iris
- Golden Creeping Speedwell (*Veronica repens*): forms a nearly-flat carpet of small round leaves and blooms with light blue flowers
- Hosta 'Green Ice': dormant in winter, two inch tall, green spear-shaped leaves
- *Orostachys iwarenge*: one inch tall sedum which forms attractive ground cover
- Miniature Fairy Garden Lawn - *Schleranthusuniflorus*: a native of New Zealand, found in rock and alpine sections of many nurseries. Tends to grow in cushion shapes but can be flattened and used for small lawns and rustic hummocks
- Ellwood's Pillar (*Chamaecyparis lawsoniana*): columnar dwarf evergreen which resembles an Italian cypress. It grows approximately three inches each year and reaches a height of around three feet, which gives a good few years until it is too big for a miniature garden
- Jean's Dilly (*Picea glauca*): miniature spruce tree
- Dwarf Hinoki Cypress (*Chamaecyparis obtusa*): 'Just Dandy'
- Asparagus fern grows like a very elegant, upright and green young tree You might also wish to use bonsai trees
- *Picea Abies* (Diffusa) is a little dwarf spruce which only grows a few centimetres a year

- *Taxus baccata* (Icicle) is a creamy white colour in winter and golden yellow in summer and only grows two feet in total in ten years
- Sedum (Atlantis) is a pretty, dainty plant of variegated green and yellow frilly leaves which finally matures to about 6 x 12 inches
- Erodium (Bishop's Form) spreads up to ten inches but only grows two inches tall. It has tiny, scalloped, deep green, frilly leaves and deep pink flowers.
- Sempervivum 'Zeitlauf': tiny green and dark rad edged leaves.
- *Mazus Albul*: sprawling tiny green leaves; flowers white in late spring and early summer

SLOP-STONES, GARDEN POTS AND TREE STUMPS

I first had a miniature garden when I was a small child. My mother helped me to make it in an old slop stone sink which must have originally been installed in our cottage. These sinks were not usually plumbed into any water supply or drainage system. The cottagers carried the water in from the well in a bucket and it drained away again through a plughole into another bucket set beneath the sink. When we arrived at the cottage in 1959, we discovered this old domestic utility carelessly discarded out in the garden. It was covered in a brown-red glaze which was quite pretty. It made an excellent outdoor container for a miniature garden being sturdy and thick walled and with the distinct advantage of a ready-made drainage hole at one end. The downside was that it was relatively shallow, unlike the deep white glazed Belfast sinks.

I cannot remember much about the plants in that miniature garden now. Hazy recollections of saxifrage and other small foliage waver at the corner of my mind – after all, I was only about four years old at the time and it is nearly sixty years ago! But what did make an impact on me was the small circular mirror which my mother gave me to press into the soft earth to make a 'pond', and the little china house which we placed beside it. How I wish that I still had that slop stone now!

I used to love making tiny gardens in small terracotta pots filled with damp sand. I would gather the flower heads of dandelions, plantains and daisies and display them artistically in pleasing groups with little paths curving in between which I fashioned from tiny flat pebbles from the stream. But these were too transient for my liking and I got very upset when the flowers finally wilted.

My next real adventure into making something natural was when I was just six years old. I always listened to 'Children's Hour' on the radio at teatime and in the February of 1962 the BBC broadcast a story in five episodes called 'Mossy Green Theatre'. It was serialised from a book of the same name by Mary Dunn, illustrated by Astrid Walford and published some years earlier in 1949. The story was about a woodland theatre which the little animals fashioned for themselves and the adventures that they enjoyed there. I was utterly enchanted by this whole concept and nothing would satisfy me until I had one of my own.

It was my mother who suggested that I utilise the old willow on the bank above our stream. At some point in the past the tree had fallen, re-rooted and regrown, forming a small living archway of branch from which many smaller branches now grew. Beneath this natural proscenium the steep bank had become hollowed out while the original stump provided a serviceable roof. With a little judicious wielding of a small trowel I managed to enlarge and flatten a clay area for a stage and collected soft cushions of velvety moss on which to seat my imaginary audience. I spent hours sitting beside it, imagining all the little animals and insects that might come and enjoy it, but try as I might I never actually saw any. Still, it was very pleasant sitting in the green shade among the ferns below the holly tree, listening to the water which chuckled and gushed over its stony bed on its way to the river.

In some respects I was a true child of the '60s and the coming of the plastic age, for my parents gave me a boxed set of 'Britain's' Garden one Christmas, including an oblong of green flock lawn, stone walls, cardboard crazy-paving paths and flower beds with daffodils and tulips which you planted by sticking the little handle with a metal ferule on its end into the plastic cup in the centre of the flat plant and then into one of the ready-made holes in the plastic soil of the flower bed. As the plant was inserted it suddenly came together in a most appealing and life-like bunch of stems and flowers. The beauty of Britain's garden range - apart from the exquisite detail - was that many items could be bought individually and in time I added a pond, rose garden, wrought iron fencing and gates, apple and silver birch trees and a greenhouse with tiny pots and seed trays which could also be individually planted. I spent many winter evenings engrossed in designing various gardens and even extended it by throwing a piece of green velvet material over scrunched up newspaper 'hills' on which I then carefully balanced my trees and flower beds.

It is nearly twenty years since I last made a simple outdoor garden in a deep square terrace pot. I wedged two tapering, triangular shaped slates horizontally into one corner and against these I built a 'hill', with a small cypress tree at the top and little stone-faced steps curving around down its sides to a pond at the bottom. At the time my son had been building himself a small life-sized pond in the back garden, so I was able to filch a corner of black pond-liner with which to insulate it. (Sadly, it always leaked!) I covered the hill in emerald green, velvety moss and put in one or two little thyme plants and other sedums and a miniature bench by the pond. It was constructed hastily as part of an experiment and illustration for an article I was writing for an international dolls house and miniatures magazine. Again, the garden has vanished into the soil it was made from but the little tree (which is now about two feet high) still flourishes in its pot.

One day I plan to design and plant a miniature garden somewhere out in the sunshine of my garden at home. The tiniest alpines, succulents and houseleeks mixed with small-leaved herbs never cease to set my imagination in a whirl... meanwhile, I continue to dream...

Chicken and Mushroom Pie
1970

There is nothing more comforting after being outside in bitterly lazy March winds, or after spending an exhausting day vigorously spring cleaning one's home, than to sit down to a hot, rich chicken pie, with soft, savoury crust and lots of creamy, thick gravy!

Ingredients

1 lb (500 g) chicken – portions or pieces or even left-overs from a roast chicken (a tray of chicken wings also works well)
¼ lb (110 g) of mushrooms, wiped clean and chopped in halves or quarters
1 onion, peeled and chopped.
1 – 2 oz / 25-50 g flour
Seasoning

For the pastry:

Two parts self raising flour to one part lard or butter
A little water and seasoning

Method

- *Place chicken, onion, mushrooms and seasoning in a pan, barely cover with water, place lid on pan and bring to boil, then simmer until meat is tender.*
- *Drain liquid off meat and thicken with 1 – 2 oz flour – cornflour will give an attractive glossy effect.*
- *How much pastry you need depends on how much you want. Are you after a pie with a top and a bottom? Or a pie with just a lid? Or would you prefer a cobbler crust which consists of no bottom and a top made from overlapping circles of pastry?*

- *Make pastry by rubbing fat into flour (with a pinch of salt if preferred), mixing with a little water until it is the consistency of soft plasticine (modelling clay) and roll out to ¼ inch thick*
- *Grease pie dish*
- *Combine meat, veg and thickened gravy and place in dish. Cover with pastry lid of your choice. Paint with milk and cook in hot oven for 20 minutes of so, until ingredients are properly heated through and pastry is just beginning to tinge golden. (This pie is not the kind to have light, flaky, golden pastry but be thick, soft and pale.)*
- *Serve hot with mashed carrots and swede and/or a pile of savoy cabbage – both well buttered and peppered.*

THE BENEFITS OF SPRING CLEANING

There comes a point when the impulse to have a clean sweep through our dwellings becomes irresistible. So, don't resist it. It is another seasonal activity which is absolutely normal and necessary. Throughout the cold dark months, items and energies have accumulated and stagnated within the walls of our homes. Wait until a really fresh breezy, sunny day. Throw all your doors and windows wide. Sort through junk mail, and the accumulated bits and bobs which tend to fill up every fruit bowl and surface. Check piles of books for any which you might donate to charity shops. Fling open cupboards and ruthlessly dispense with out-dated packets and tins and those half-eaten jars of heaven-knows-what. Use lashings of soap and hot water and scrub, scour and wipe. Wash curtains and see them billowing on the line. Cut up old frayed towels for floor cloths and threadbare sheets for dusters. Clean windows. Scrub floors. Plan which walls need a fresh coat of paint or which room(s) might require completely redecorating. (If you are going to give any parts of your home a total make-over, this is another 'planning' job for earlier in the spring. At this stage we are into physical action.)

While we sweep through our surroundings like the sorcerer's apprentice on speed, it reinvigorates us too. Physically it gets our blood pumping. Psychologically it empowers and enables us and brings to an end all the threatening detritus of winter which can become so oppressive. Emotionally it lightens our hearts and can in itself bring new clarity and direction into our lives. Spiritually it is refreshing and inspiring.

Something else which might make a huge difference to you – and your environment – is to ask yourself what cleaning products you use in your home? How environmentally friendly are they both for your house and yourself?

In our quest for cleanliness we regularly ere on the side of sterility and use many products which are filled with highly damaging chemicals and corrosive ingredients. We use a whole plethora of cleaning products – wipes, disinfectants, sprays, de-greasers, agents to 'melt' burnt food from our pots and pans and ovens, – as well as fabric softeners, washing up liquid, laundry liquid and bathroom disinfectant. Many of these simply aren't necessary. Most of the time all we really need is soap and hot water and a bit of elbow grease and fresh air. In the kitchen often all that is needed is a damp cloth left on the burnt-on food, or water left in a pan or dish to soak for half an hour while you eat your meal. A freshly sterilised (boiled) cloth and a little vinegar or lemon juice and water or a few drops of tea tree essential oil with mint or lemon are equally as effective. They do absolutely no harm to the environment, and incidentally, cost a lot less.

So, please have a look at exactly what you use around your home. Ask yourself whether it is really necessary, and then investigate which eco-friendly products are available and (as far as you can tell) are also truly safe. What can you formulate/ make to substitute for yourself? Scrutinise your supermarket shelves. Go online. Ask questions. Don't be afraid of looking a bit silly or ignorant – this is OUR world and each and every one of us has a right to say what goes on in it!

It doesn't matter what part of the world you live in, or how much or little you manage to find out. Make the effort to take responsibility for your own household, for all the chemicals we use which then drain into the sea and onto the land, which in turn run off the land and eventually find their way into our streams and rivers and finally into the sea anyway. They certainly find their way into our food chain and drinking water. Manufacturers will not continue to produce such detrimental products if we do not buy them. Do not endorse them with your money.

Chapter Seven

The March of Mothers

"Tossing his mane of snows in wildest eddies and tangles,
Lion-like March cometh in, hoarse, with tempestuous breath..."
William Dean Howells

"Can you finish work a bit early today? I want to go and look at a field."
My husband has long been accustomed to unusual or seemingly
random acts on my part and, and to give him full credit, he hardly
missed a beat as he kindly replied that, yes, he would be with me by
half past four. He did not enquire why I should so urgently need to
drive seventeen miles from our home on a damp, grey afternoon in
early March. Bless him, he simply collected us in the car as my son and
I enthusiastically jumped in beside him and waited for me to explain
as he drove.

THE FIELD OF THE NUN

I had spotted this particular parcel of land for sale in the local newspaper
one Saturday evening: 'Field, 4.9 acres, with stream. Suitable for
grazing horses.' At the time I was not looking for land — or indeed any
other property – merely idly glancing down the columns of classified
advertisements while I ate my supper. For some inexplicable reason,
this stark little notice leaped out at me and I suddenly experienced a

great wave of excitement. It was almost as if I unconsciously recognised what it signified, as if I had found something precious that I hadn't even realised I was looking for.

We had no difficulty finding the field. The directions and map which the estate agent had emailed to me that Monday morning were explicitly clear. Being early March, and a dull day with lots of low cloud, the daylight was already gloomy by the time we drew up beside the gate. It was obviously some time since anyone had opened and entered that way. Secured with a rusty chain and padlock and half obscured by gorse, nettles and brambles which had threaded their way through and around its metal bars, there was no way we could gain access through it. We all made short work of climbing over it, only to find ourselves wading thigh deep through well-established tussocks of grass, two feet high and hard as iron, topped by several summers of dead grass which formed lethal barriers, making it impossible to stride – or even step – out easily in any particular direction. Worse, just below the surface underfoot, lay standing water which sucked cloyingly at our boots.

The spirit of Boadicea was with me that day as I strode purposefully towards the end of the field where the stream ran onto the land. 'Yomp' is probably a better word to describe the curious action of raising one's feet and striding out high and far to clear all obstacles while still propelling oneself forward, only to bring them splashing down again. I was wearing a calf length skirt and it is just amazing how icy water has the propensity to shoot straight up the inside of one's legs!

Frequently stopping to look around me, I observed the high ridge of craggy hills towards the coast which acted as a sheltering barrier from the worst of the wind blowing in from the sea. On one side the lane ran along the boundary hedge, on the other three sides lay undulating fields where cows and sheep stood watching us with curiosity. Visibility was too grim for me to be able to appreciate the panorama of mountains hidden in the distance, but on clear days we can see up into Snowdonia and right across into Meirionnydd. Nor could I see the band of silver sea as it sweeps along the southern coastline of the peninsula across from which Harlech Castle perches upon its craggy rock and guards that stretch of the coast from which the seas receded long ago. As I made my way slowly up the gently sloping land I breathed deeply and listened to the intense silence of an early spring dusk. I fell flat on my face at least twice in the process and at one point lost a boot, but I eventually found the chuckling stream which flowed beneath the hedge onto the land and then merrily danced all across the top of the field before flowing out under another hedge at the opposite side.

Water, wind, the brown dead stalks of the previous summer, cold, grey, wet – I was in love - our lives would never be quite the same again!

My husband took longer to reach the stream. He simply kept standing looking about him in obvious confusion and bemusement. At that point, I had absolutely no idea what I was going to do with this field, but the feeling of excitement and raw potential was making my heart sing and gleeful laughter spontaneously bubble to my lips. I was under no illusion that there was absolutely no way I could take this land on – and whatever activities it led to – without the full co-operation and support of the rest of the family. Since that first fateful visit, we have all fallen deeply in love with this little corner of largely undisturbed heaven, no one more so than my initially doubtful husband. Indeed, at one time, I could hardly prevent him from driving off to spend time there on the flimsiest of pretexts, even when there were jobs which desperately needed attention at home.

As my son and I blundered our way down the far hedge, my off-spring suddenly said to me, "This is *Cae Non*, mum, if you buy it, that is what you should call it – that is what it will be." For in Welsh *cae* means 'field', and *non* means 'nun', and my middle name is Nonita, which is one of the Latin forms of 'nun'. If I owned the field, it would literally be 'the nun's field'.

The very next morning I contacted the estate agent and put in my offer. I was quite prepared to go and withdraw the cash from the bank and make the exchange there and then, but it took another three nail-biting months of offers and counter offers before the land finally became ours in early June - or to be more precise, I should say that the land was allowed to officially adopt us.

In the intervening years, we have made an island and planted lots of trees which have begun to suck up the water from the surface of the clay, produce leaf mould and compost and rid us of the mammoth grassy tussocks. We have planted willow structures – a dome, and a labyrinth – and cut smoother paths around the land. We have built a small *Hafod* (Welsh for 'little home' which shepherds and their families used to dwell in up on the high pastures during the summer months). It is only tiny, ten by twelve feet, but contains a wood burning stove and gravity water filter and equipment to produce hot meals. It can also sleep three. Outside there is a firepit where I like to bake loaves of flat bread in a heavy cast iron pan hanging from a metal tripod – real gypsy style! – and picnic table and benches. We have fashioned steps down to the stream so that we can more easily draw our drinking water. We have built a compost loo up behind the Hafod. We are — and will remain by choice – completely off grid.

To the side, my son has cleared the land and has a selection of herb beds growing produce for his medical herbal practice. Here, we run courses and workshops for the general public. We do have wider gates at the entrance, where we also had seventy tones of stone put down to provide hard standing for at least four or five cars. But the gates are no longer locked. Anyone is welcome to come onto our land and also enjoy it, for it does not really belong to us, we are merely guardians, watching over it, sensing how it might next like to grow and express itself, facilitating how it might achieve and fulfil itself.

It is a place of deeply profound peace and serenity. Everyone who comes there is deeply affected and healed by it. And it is most glorious in spring! From April to June, the land is filled with a myriad of wildflowers. Little cream and brown willow warblers perch in the tops of the alder, poplar and willow trees, (some of which are now over twenty feet tall), and sing beautiful choruses to us, or squabble melodically in the original bushier field willows which grow by the Hafod door and beyond the herb beds. Lizards and newts sun themselves on logs beside the path, ducks nest in the channel around the island, grouse strut across the neighbouring field and the fox crosses Cae Non so frequently that he has worn his own path. Mr mole mines his way through the clay and earth and slow worms disappear silently into the herbage. Frogs and toads abound. At least nine different species of wild bee make their home here, including carpenter bees. By day, the buzzards spiral on the thermals above us and at night an owl swoops silently over the darkened land giving the numerous indigenous mouse population little respite from their hunting.

It is worth noting that the flora and fauna are so rich and prolific because they have been left alone to get on with their lives unmolested by the blundering interference of mankind.

Sunlight dappling on water, the myriad swelling and unfurling buds of red, cream, coal black and pale green, the bleat of lambs and the symphony of birdsong… the feel of the strengthening spring sunshine beating down upon one's head and back, the rich aroma of the earth… It is rather extraordinary that the natural world can bustle about its all important affairs of growing and reproducing and yet simultaneously engender such stillness and peace. This is truly a Welsh springtime at its very best!

Glamorgan Sausage
1980

These vegetarian sausages can be eaten hot for breakfast or cold for lunch. They are a delicious tasty cheese sandwich all rolled into one – great for picnics, barbecues or simply to pop into a food bag and stick in your pocket when you go walking.

Ingredients

½ lb / 250 g breadcrumbs
½ lb / 250 g finely chopped onion
½ lb / 250 g grated cheese (a mature cheddar is good)
1 teaspoon dried mustard powder
2 eggs

Coating:

1-2 beaten eggs
Fine or medium oatmeal

Method

- *Mix all ingredients together thoroughly in a bowl.*
- *Form into six large or twelve small sausage shapes.*
- *Beat eggs to coat in a wide/flat bowl and tip some oatmeal onto a plate.*
- *Dip the sausages into the beaten egg and then roll in the oatmeal.*
- *Fry in a little vegetable oil until golden brown on all sides.*

Serve with fresh green salad or thickly sliced tomatoes or a homemade tomato sauce.
Can be frozen. Can be kept in the fridge for up to three days. Can be reheated.

SEARCHING FOR THE MOTHER

We all have parents. Whether we know who they are and whether we get on well with them or not, we could not, would not be here if they hadn't existed first. Everything in creation has a source which it has sprung from. Everything in this world has a common denominator; everything here around us shares something – we all belong to the Earth. Physically, we are generated out of matter belonging to the Earth. Every plant, animal, bird, mountain, river and sea is also created from this physical matter contained here upon and within this globe. Our spiritual input is something else, but for now, we are simply considering the practical issues of existence.

As a species, we tend to personalise things. Historically, we refer to the Earth as our Mother and to the Sun as our Father. Put these two factors together and we have life in all its many wondrous and diverse forms. Take either one of these factors away and it all falls apart. We need input from both. We need to learn to balance these various energies so that we can learn to live in harmony, with everything around us and with ourselves.

Springtime is a good season to seek out the mother figures in our life, whether that be our genetic parent, past teachers and guides or the very Earth herself – or ALL of them. Mother figures have always given life, support, nourishment and nurture… provided inspiration and the building blocks with which we have at least begun to form and develop our lives.

This is the season of birth and rebirth, of anticipation and plans well laid, of fresh growth and new beginnings. This is our annual chance to 'begin again' and for that we might wish – or need – to turn to our Mother.

On the human level, springtime has many celebrations of the feminine and the mother figure so you may wish to concentrate on one or more of these to give your activities structure and focus.

Or you may wish to generalise. Unfortunately, some of us have had negative experience with our mother figures and may be put off, offended or frightened by the thought of opening ourselves up to contact with, or the emotional implications of connection to any form of 'mother'. All the more reason to turn to Mother Earth for support; she can be very gentle with her wayward offspring and generously provides unique succour and healing for us all.

There are many very basic ways in which we can become more aware of and closely in tune with the Earth Mother – things which we can integrate into our ordinary everyday activities.

It all begins with one small action. Stop. Stop whatever it is you are doing and thinking. Look around you. What can you see? Allow yourself to feel gratitude for the things in your life which help you to live in some degree of comfort – the clothes on your body… the shoes which protect your feet… the walls and roof which shelter you… the food already in your belly. Encourage yourself to feel gratitude for all the basic ingredients of life; the fresh air that we breathe, the clean water which we drink. Be grateful for the body that you have. No matter how you might not be satisfied with it, or how much pain or illness it puts you through. It is your body and it functions and gets you around through your life like any vehicle that is sometimes driven badly and abused, but still keeps going and serves us well.

In noticing what is around you and what you can feel thankful for you are beginning to generally tune in to yourself.

Now I want you to go and stand outside. Breathe in deeply. Feel the air on your face, your skin. Really become aware of where you are – the streets and buildings… the people… the birds nesting in the gutters, the cat prowling… the dog barking… your garden… the fields and woods… the heat or cold, dryness or wetness of the weather… feel ALL these things.

In the grand scheme of things you are now connecting to your siblings.

Sense the ground beneath your feet – even if the living earth is many metres below you through concrete. Feel your feet really making contact with the Earth and sense that there are roots growing out of the soles of your feet, burrowing deep into the ground, stabilizing you and drawing natural nourishment up into you.

Now you are connected to the Earth… to your Mother… and she will hold, support and nourish you for as long as you need. In fact, she supports and nurtures us constantly, we are usually just too busy to notice and appreciate it. Send out your love to Her and come home to your wonderful reality.

Lastly, send out your love – pure unconditional love – just let it go from you to anywhere and everywhere. Now you are connected to the universe and all that is.

Welcome home.

THE CELEBRATION OF WOMAN

What better time of the year to celebrate womanhood and one's femininity – or feminine side – than in the spring… on the 8th March to be precise. There are many ancient festivals and celebrations which, throughout history, have done just that, but in recent times they have become misunderstood and fallen by the wayside of our modern society.

This modern incarnation of celebration originally began in the United States in 1909 when the Socialist Party of America took to the streets in support of garment makers who had protested against inhumane working conditions the previous year. They called it the National Women's Day and, keeping it to springtime, it took place on the 28th February.

Following suite, in 1910, during the Second International Conference of Woking Women in Copenhagen, (Denmark), the 8th March was established as the International Working Women's Day to particularly celebrate those working for women's working conditions and rights and universal suffrage. In 1911, Austria, Denmark, Germany and Switzerland celebrated the first International Women's Day on the 19th March when over a million people attended rallies focusing on suffrage, representation, education and workers' rights. Over the next few years, more countries in Europe began to mark the holiday on the 8th March.

It wasn't until 1975, during International Women's Year that the United Nations sanctioned it as an official holiday which celebrates women's contribution to society, raises awareness about the struggle for gender parity and inspires support for organisations which help women globally. Since then, the occasion has gained awareness around the globe as a way of recognising and honouring the feminine side of our society.

Each year there is a different theme for the occasion such as 'Be Bold For Change', 'Press For Progress', 'Balance For Better' and the 2020 focus of 'Each For Equal'.

Whether one feels the need to be militant or simply rejoice in one's feminine side (and we all have them, even the men!) this is an excellent opportunity for letting one's hair down with the girls, doing something really positive and meaningful with one's children, gathering with our sisters in a cosy nurturing space or venturing out upon the land to commune with our Earth Mother. Another 'special day' which you might like to make your own. How would you celebrate the woman or women in your life? Or celebrate your own femininity?

COMMENT FROM JOAN: LATE MARCH 1960

There are times when it is very obvious that men and women simply do not view an event or situation in the same way with the same degree of relevance or urgency. The passage below was taken from my mother's journal, written in late March, 1960, which was to be a second summer of drought. The first summer that we were at the cottage, in 1959, the whole neighbouring wood was set alight and this made my parents very nervous, especially as there was no real firebreak between the surrounding countryside and our home. My mother's sense of urgency and panic is almost tangible, although I was frequently an observer of this kind of misunderstanding and, I have to confess, often could hardly refrain from having a quiet chuckle.

It was almost 10:30 p.m. when we arrived here from the shop because I had a dog-trim - Rover Blackledge, Park Mill - and he was quite awkward. Then, by the time Jim had finished some of the Preston dolls and we had called at Mrs Monks' for Jill, time was getting on.

When we were coming down the bumpy part of the lane below Farmer Hough's new gate (which we eventually named 'Rocky Hill') I saw a light in the hedge and immediately yelled 'Grass fire!' Ricky stopped the van. Jill's nervousness of fire kept her in the vehicle. I got out and was amazed to see, not burning grass, but complete trunks six inches in diameter of the hawthorn hedge, glowing red and sparking. Fortunately, there was no breeze, or they would obviously have been flaming.

We got back in the van to continue to the cottage for buckets, etc. and as we drove past the hedge we could see one after another of the trunks alight in this way. Whether Farmer Hough had been doing something to purposely burn them in this way, or firing grass – although it's late and dangerous with everything so dry – or it was instantaneous combustion… or as usual, a carelessly thrown cigarette end, we couldn't decide.

Anyway, Jim and Ricky gathered every bucket in sight, even emptied the coal buckets. Ricky, in his usual exasperating manner sat on the settee phlegmatically donning his wellingtons, almost driving me, as usual, to a pitch of frenzy with his lack of speed. When provoked to scathing remark, he only looked up, most deliberately taking even more time, and replied, "Look here, it's like this, if it gets so bad that I have to hurry I'll just get the fire brigade, that's all.

Restraining myself to prevent further delay, I was very glad when Jim and he went out but was startled at least five minutes later when I went collecting clothes which I had washed earlier this morning from the line, to find Ricky Evans patiently uncoiling the rubber hose from one of the stirrup-pumps from the potting shed. I wouldn't care but they seemed so slow last year during the drought when Jim and Ricky pumped water from the river for degging.

Saying this, Ricky replied that it was possible to direct the water with said pump, so I again swallowed hard and waited quietly by the buttery door so that I could watch while he turned the van around, to make sure that none of our nine cats were run down in the process.

I have come to bed.

MOTHERING SUNDAY AND MOTHER'S DAY

Life is full of little anomalies and the confusion between Mothering Sunday and Mother's Day is just one example. The two titles are frequently used interchangeably but in fact, they are not the same thing at all, do not fall on the same day and belong to different continents.

Mother's Day began in the United States at the instigation of Anna Jarvis, whose own mother had expressed a desire for the establishment of such a holiday. After her mother's death, Anna led the movement for the funding of Mother's Day and on the 5th May, 1908, three years after Anne Reeves Jarvis died, her daughter held the first memorial ceremony to honour her mother and all the mothers at her church.

Anna Jarvis adopted the white carnation as the emblem of the movement: '… *Whiteness to symbolise the truth, purity and broad-charity of mother love, its fragrance her memory and her prayers. The carnation does not drop its petals but hugs them to its heart as it dies, and, so too, mothers hug their children to their hearts, their mother love never dying.'*

Unhappily, Anna Jarvis became increasingly distressed by all the commercialisation which was attracted by her simple intention of honouring her mother and women like her. She tried various ways to counteract it and never directly profited from it. It is ironic that it was the companies in the floral and greetings card industries who actually paid for her care in later life.

Mothering Sunday is celebrated by Christians in the United Kingdom and Ireland and some other countries with strong connections to the British Isles such as Canada and Australia. It is generally observed in parishes of the Roman Catholic Church, the Church of England and Anglican parishes throughout the world. To begin to explain what it actually is we need to look back a few hundred years.

On Mothering Sunday, people were expected to return to their mother church for a particular service which was held on *Laetare* Sunday, the fourth Sunday of Lent, just three weeks before Easter Sunday. One's 'mother church' was the church where one had been baptized, the local parish church or the nearest cathedral. Anyone doing this was said to have gone 'a-mothering'. This practice only came about after King Henry VIII's break with Rome.

More recently, domestic servants were given the day off from their work, (an extremely rare occurrence!) to enable them to visit their mother church, usually with their own mothers and other family members. It was often the only opportunity for the entire family to get together due to the pressure of conflicting working hours. Youngsters 'in service' were given the day off so that they could visit their families. It was sometimes the only day in their year when they might get to see and spend time with their mothers. The children often picked wildflowers along the way to place in the church or present to their own mothers.

By the 1920s the tradition had begun to lapse. In 1914, inspired by Anna Jarvis' activity in America, Constance Adelaide Smith created the Mothering Sunday Movement. Also known as C. Penswick Smith in her published works, she wrote a book in 1921 advocating the revival of the festival. The tradition of Mothering

Sunday which was still practiced by the Church of England and the Church of Ireland eventually merged with the newly created traditions from America and celebrated in the wider Catholic and secular society. Predictably, the merchants in the United Kingdom were no less keen to capitalise on this new commercial opportunity and have continued to relentlessly promote it.

Traditionally there is a relaxation of the strict Lenten vows on this fourth Sunday of Lent in celebration of the fellowship of family and church. Unsurprisingly, there are therefore many colloquial names for Mothering Sunday which appertain to food, Simnel Sunday, Refreshment Sunday and Pudding Pie Sunday to name just three. Simnel Sunday is named after the practice of baking simnel cakes to take as a gift for the mother of the family, or in celebration of the reuniting of families during the austerity of Lent.

Whatever the origins of Mothering Sunday or Mother's Day, it is a lovely time of year to acknowledge, honour and celebrate motherhood. What aspect of this festivity attracts you – resonates with you – most? How might you celebrate this day?

I have to admit that, personally, I feel that any occasion which can bring family or the wider community together has to be a good thing and I wholeheartedly support. My apologies to the various industries implicated in this celebration, but you do not need to spend money to have a warm and happy gathering of family, or simply quality time spent with your child or mother. Use your imagination and open your heart to enliven the true meaning of celebrating motherhood.

WHAT IS A SIMNEL CAKE?

Dating back to mediaeval times, the origins of this cake can be found in yeast-leavened flat bread which was made from very fine-ground flour known as *simila*, the Latin name from which we also derive the word semolina. By the Seventeenth and Eighteenth Centuries, the bread mixture had been replaced by a batter mixture, enriched with dried fruit, almonds and spices, and boiled like a pudding in a dish or cloth. When cooked it was wrapped in pastry, glazed with a beaten egg and baked in the oven until a hard crust had formed, similar to the Scottish black bun.

By the Nineteenth Century it began to more closely resemble the cake we know today. Different regions boasted individual recipes and designs varying in contents from currants, lemon peel and saffron to heavier nuts, cherries and dried fruit. Some recipes had a layer of marzipan baked through the centre of the cake whilst others were only decorated on the top. Some cakes were baked in the shape of a star, others in varying sizes of rounds.

More common in the north and west of England, this tradition was slow to spread and only became more popular when the recipe was modified into a light fruit cake formula. It was towards the end of the same century that simnel cake began to lose popularity as a celebratory dish for Mothering Sunday and started being eaten at Easter too.

It was only in the Twentieth Century that the familiar marzipan layers and decorative marzipan 'disciples' appeared. Traditionally, the layer of marzipan covering the top of the cake is browned (grilled) lightly or finished off with a layer of sugar icing. Eleven, twelve or thirteen balls of marzipan are then arranged in a circle around the edge of the cake to represent the eleven faithful apostles, with or without the addition of Judas and Jesus.

Sadly, and similar to the tradition of eating Christmas Pudding on Christmas Day, the serving of simnel cake at Easter seems to be in steep decline. For those who do still uphold the tradition, modern forms of the cake are often also decorated with spring flowers, Easter chicks and little chocolate Easter eggs.

It is wonderful in this day and age that we are not so bound by convention and can happily choose what we eat and when we wish to eat it. But I wonder if we are in danger of metaphorically throwing the baby out with the bath water? As demonstrated within the chapters of this book, there are so many occasions which we can choose to celebrate, why not utilise some of the other wonderfully mouth-watering cakes and desserts for these events, and still preserve one of our traditions by baking or buying a simnel cake? It is only once a year. Hardly often enough to become jaded by the taste and tired of it. Think about it.

Simnel Cake
1964

My mother did not have a specific recipe for simnel cake – she tended to use her rich fruit cake recipe which she also used to make the Christmas cakes from, with the addition of the marzipan layers. To give a more representative recipe, I have taken some measurements from Joan's 1950s edition of '*A Good Housekeeping Cookery Compendium*'

Ingredients

6 oz (170 g) soft brown sugar
6 oz (170 g) butter
8 oz (225 g) self-raising flour
Pinch of salt
½ teaspoon grated nutmeg
½ teaspoon ground cinnamon (or teaspoon mixed spice)
12 oz (340 g) currants
4 oz (110 g) sultanas
3 oz (85 g) chopped mixed peel
3 eggs
Milk to mix

For the marzipan:

½ lb (250 g) ground almonds
1 lb (500 g) sifted icing sugar
2 tablespoons sherry
1 tablespoon lemon juice
2 egg yolks
2 tablespoons apricot jam (to stick marzipan to cake with)
Glacé icing (optional)

Method for making marzipan

Mix all ingredients in a bowl, bind with unbeaten egg yolks, turn out onto a board sprinkled with a little icing sugar and knead well. Divide into one third and two thirds.

Method to make simnel cake

- *Preheat oven to 170°C, Gas Mark 3. Grease 8" round cake tin with butter and line with baking parchment. Tie a couple of layers of brown paper around the outside of tin so cake won't become too dry of burn.*
- *Sift flour, salt and spices into bowl.*
- *In another bowl, cream butter and sugar thoroughly and beat in one egg at a time very thoroughly.*
- *Stir the flour and spices into the mixture and then add the fruit, adding a little milk if required to give a dropping consistency.*
- *Put one half of the cake mixture into the cake tin and smooth top. Cover with the round of marzipan on top. Put rest of cake mixture into tin and smooth leaving shallow well or indentation in top of mixture (helps to keep cake top level).*
- *Bake, covering top of cake after one hour to prevent burning, for 1 ¾ hours or until cake is risen and spring to the touch. A skewer inserted into the centre should come out clean – although the marzipan can sometimes be sticky while hot – don't be tempted to test too early or cake may sink. Once cooked, take out of oven and leave to cool completely in tin.*
- *Remove cake from tin, peel off parchment and place on serving plate.*

To decorate

- *Dust work surface with icing sugar and roll out 2/3 of marzipan until almost large enough to cover top of cake.*
- *Heat jam with 1 teaspoonful of water in a small pan over a moderate heat until runny.*
- *Brush top of cake with jam, lay marzipan circle on top and gently run rolling pin over it to press marzipan into position and bring it right to edges of cake.*
- *If preferred, use a small knife to make diamond pattern on top of cake. You can also crimp the edges with your finger and thumb to emulate the crenulations that used to traditionally decorate the simnel cakes made in Shrewsbury.*
- *Roll remaining marzipan into however many equal-sized balls (11, 12 or 13) you want. Brush undersides of balls with jam or water and stick on top of cake.*
- *Brush marzipan top and balls with a little beaten egg and brown in a quick (hot) oven or under the grill. (A salamander would have originally been used for this.)*
- *If you like, a little glacé icing can be run into the centre of the cake with additions of preserved sugar flowers, little chocolate eggs and/or chicks.*

LADY DAY

Beginning in the year 1155, the 25th March was celebrated as the start of the New Year in England. By the time the Tudor monarchs came to power at the end of the Fifteenth Century, this date was referred to as 'Lady Day' because in the church, this was the Feast of the Annunciation, the day it was believed the Virgin Mary learned that she had immaculately conceived the baby, Jesus. (Christmas Day, the 25th December and the day of Jesus' birth being exactly nine months later.)

The 25th March was the first of four quarterly dates in the English calendar when, traditionally, servants were contracted to work, legal agreements were made and students began a new term of study. The other three dates were the 24th June, the 29th September and the 25th December. The autumn term in higher education is sometimes still referred to as the 'Michaelmas term', after Saint Michael's mass on which the autumn quarterly day fell.

Taking the Christian definition, perhaps this should be celebrated as a particularly special day for all pregnant females when any expectant mother is feted and given treats and taken especial care of. In this case, not a baby shower, but a day when the mother is the main focus and showered with little gifts with which to pamper herself or make the rest of her pregnancy more comfortable. Thought might also be given to her welfare after the birth of her baby and some gifts aimed at supporting and pampering her in the months to come.

As always, these gifts do not need to cost any money, but place time, care and effort to the forefront – a pledge of regular supportive company after the baby's birth, or to watch over the baby while the new mother has a good sleep or gets some fresh air might mean far more than the most lavish token.

Keep your eyes out for expectant mothers among your friends or the children of your friends or even within your wider local community and make Lady Day a time for showing thoughtful love, care and support. And if Lady Day is too early in the first trimester or does not fall within the term of pregnancy at all, then consult with family and friends and arrange another date to be the expectant mum's special day.

Become aware of what is happening around you in your local community. Set an example of reaching out, extending a loving helping hand to another person who might be struggling or simply appreciate the consideration. We are all aware of not wanting to be considered bossy or nosey, but as long as you are prepared for a rebuff, try it anyway. Aim for light-hearted generosity. Just be careful how you word your enquiry, how you smile or respond. I am not a particularly Christian person, but as it says in the Bible, cast your bread upon the water – you never know just where it might end up or who it might feed or what comfort it might bring.

A TAXING TIME

Anyone looking at or studying our calendar will soon begin to notice various oddities and inconsistencis about certain celebrations and dates, so I feel that something should be said about how it has been changed over the years, and why.

There are many different calendars in use in the world today: Hindu, Buddhist, Islamic, Jewish, Persian, Chinese, Coptic, Ethiopian, Mayan and so on. The calendar most widely used is the Gregorian calendar – sometimes referred to as the Western or Christian calendar.

Before 1752, here in Britain we used the Julian calendar. Unfortunately, this calendar had an inbuilt error of one day every one hundred and twenty-eight years due to a miscalculation of the solar year by eleven minutes. Among other things, this began to have an effect on the date of Easter as it began to move increasingly further away from the Spring Equinox with each passing year.

To bring everything back into line, the Gregorian calendar was introduced in 1752. This is a solar calendar based on a 365-day year, divided into twelve months. Each month consists of thirty or thirty-one days, with one month, February, consisting of only twenty-eight days – twenty-nine days every four years (which gives us our 'Leap Year') when an extra day is inserted to keep everything literally up to date.

> *"Thirty days hath September, April, June and November,*
> *All the rest have thirty-one -*
> *Except February which has twenty-eight, and twenty-nine in a Leap Year"*

Children's rhyme

Authorities faced with the problem of aligning the new Gregorian calendar with the old Julian calendar found it necessary to correct it by 'loosing eleven days. In order to do this, it was decided that Wednesday, 2nd September would be followed by Thursday, 14th September. At the same time, the date for the beginning of the New Year was now set at the 1st January.

As the new (and the old) calendars had both been instigated by the Pope, the head of the Roman Catholic Church, it is not surprising that the first countries to adopt this new calendar were France, Italy, Spain, Portugal and Poland. The last country to adopt the Gregorian calendar as from the 1st January 1927 was Turkey.

Predictably, not everyone was happy about these changes. Many people mistakenly believed that they had truly 'lost' eleven days and as a consequence that their lives would ultimately be that much shorter. Some people were also unhappy about the apparent moving of saint's days and holy days, including the date for Easter. This reflects just how many or our religious and cultural 'special days' have been – and remain – closely allied to what is happening in both the astrological and natural worlds where the abrupt variance of nearly a fortnight could make a huge difference.

The fact that the tax year in Britain begins on the unlikely date of the 6th April is also due to this calendar change. The official start of the year on the Julian calendar used to be Lady Day, the 25th March, and was also the day when taxes were due to be paid. To avoid the loss of eleven days of tax revenue the date of payment changed from the 25th March in 1752 to the 5th April in 1753. A further adjustment was made in the year 1800 which would have been a Leap Year in the Julian calendar but wasn't in the new Gregorian calendar, which meant that the tax year was once again extended by another day, bringing the date of the beginning of the new Tax year to the 6th April where it remains to this day.

Originally it was because of the New Year beginning at the end of March that we now erroneously name some of our autumnal months as we do. March was considered the first month of the year and was referred to as such; April was the second month, and so on. Which is why, in Latin, September means the 'seventh month', October means the 'eighth month', November means the 'ninth month' and December means the 'tenth month'.

LEAP YEAR

The proper term used for inserting extra time into calendars is 'intercalation', which is a bit of a mouthful to say. 'Leap' is much easier to articulate and also more easily conveys what it means – the fact that every four years, after the end of February, each date on the calendar jumps ahead by not one but two days of the week.

Have you ever wondered what a person does if they are born on the 29th February? Technically, they are only entitled to an actual birthday every four years. For example, like the character, Frederic, in the Gilbert and Sullivan operetta, 'the Pirates of Penzance'. The story goes that he was apprenticed to the pirates until he was twenty-one years of age, but because he was born on the 29th February, he would only attain his majority when he was in his early eighties! Happily, in Britain, for those born on Leap Year Day, they may officially take the 1st March as their true birthday. Other countries, such as New Zealand, designate the 28th February as the official birthdate.

The natural world, the land, the spring season and agricultural activity, the annual festivals - this time of year is definitely orientated towards the celebration of the feminine, motherhood and new life. In a similar vein there is much more to come, too, and in the next chapter I want to turn our attention to the celebration of the Spring Equinox, upon which our major spring activities all hang.

Chapter Eight

The Spring Equinox

"...A portion of land not so very large, but which should contain a garden, and near the homestead a spring of ever-flowing water, and a bit of forest to complete it."

Horace

Like the Winter and Summer Solstices, the Spring Equinox is a solar event, and also one of the eight festivals around the yearly cycle which we, as a family, (along with many other people), love to celebrate. It is regarded by many as the point when we leave Winter behind and enter into the light summer half of our year.

WHAT IS THE VERNAL OR SPRING EQUINOX?

The word equinox comes from the Latin *aequus* (equal) and *nox* (night). The equinox occurs at two specific moments during our yearly cycle, around the 21ˢᵗ March and the 22ⁿᵈ September, and are the only times in the year when the centre of the visible sun is directly above the equator, moving northward in March and southward in September.

Generally referred to as the Vernal or Spring Equinox in March and the Autumnal Equinox in September, this only actually applies to the northern half of our planet. In consideration of our brothers and sisters in the Southern Hemisphere where their seasons are reversed to ours and autumn begins in March and spring in September, it is perhaps easier for everyone to refer to them by the name of the month and the not the season, making them the March and September Equinoxes.

Day is usually defined as the period when sunlight reaches the ground in the absence of local obstacles. On the date of the equinox the centre of the sun spends a roughly equal amount of time above and below the horizon at every location on earth, which means that daytime and night-time are of approximately equal duration all over the planet.

In the northern hemisphere, the vernal or spring equinox conventionally marks the beginning of spring in most cultures and is considered the start of the New Year in the Assyrian, Hindu, and Iranian calendars. However, I would question the logic of this and suggest that spring actually begins much earlier, any time from the beginning of February onwards in fact. In support of this one only has to look at the activity going on within the natural world. As I have already pointed out, if spring only begins around the 21st March, the snowdrops, crocus and many daffodils are actually winter flowering, not spring flowering plants, and some of our trees like the elder, actually come into leaf in winter, not spring. To me, it doesn't make sense and supports the practice of celebrating the start of the seasons when nature actually performs certain actions and not when mankind decides it should be so. When does springtime begin for you in your part of the world? How do you define its beginning?

WHAT DOES THIS MEAN FOR US?

In reality, the Spring Equinox is a fleeting moment in time, a single day when, globally, so much is momentarily balanced in perfect equality; night and day, daylight and darkness. As a solar celebration, this is the precise point in the year when the waning energies of winter are evenly matched by the waxing energies of summer.

Balance is what is celebrated at this time, yet it is so difficult to achieve and can only ever be transient – we wouldn't want it any other way. If we existed in perfect harmony all the time, we would never learn anything, never progress. It is only in the wild swinging from one extreme to the other that we experience all the stages of life through which we pass, including the fleeting moments of perfect balance and harmony.

The Spring Equinox (and similarly with the Autumn Equinox in reverse) can be seen as a threshold between summer and winter, a halfway marker when both season and conditions hold equal sway. It gives us a brief moment in which to stand and acknowledge the passage of time and the turning of the seasons, to really experience what this pivotal point feels like in our everyday lives. If one regards the winter as a time of rest, stillness, introspection and contemplation, of time spent around the hearth of the Holly King, then this is the time when we begin to move further away from the days of inactive darkness out into the light half of the year when all is bustle, energy and time spent focused on activity out in the fresh air of the realm of the Oak King.

We need to pause at this precise time so that we can gather all the thoughts, plans and intentions that we have been formulating and brewing within us throughout the dark months, ready to spring into action with the growing light and warmth of the new season. It is a time to take a deep breath, like a swimmer about to leap from the highest diving board into the very different and exhilarating environment of the water, so we stand poised to enter a whole new phase of our lives with the coming summer.

Now we can also begin to truly appreciate the great energy of this youthful season – the tremendous potency and power of new life as it surges up through everything – including us – on its unstoppable way to creating new life and the continuation of *all that is*. For here is where the sovereignty of the land itself comes into its own and is made obvious. Whether it be the dark deadly forces of death and regeneration of the winter or the light, bright energies of growth and fruition of the summer, the land responds and replies to it all.

There is a saying that 'when gorse isn't blooming, kissing's out of season', because of course, there is never a time when people don't kiss; similarly no matter how dire the winter weather, if you look hard enough you will always be able to find a little gorse in bud or blossom somewhere.

GORSE BLOSSOMS

Across the wide green spaces
All over the common land,
Burning bushes of fragrant gorse
In bright battalions stand.
It's glorious, that colour,
Among black prickles blent,
Wonderful the richness
Of the gorse bloom's almond scent.
For it brings a gladsome message
through sun and driving rain;
Winter's dark days are over,
Spring draws near again!
I know a place with bushes
Higher than my head,
'City of Golden Streets' we called it
When every care had fled.
And we stuffed our many pockets
Full with blossoms sweet,
Now only memories walk besides me
Along those 'Golden Streets'.
Years fly swiftly past,
On the breeze, faint voices call
Across the yellow gorse blossoms,
Dearest flowers, to me, of all.

Agnes Gore Green

Gorse Wine
1993

There is nothing finer on a blowy, sunny spring day, than to take a basket
and go gathering gorse blossoms. Early bees are bumbling among the
colourful flowers and the heat of the sun beats down on one's shoulders.
Out on the open moorland or mountainside where the best gorse is
found, birds of prey will wheel and cry out overhead and sheep with their
lambs can be heard talking to each other in the distance.
Neither my childhood home of Drybones, nor my mother's former
home of Cumberland House were situated in areas where gorse grew.
Therefore, I am supplementing her recipes with one of my own from my
current homelife in the mountains of Snowdonia.

Ingredients

2 generous pints (1 litre) of gorse blossoms (by volume)
Rind grated and juice squeezed from 1 lemon and 1 orange
1 lb (500 g) sugar
1 gallon (5 litre) water
1 sachet of yeast for white wine
A large bowl or container
A length of plastic syphon pipe
Glass wine bottles (save the ones you buy in and recycle!)

Method

- *Gather your gorse blossoms on a dry sunny day. Be very careful how you
do it as gorse comes armed with two-inch-long spines which are very
painful to soft fleshy hands! You may try wearing gloves but it makes
plucking the flower heads difficult, so my advice is to just aim for the
blooms at the tips of branches and develop a dexterous and nimble style
with your fingers!*
- *Once home, place in a large bowl, pour over a gallon of boiling water,
cover and leave for three days, stirring every day.*

- *After three days, strain liquid off gorse blossoms (which you can now relegate to your compost bin) and place liquid in large pan with the sugar and lemon and orange zest. Bring to boil and the simmer for twenty minutes.*
- *Allow to cool to blood heat (same temperature as your little finger) and then stir in your fruit juice and wine yeast – you may have to activate this first, follow instructions on packet.*
- *Pour into glass demijohn and place airlock in top.*
- *Stand somewhere not too hot or cold and out of bright light. Within a few days the wine should begin to ferment (you will be able to see lots of tiny bubbles rising to the surface and every so often the water in the airlock will make a gloop-gloop sound. This means that the yeast is working. If this doesn't happen, try placing your demijohn somewhere*
- *a bit warmer.*

  It can take anywhere from a few months up to a year for the yeast and sugar to do their magic. When the wine has stopped fermenting, carefully syphon the liquid off the cloudy 'must' in the bottom of the demijohn into clean, dry, sterilized bottles – screw tops can be used, but if you want to use corks you will have to buy a little device which I know by the old colloquial name of 'floggle-toggle' (I have no idea what it might be known as now) to help you insert the corks into the necks of the bottles.

SIGNS OF SPRING

As a child I was always encouraged to be on the look-out for signs of early spring. I soon began to spot messages of the spring-to-come in the newly formed buds on the otherwise leafless trees in late October and November, the first dark green spears of daffodils to emerge above ground in December and the partially unfurled leaves on the elder in late January.

My mother would point out where birds were nesting and set me to quietly watch them for a while as sparrows and tits dipped in and out of the house guttering and robins and blackbirds found snug havens in the dense hawthorn. Later I would walk around the garden and woods watching frazzled parent birds flying to and fro with the speed of little arrows in an endless attempt to keep their newly hatched and very demanding off-spring adequately fed.

Moorhens and ducks would begin building twiggy residences on handy branches precariously stuck in the deep mudbanks of the river below the cottage – one good downpour of rain, the river would rise and all would be swept away and the poor souls would have to begin all over again. I learned to sit as still as a stone for hours on end watching the water voles popping in and out of their holes along the river bank or sitting washing their whiskers in the sunshine on the short-cropped grass of their little lawns. I used to think that the character of Ratty from 'The Wind In The Willows' was our ratty on the banks of the Yarrow, and that the huge old willow tree which leaned out across the water was the tree through which the wind in the title of the book blew. I often waited for Mole to also appear, but despite the numerous little hills of freshly excavated soil further up the bank, I never caught sight of him.

One spring, we were enchanted to discover that a pair of tawny owls had nested in a hollow alder tree on the riverbank opposite my parent's bedroom window. Whole evenings were spent with all of us sat like statues, silently crowded at the window watching the miracle of new life unfold before us, from the usual building procedure and then seemingly an age of waiting until feeding suddenly commenced and we knew that the eggs had finally hatched. As the owlets grew, we began to be able to see them in an untidy feathery heap in their wooden hollow. The most exciting moment was when the first chick ventured out onto a neighbouring branch, finally followed by his siblings. There they sat; a little row of fluffy, feathery balls, squawking and chuntering to their parents and each other. Their first flight was felt as a triumph for us all, only marred by the knowledge that they would so soon be disappearing into the night-time woods, to be heard but rarely seen, and never again on such intimate terms as we had enjoyed those few short weeks.

Occasionally, Farmer Hough would bethink himself and unbend his natural reserve far enough to invite me to the farm to see the first of the new-born lambs. The first time I stroked a youngster I was shocked by how wiry and tough their soft-looking coats really were!

I actually got far more pleasure from the calves after they had been separated from their mothers. I used to climb through the hedge into the field which separated our valley from Mr Hough's farmyard. There I would play at cowboys with the 'child-sized' animals. They weren't very good at co-operating and I never did manage to 'round them up' as in my favourite westerns, but I enjoyed myself immensely. I do wonder, though, that farmer Hough didn't come out and object – he must have noticed me cavorting around his land after his animals, but never a word passed his lips.

BEFRIENDING A SWAN

On walks along the banks of the nearby lodges (industrial manmade lakes) I would delight in finding the huge nests of equally hard-working swans and, later in the spring would watch carefully as eggs were laid and hatched and count the number of fluffy grey signets.

When I was around seven years old it was one such nest which was vandalised by youths from the nearby village. They had thrown large logs of wood onto the nest where the cygnets were sheltering. One of the babies had a permanently damaged wing and couldn't fly. He survived his first winter and underwent the transformation from ugly grey-brown cygnet to regal snowy-white swan but was always alone and rejected by the rest of his kind around the lake. Two men from the R.S.P.C.A. came and had a considerable tussle to apprehend Swanny, attach a tag around his leg and then carry him up through the wood to Drybones.

My mother was somewhat stunned when the trio arrived at our cottage unannounced and invited the exhausted officials to temporarily incarcerate the furious bird in her old shooting-brake. Even as I was aware of the terrified bird's distress, I had to have a chuckle as I watched him glaring through the passenger window like a hugely unimpressed motorist, whilst periodically hammering on the glass with his beak. Meanwhile we revived the R.S.P.C.A. fellows with a cup of tea and they and my mother discussed what would be best to do with the injured swan. It was far too late to treat the damaged wing – it had long ago set too crookedly. So, it was decided to release him onto our stretch of the river where it was quieter and where we hoped he would settle and we could keep an eye on him. When all was ready, the men carried Swanny down the polyanthus path to a secluded stretch of the Yarrow where he was finally released. There Swanny was left in peace to recover his dignity and equilibrium.

A few days went by when, one morning, my mother glanced out of the back kitchen window which overlooked the river and, to her delight, spotted the recalcitrant swan busily preening himself on the little island of sand and tall grasses which had formed just below our huge ash tree. It was perfect for him. Sometimes we would give him treats to eat and I loved to go down onto the bank to talk to him and throw bread into the water and watch him feed. I spent hours in his company. Always a little cantankerous (he had nothing to particularly thank the human species for) he would march up to our back door on cold winter mornings and boldly bang on it with his beak, demanding his breakfast. He was with us for about three years, and then one day we found his body floating further downriver, but my relationship with this brave snowy-white king of the birds was something I treasured and which has given me a life-long love of swans… and a habit of sitting talking to them wherever I come across them.

CELEBRATING THE EQUINOX

These days, my family and I might celebrate the Spring Equinox in various natural locations, largely depending on the state of the weather. We might go out into the awakening woods, or besides a lake, onto a sunny hillside or even higher up onto the lower slopes of Mount Snowdon. This year, we plan to go to the beach. If it is a day of wind and rain, we might be confined to remaining indoors, but it is quite remarkable how rarely this happens, regardless of the time of year.

To mark this particular time of year we take little pots of soil and seeds to mindfully plant; usually something like sage thyme or even lettuce which are going to be useful in the garden later in the season. We sit or stand and deeply connect with the Earth, literally feeling the soil with our hands, sensing Her awakening... Her marvellous breaths and shudders as She bursts forth into increasingly exuberant activity and life. We have little contests which involve literally balancing our bodies in sympathy with the whole balancing experience of the planet on this day and discover – and discuss – what it means for us to be 'in balance', in harmony – similarly, what it also means for us to be out of balance, which is not necessarily always a bad thing.

We also incorporate some of the elements of Easter into our activities, especially those involving chocolate! On occasion, the traditional carraway seed cake gives way to a huge chocolate 'nest cake' – the kind made from breakfast cereal coated in chocolate – but this being large enough to cut into many slices, piled high with gaily coloured mini-eggs in its centre. (Recipe in Chapter Eleven.) Sometimes we spend the day with a friend who lives in the Conwy Valley and who has constructed her own full-size stone circle atop a breezy little hill with a breath-taking view of all the mountains around the valley. Exposed to the sometimes remarkably hot sunshine, (for so early in the year), I have known us to have problems with our chocolate cake as it rapidly began to melt whilst waiting to be shared out and us having to eat the collapsing portions with spoons!

With all the connotations of new life and rebirth, we also decorate hard boiled eggs and have rolling competitions down grassy slopes, or simply take them home with us as symbolic reminders of this amazing time of year when the season begins to pick up speed and new growth and birth is beginning to erupt and flourish all around us.

Basic Sponge Cake
1964

Ingredients

5oz (140 g) butter, margarine or dairy free spread
5oz (140 g) sugar
8oz (225 g) self raising flour
2 – 3 beaten eggs
A little water to mix

Method

- Pre-heat oven to 355°F/180°C, and grease and line a 7" - 8" cake tin
- Cream butter and sugar, gradually add egg (and a little flour if you wish, to prevent curdling)
- Fold in rest of flour, add a little water until mixture is soft, but you can see the track of your spoon left standing in it
- Pour into tin and bake for approx. 30 minutes or until golden and cake has left sides of tin (test by inserting a skewer into the cake; if it comes out clean it's cooked, if it comes out sticky it needs a bit longer.)
- Remove from tin and place on a wire rack to cool.
- To finish: Cut in half and spread bottom half with jam. Replace top half and dust with castor sugar.

Variations

- **SEEDY CAKE:** To your sponge cake mixture add 1 oz (25 g) caraway seeds – or more if preferred. This is an old ingredient which was very popular in the Victorian era in the Nineteenth Century, but is an excellent choice if you wish to make an appropriate cake with which to celebrate the March Equinox and the planting of the new season's seeds.
- **CHOCOLATE CAKE:** Add 1oz (25 g) of cocoa powder to basic cake mixture when combining the flour. (You may wish to only use 7oz (200 g) S.R. flour, but it doesn't really matter.)

When cake is cool, cut in half and spread one half with jam and/or chocolate butter cream, sandwiching the two halves together again. Make chocolate icing by adding two teaspoons of cocoa powder to some icing sugar and mix with a little water to form a thick but spreadable paste. Spread icing on top of cake and decorate with glacé cherries, grated chocolate, sprinkles or grated nuts.

- **COFFEE CAKE:** Use basic cake recipe but this time substitute 2 - 3 teaspoons instant coffee granules melted in a little boiling water and added as you fold in the flour. When cake is baked and cooled, slice horizontally in half and spread coffee butter icing containing 1 oz (25 g) chopped walnuts over one half of the cake and then sandwich back together again. Spread top with glacé icing made from some icing sugar and 1 – 2 teaspoons coffee granules melted in a little hot water. Decorate iced top with walnuts and glacé cherries or a circular border of chopped nuts.

- **CHERRY LOAF OR COCONUT LOAF:** For the cherry loaf add two ozs/50 g of glacé cherries (cut in half and rolled in a little flour) to the basic cake mixture. For the coconut loaf, add 1 - 2 oz (25 - 50 g) of medium desiccated coconut to basic cake mixture. Bake either cake in a 1 lb (500 g) loaf tin instead of the circular cake tin.

- **ICED COCONUT CAKE:** Add 1 - 2 oz (25 - 50 g) medium desiccated coconut to basic cake mix and bake in usual way. When cake is cool, mix icing sugar with juice of half a lemon and ½ oz (12 g) desiccated coconut and spread evenly over top of cake – will set very firmly.

- **ORANGE OR LEMON CAKE:** Basic cake recipe but grate and squeeze orange or lemon, (one orange or lemon if large, two if small, and depending on which kind of cake you are making). Add to zest to cake mix while adding flour before baking. When cake is cooked, turn out on wire rack to cool. Stir two ounces or fifty grams sugar into squeezed juice and warm to melt in a small pan, but do not boil. When cake is cool, pierce top all over with sharp fork and then paint juice mixture all over top of cake using a pastry brush until juice mixture is all used up. Finally, sprinkle with ordinary sugar or castor sugar, as you prefer. Either makes a makes a nice tangy fresh alternative.

- **LEMON CAKE:** When basic lemon cake is baked and cool, cut horizontally in half, spread generously with lemon curd and sandwich two halves back together. Make lemon icing using icing sugar, lemon juice and enough yellow food colouring (added one drop at a time) to make a pale yellow primrose colour, and spread over top of cake. This may be further embellished with pieces of candied lemon or a border of fine desiccated coconut.

- **LIGHT FRUIT CAKE:** To the basic cake mixture add ½ lb/250 g mixed dried fruit (or more if you wish) and 1 -2 teaspoons ground mixed spice or cinnamon, or a grated nutmeg if you prefer.

- **ICED SPONGE CAKE:** Bake cake using basic cake mixture. Cut horizontally in half, spread with raspberry or strawberry jam (or any other jam you prefer) and sandwich two halves of cake back together. Ice top with glacé icing and decorate around edge with halves of glacé cherries.

  The basic sponge is a quick and easy recipe which usually turns out well every time and can easily be mixed and popped in the oven while you are clearing the table from breakfast or lunch and doing the washing up.

NOTE: If you substitute dairy-free spread for the butter and/or gluten-free self-raising flour for the ordinary self-raising flour it is suitable for anyone with gluten or dairy intolerances.

These are just a few ideas – I am sure that you can think of lots more variations! Thursday was usually my mother's baking day ready for the weekend. She would often mix two or three times the quantity of cake mixture and divide it into three separate bowls, adding other ingredients to quickly end up with three totally different cakes. Some cakes are best eaten absolutely fresh, others, like the chocolate or coffee cake, are greatly improved for being kept to 'mature' in an airtight container for a day or two. This is a time and energy effective way of filling your cake tins – or providing an impressive spread with relative ease.

Something a little different – Sigils

A sigil is an original artistic creation, produced by conceiving a word, phrase or sentence that expresses a wish, desire, quality or intention and which converts those words into a pictorial representation.

Sigils are monograms of thought – a glyph used as a means to bridge the gap between the conscious and subconscious mind. The strength of focus they represent is deeply potent in its distilled essence.

- First of all, you need to decide what inspirational word or phrase you want to portray. You may wish to use capital or lower-case letters or mix the two; there are no hard and fast rules, the aim is to be artistically pleasing as well conveying a message. To begin with, use a piece of scrap paper until you have worked out a design you are best satisfied with.
- To begin with I have chosen the word 'love'. Write the word out in the form you wish to use. If using lower-case you will write l o v e. If mixing capitals and lower-case you might write L o v e. If using all capital letters, you will need to write LO V E. See *Fig 1*.
- As you use each letter in your sigil design, cross it out of the word you have written above – in longer words and messages it is easy to forget where you are up to and leave a letter or two out. No matter how many times a letter appears you only use it once in writing your sigil . Using the word written in lower-case, begin by writing the tallest straight letter, which is 'l'. Next, write the 'o' against the bottom right hand side of the letter 'l'. The 'e is almost the same shape as the 'o' so write it over the top of the 'o' see *Fig 2*. Lastly, the 'v' doesn't obviously share a similar shape with any of the other letters, so it will have to stand out on its own – I have chosen to place my 'v' besides the 'l' and just above the 'o/e' letter, in two slightly different positions – *Fig 3*. Or you might choose to place it with one of its lengths along the vertical stroke of the 'l' with the other side of the 'v' jutting out at a tangent across the 'o' and the 'e', see *Fig 4*.

- Look how the shape of the word changes if you use a capital letter 'L' with the rest as lower-case letters. See *Fig. 5*. If you use all capital letters, the shape and appearance of the word is drastically altered, see *Fig 6*. Which do you prefer? Which shapes of letters best or more appropriately convey to you the feeling of 'love'? What truly speaks to *you*? This is why I suggested that you doodle about on scrap paper first. When you have your preferred design, copy it out onto fresh white or coloured paper or card.

- Just to really jazz things up, you can also write letters lying on their backs or fronts or upside-down. So you might write 'Love' as *Fig 5*. You might wish to simply use a black or blue pencil or pen to write your sigil. In the diagrams I have not superimposed all the letters on top of one another; instead I have drawn the letters very close to one another so that you can more easily see where they go and how they fit together. You might also wish to write them this way and make each letter stand out individually by using a different colour for each letter.

- Making one letter larger than the others and using it to encapsulate the rest of the word can give the word shape added clarity and definition, as in *Fig 8* with the word 'sympathy'.

Apart from making your own affirmations and pictorial reminders, sigils can be used as patterns and decorations with extra relevance and meaning. You can draw or paint them on homemade greetings cards or bookmarks or embroider them as wall hangings or other forms of decoration – their application is endlessly various, relevant and attractive (interestingly the company logo for the car manufacturer Toyota is devised from a sigil).

love   Love   LOVE

Figure 1

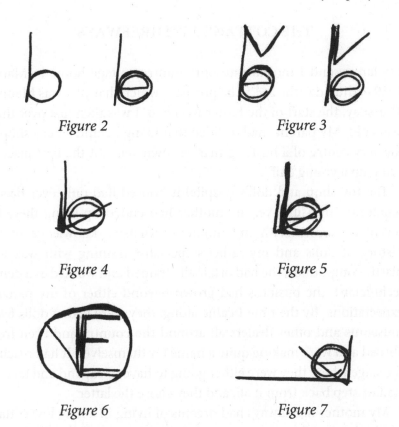

Figure 2   *Figure 3*

Figure 4   *Figure 5*

Figure 6   *Figure 7*

Figure 8: *The seven stages of building up the word* Sympathy

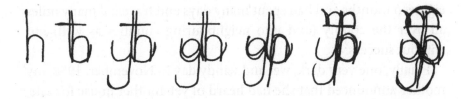

Can you work out what word this sigil represents?
(Find the answer at the back of the book)

THE COTTAGE AT 'THREEWAYS'

My family and I moved into our country cottage home in March, 1959 – Thursday the 26th to be precise – which that year was Maundy Thursday, the start of the Easter weekend. I was then just over three years old. My parents had decided that living behind a busy shop in the very centre of a bustling market town was not the best place to bring up a young child.

The toy shop and doll's hospital it housed had only ever been a temporary measure, yet my mother had ended up living there for seventeen years. With my mother's extensive knowledge of the history of dolls and my father's specialist training with wax and plastic compounds, (he had originally trained and worked as a dental technician), the business had grown beyond either of my parent's expectations. By the time I came along, they were taking dolls from museums and other dealers all around the country and even from abroad and were making quite a name for themselves. It had reached the stage where they were either going to have to expand and take on staff or step back from it all, and they chose the latter.

My mother had always had dreams of living in a long low cottage on the banks of a river surrounded by a huge garden. She wanted to grow things and spend days in a big kitchen with old fashioned pancheons of bread and brightly shining copper pans bubbling away. My parents had been looking for somewhere suitable for over eighteen months and had spent many days and travelled many miles all over the county (and into neighbouring counties as well) but without success.

Finally, one very dark, wet and windy day in November, 1958, my mother announced that she had heard of yet another house for sale, only three miles from where we were living and she wanted to go and see it as soon as possible as the vendors wanted to move before winter really set in. My father was unable to take her – and at that time my mother didn't drive a car – so it fell to my uncle to act as chauffeur, but he was late picking her up and it was well and truly dark by the time they set out.

The wind was roaring overhead, blowing the torrential rain almost horizontal and the night was black as pitch – especially after they left the tarmacadamed road and streetlights behind and plunged down a narrow and extremely bumpy lane full of ruts and potholes. Not surprisingly the intrepid pair had quite a time finding the property. For some reason which I never quite understood, my mother and uncle decided to park up and leave the car and take a short cut through a small wood. It was only later that they discovered that the path which they had followed was actually perched along the edge of a fifteen foot drop above a small stream which that evening was swollen to a roiling, foaming frenzy. The one little torch they had with them hardly produced enough light to penetrate even a couple of feet in front of them. Nor in their questionable wisdom had they equipped themselves with waterproof footwear, my mother slipping, sliding and turning the occasional inelegant pirouette in four-inch-high heels which soon became swamped in freezing cold mud. Finally climbing the last style and crossing the mini raging torrent via a little bridge made from a single massive slab of stone, they relocated the lane and the big, five-barred gate to the property they were searching for – 'Threeways'

After that night, there was never any doubt in my mother's mind. After combing the available properties in three counties she had finally and very definitely found exactly what she had been looking for just three miles from her own front door. She certainly didn't see it at its best that storm torn November night – hardly a 'roses round the door' experience. But the cottage, which was well over three hundred years old, was long and low with black oak beams and even though my mother couldn't actually see them that first evening, she was also told that the cottage was set in over an acre of land and that there was indeed a river flowing around two sides of it. Without my father even seeing the cottage for himself my parents put in an offer and it was immediately accepted.

At that time, my mother was the president of the local historical society and they had been investigating the history of an old property which seemed to have vanished, believed to have been demolished.

The name of this ancient place was Drybones and local tales abounded as to how it might have come to earn its rather gruesome appellation. Speculation was rife, both as to its origins, its location and its fate and various members of the historical society had been delving into the scanty facts for several months.

When my parents went to see their solicitor about arrangements for the purchase of Threeways, they were somewhat bewildered by his barely concealed amusement. He was also an active member of the same local historical society and while Joan and Jim were still sitting feeling bemused, the solicitor grinned at them and asked, "Do you know what property you want to buy?" My mother replied that of course she did. "But do you know what it is called?" the solicitor persisted.

"Yes," my mother replied firmly, "It is called Threeways".

"Ah, now that is where you are wrong" he grinned, "That is only the name the last owners gave it because they didn't like the original – in actual fact, you are buying Drybones!"

The mystery of the missing cottage was solved, as was the lurid name for it, for in their decision to rename it, the previous owners had hit upon the very meaning of 'Drybones'. The cottage was built on an ancient site – a Canadian professor once told us that he believed one of the sinuous, curving beams in the dining room had originally come from a Saxon barn – and the name was derived from the Anglo Saxon words *dree bahn* meaning 'three ways'. Indeed, there are three ways to approach the cottage which sat at the far end of its own little valley; the lane leading from the town, the path which my mother and uncle took through the wood that fateful November evening and another path which winds its way besides the river and leads to a waterfall, some manmade lakes beyond and, eventually, the next village.

It was to be another four months before I first saw my new home, and by that time winter had come and gone and the first soft touches of spring were just beginning to colour the countryside.

COMMENT FROM JOAN: APRIL 1964

My father always said that work is only work when there is something else you would rather be doing; well according to that, I must be the laziest person on God's earth. Of course, maybe he only quoted and got it wrong? Whichsoever way it is, I am busy not working for eighteen hours out of every twenty-four. Instead I look after my husband, eight year old daughter, brew, bake, bottle, garden; all the time accompanied by my five Alsatian dogs and two cats who in turn expect me to feed, exercise, love and save them from each other at regular intervals.

Take gardening – I wish you would – the word to me conjures up pictures of weedless perfection, regular shaped beds of packet-picture flowers, vegetables of correct size and soilless when pulled. Or a herb garden, a knot garden straight from the Elizabethan manor house, each bed with its edging of violets. Far away from worldly cares is a lawn complete with table laid for tea, sparkling silver, scent of roses and cooing of pigeons nearby in the woods. Well, we all have our dreams!

In reality my garden consists of trying to bring under control two acres of jungle that has been 'let go'. When in desperation I turn to my gardening books for solace I read that it is better to start with a completely new garden than face the heart-breaking task of slow rescue and renovation, especially as I am so soft hearted, not to mention soft in the head. But I discovered my very own paradise here (after all, the word paradise is only Persian for 'park' or 'garden'.

Stoically I eschewed the advice of friends:

"Joan, you need a five year plan."

"Use a flame-thrower."

"Cut down all the trees."

"Hire a bulldozer and flatten the lot."

"Move!"

I went out one pale green April morning and became a slave, literally a slave, because as far as I can see everything – except the plants I buy in and plant out – grows with such amazing rapidity and vigour that my whole and entire life must be dedicated to attempting unsuccessfully to merely preventing the jungle encroaching anymore and covering the cottage completely. So, the mental picture of my carefully tended garden becomes a mere figment of my imagination. Friends call and run me to earth fittingly dressed (for what, I wonder) in an old tweed coat (much tree-torn) , shod in gumboots (heavy gauge) wielding my own pet bow saw which accompanies me everywhere like some pet lapdog.

Boldly I face them - the friends, I mean – well, maybe not quite boldly because I must first unbend myself in easy stages, hair pulled on end by recalcitrant trees that I've been working under. Before the unbending has commenced I think that I must look like a character I often saw on the films when I was a child before World War Two – this man used to actually play two parts and became disguised as Lord Epping by means of hunching himself and his shoulders into the most unlikely posture. Now I know that the actor must have been a gardener because I daily 'Lord Epping' it up and down my overgrown paths and I have developed great proficiency in the posture. There, as I face friends and family I am greeted with exclamations of "Good God, she's gone bush!" or at the very least, "I suggest, Joan, that you work out a forty year plan like the Russians."

I bravely ignore such remarks and elegantly wave with my heavy leather gauntlets in the direction of masses primroses at the edge of the wood, clumps of forget-me-nots as blue as Grecian skies by the stream. I point out the aesthetic value of the sudden sight of these various delights while walking in the garden and the strange content and peace of mind engendered all the time by such unexpected surprises. Like the Easter Sunday morning I drew the bathroom curtains back just as two swans flew by right outside – I could imagine no more joyous or appropriate start to the day.

Chapter Nine
The Magical Hare

"My soul can find no staircase to heaven unless it is through earth's loveliness."

Michelangelo

Not everyone realises that there is such an animal as a hare which is distinctive and quite different from its similar looking cousin, the rabbit. The hare is larger than the rabbit. It has amber eyes, long, black tipped ears, a brown back and much larger back legs. When running, the rabbit holds its scut (tail) up and moves with a hopping, lolloping motion, whereas the hare holds its tail down when running and has a loose, gangly stride which can develop into great swiftness and speed.

Little did I realise as a very young child arriving at my new home of Drybones for the first time that in the coming months and years I would be a privileged spectator to hares boxing in the field across the river behind our cottage. I would sometimes see this shy creature with the long ears and powerful back legs silently appear before me on my solitary walks along our lane and I would also regularly see hares jauntily crossing the wide open sweep of pasture on which our dining room and kitchen windows looked out. Occasionally I was treated to the vision of a hare streaking at lightning speed over the meadows, but that was only if it had been frightened; more usually they simply melted away – vanished before my astonished eyes. They became a fact of my life which always fascinated and enchanted me – a handsome and truly magical animal who I grew to love and deeply respect.

However, at the tender age of three and a half, I had absolutely no idea of all the wonderful adventures and experiences which awaited me in my new home...

THE HARE AS SACRED

Unlike the rabbit, the Hare has a long tradition of featuring in various spiritual belief systems all around the world and throughout history. My mother brought me up to greatly respect and revere this shy, magical animal. In many ancient cultures the Hare was regarded as a mystical animal linked to the Moon. As the cycles of the Moon rule the Earth's waters, and also influence the female reproductive cycle, so the Hare became an archetypal symbol of the divine feminine, fertility, longevity, rebirth and the lunar cycle from new to full and waning to dark; from conception to gestation; from growth to decline and death. Until relatively recently, the hare was thought to be androgynous and was representative of the way the Moon was perceived – in some cultures the waxing Moon had a masculine aspect and the waning Moon a feminine aspect. Even today, hares remind us of these ancient ways; they embody the natural rhythms – the very spirit – of life and such concepts as spiritual fulfilment and enlightenment.

The Hare is often seen as a messenger of the Great Goddess, moving by moonlight between the human world and the realm of deity. In some traditions the Hare is a god or goddess in his/her own right. Others demonstrate a belief that the Hare was somehow disgraced or denigrated, either out of jealousy or as a result of its own bad behaviour. However, there is always a very contradictory and paradoxical element to the Hare, simultaneously seen as a symbol of cleverness and foolishness, courage and cowardice, rampant sexuality and virginal purity, femininity and androgyny, a sacred world creator and wily deceiver all rolled into one. Perhaps this element to the Hare's sacred character only goes to reflect the generally amoral and untameable character of the elemental natural world?

Julius Caesar recorded that hares were taboo food for the Celtic peoples, although they were implicated in various rituals and remains have been found ceremonially interred at various sites. Perhaps this was because of the sacred connection between Hares and various goddesses, warrior queens, female fairies and the 'wise women' who were purportedly able to shape-shift into the form of a Hare by moonlight. Some of these beliefs have lingered on and until relatively recently, in County Kerry, it was believed that to eat hare meat was to eat one's own grandmother.

There is a legend that the Celtic warrior, *Oisin*, hunted a Hare and wounded it in the leg, forcing it to seek refuge in a clump of bushes. When *Oisin* followed it, he found a door leading into the ground and eventually he emerged into a huge hall where he found a beautiful young woman sitting on a throne bleeding from a wound in her leg.

In Teutonic myth, *Holda*, (*Frau Holle* - or Mother Holly - of Midwinter), the earth and sky goddess and feminine leader of the Wild Hunt, was sometimes depicted soaring across the sky followed by a procession of hares bearing torches. *Freyja*, the headstrong Norse goddess of love, sensuality and women's mysteries, was also served by hare attendants.

In other areas, such as western Siberia, the shape-shifting moon goddess, *Kaltes*, was thought to like to roam the earth in the form of a Hare and was sometimes pictured in human form wearing a headdress with hare's ears.

In Ancient Egypt, the god Osiris, had hare's ears up the sides of his crown or headdress. It is Osiris who was annually sacrificed to the Nile in the form of a hare. As principal god of the Egyptians, Osiris ruled the heavens with the god, Ra, the Sun God. They presided over night and day respectively, Ra governing the bright light of daytime and Osiris ruling the night as the personification of the nocturnal moon, (and, also by association, the god of the underworld and the

dead). Osiris, the hare-eared god, was seen as the bringer of Light –
and enlightenment - as he symbolically presented Ra, the Sun God,
to the darkened world each morning at the end of his nightly reign.

Also in Ancient Egypt, the hare-headed *Unnu't* or *Wenet*, was
worshiped as a moon goddess and there are pictures of her on
the walls of the temple of Dendera. In many parts of the world,
including China, Tibet, India, Sri Lanka, Mexico, parts of Africa and
across much of North America, the shadows on the surface of the
moon are thought to bear a strong resemblance to a hare and are
known as 'The Mark of the Hare'. As the full moon passes its highest
point in the sky, a hare appears to be at full stretch, leaping upwards
and towards the right. Earlier in the night it more resembles a sitting
hare, or the Hare that holds the Cosmic Egg. In Hindu and Sanskrit
belief, the Cosmic Egg was created by Shiva; when it cracked and
expanded it formed the universe, including our own solar system.

In China, the story is told of three fairy sages who turned
themselves into pitiful old beggars and asked a monkey, a fox and
a hare for food. The monkey and fox both had food to give but the
hare had nothing, so he leaped into the fire and offered his own flesh
as meat to feed the beggars. As a reward, the sages gave Hare a place
to live in the Moon Palace and he became known as the Jade Hare.
Jade amulets of hares are common in China and frequently found
among grave goods.

In Japanese mythology, the moon goddess, *Gwatten*, was often
depicted holding a crescent moon as a bowl in which crouched a
white hare.

There are also Buddhist stories all over Asia featuring the Hare
and the Moon. One famous tale involves the Buddha who, when he
was a youngster, wandered into the forest far from home and grew
hungry. The natural world took pity on him and brought their own
foods for the Buddha to eat, but of course, they were not suitable.
Eventually it was the Hare who (similarly to the Chinese tale) gave
the greatest gift by sacrificing himself by leaping into a pot of boiling
water and therefore offering himself up as a meal for the Buddha. As
a reward for his ultimate sacrifice, Buddha made the Hare immortal.

In North America, it is believed that the marks upon the surface of the moon were originally caused by an angry warrior flinging his grandmother up into the midnight sky. In other areas it was believed that The Great Hare god's grandmother was the moon. In a North American creation myth, it was taught that The Great Hare – called *Manibozho* or *Michabo* – created the sun and moon and made the land from a grain of sand brought from the bottom of the primeval ocean. The Great Hare was one of the principal gods, father and guardian of the nation, ruler of the winds and inventor of picture writing and later proper writing and who taught the people how to find food and look after themselves.

Further to the east on the opposite side of the Atlantic Ocean, there is an African myth that the Moon was so pleased with the Earth that she wanted to give mankind the gift of immortality. The Moon sent her companion, the Hare, to pass on her message, but Hare got the message muddled. Instead of 'Just as the Moon dies and rises again, so shall you', the message came out as "Just as the Moon dies, so shall you'. Mankind believed it and became mortal.

Tales were also taken to the Americas by African slaves which eventually became known as the Bre'r Rabbit tales told by Uncle Remus. The clue to their real origins is that there are no rabbits in tropical Africa – the clever animal was really the Hare.

ARRIVING AT DRYBONES

It was Maundy Thursday and the start of the Easter holidays. My father had been working that day and by the time my mother had closed the shop for the long weekend and packed all the groceries and baking and personal necessities that we would require for a few days, it was already quite late in the evening.

I well remember that first short journey to the cottage. As previously mentioned, it was only three miles from our old home at the shop in the centre of town; straight up Pall Mall, left into Weldbank Lane and up the hill to the gates for Saint Gregory's Catholic church and then right into Burgh Lane which was lined on either side by nice, individually designed and built houses. The pleasant leafy road twisted and turned for a few hundred yards before its tarmacadamed surface ceased abruptly – as did the houses – and we were catapulted off onto a rough dirt track full of large potholes and puddles. In the darkness that evening I couldn't see the greening fields which had replaced the dwellings on either side of the lane, or Mr Hough's little farm perched upon the rise above the wood which my mother had intrepidly plunged through the previous autumn and which separated it from our cottage further down the valley.

I was aware of being tossed and bumped around as we drove further down into the darkness, the two bright beams from the van's headlights catching startled mice and rabbits who then instantly froze at the intrusion and refused to move a muscle. We had to keep stopping the vehicle and switching off the engine and headlights for a few moments. Turning the headlights back on would reveal a completely deserted lane empty of all its little furry creatures and then we could carry on further until the next wild inhabitants hove into view and we would have to repeat the process.

In any case we had to drive very slowly as the surface of the lane was so very rough. Further on, the track divided, the left hand fork going to Hough's Farm and the right hand fork plunging us down a little hill where the lane became even more difficult to negotiate as uneven bedrock and huge stones stuck up out of the ground and haphazardly tipped us around. (We were later to name this part of the lane 'Rocky Hill' which it most certainly was!)

Finally, we arrived at a large brown wooden five-barred gate which my mother got out and opened and then on we went down the long drive... home. At that time I could not see the proud and powerful birch, sycamore and ash trees which crowded up to our left hand perimeter fence, or know that there was a cheerful little stream which chuckled its way across our land before rushing to combine its puny force with that of its much larger cousin, the River Yarrow, a lovely river of light and dark waters with banks of shingle and sand at the back of the cottage. I could hardly make out any of the one acre of land which mostly lay to the front of the house and I certainly had no idea how many adventures I was going to have playing in its wild, untamed and overgrown jungle!

I distinctly recall being lifted up and carried out of the van and into the cottage and set down in the kitchen on an ancient red horse-hair sofa which stood along the back wall between two windows and which was very prickly and smelt a bit damp. The Elses, the previous owners, had left quite a lot of their furniture behind them when they moved out – too out-dated and out-moded for their new bungalow in the neighbouring town perhaps. In particular, they had left a dark refectory table which stood down the middle of the room and which we eventually decided to keep; here we ate our meals together for many years before the big old kitchen was divided into two smaller rooms, giving us a proper dining room as well as a kitchen.

The brick-built cottage had originally been two dwellings but had been turned into one some decades before we arrived. The front door opened directly into the living room which contained a high brick fireplace. Another door led through into the kitchen which was heated by a coal-burning bungalow range, which also served to heat our water and cook our food. Both rooms were long and low with black wooden beams in the ceiling and yellowed walls where plaster was flaking and dropping off in places. Beyond the kitchen was a little two-roomed stone built buttery.

The stairs rose up the far end wall of the living room; two steps and then turned on a little landing before another nine steps set off again at right angles to the room. Once at the top, a long corridor ran the full length of the cottage, illuminated by a tiny window which had one of the best views in the house, out over the river and the fields beyond. All the upstairs rooms led off to the right from this corridor towards the front of the cottage. My bedroom door was directly at the top of the stairs... further down the corridor was the bathroom and at the very far end was my parent's bedroom.

To begin with, I slept in my parent's room in my old baby cot with the side panel permanently removed. But the following year, the second bedroom was cleared, painted a soft pink and divided (with the contrivance of a judiciously placed wardrobe and a very large bookcase!) to form a little nursery for me where I could play and keep all my toys and beyond it, a larger bedroom where I slept.

THE ELUSIVE EOSTRE

The modern traditional explanation for Eostre is that she was an Anglo-Saxon goddess associated with the moon and mythic stories of death, redemption and resurrection during the turning of the seasons from winter into spring. She was a shape shifter, reputedly taking the form of a hare at each full moon and also variously represented as having the ears or head of a hare. Eostre has frequently been depicted as being accompanied by a white or brown hare, a magical creature who laid brightly coloured eggs which were given out to children during spring fertility festivals.

However, all this is rather questionable as we do not have any references for Eostre earlier than the Eighth Century when the Venerable Bede wrote in his work *Temporum Ratione* ('The Reckoning Of Time') that during *Ēosturmōnaþ* – equivalent to the month of April – pagan Anglo-Saxons had held feasts in her honour. He went on to inform us that this tradition had died out by his time, to be replaced by the Christian month of Paschal, a celebration of the resurrection of Jesus.

The next reference we have to Eostre is many hundreds of years later when in 1835 the brilliant German linguist and folklorist, Jacob Grimm, claimed in his book, '*Deutsche Mythologie*', to have found evidence of Eostre in local oral traditions in certain areas of Germany. Later in the century, in a book of the same name another author, Adolf Holtzmann, claimed a connection between the springtime goddess of Eostre and the Hare.

The origins and validity of the goddess herself seem rather suspect and have generated much heated debate among academic and pagan circles alike. The author Jason Mankey writes that the historical Eostre was most likely a localised goddess worshipped by the Anglo-

Saxons in the modern-day county of Kent in South East England. Apparently, it is actually in Kent where the oldest references to names similar to that of Eostre are to be found. (Although this in itself is problematical as the word 'eostre' simply means 'east' and we are, after all, referring to a South Eastern area of the British Isles.) Linguist, Philip Shaw, argues that Eostre was perhaps a German Matrone Goddess linking a localised Eostre to the German *Austriahenea*, a matron goddess connected to the East. On reflection, the story is more likely to have its roots in a blend of Western esotericism and Eastern religions which began to popularly emerge in the second half of the Nineteenth Century.

I would suggest that Eostre herself is possibly a relatively modern invention or development. The very real and ancient relevance here is actually embodied in her companion, the Hare. In fact, I would go further and venture to say that Eostre is possibly just one northern colloquial name for the sacred Hare who has represented birth and regeneration (via the symbolic 'egg') and the rebirth of the spring season, coupled to the lunar influences upon life on Earth which have been individually developed by many peoples spanning several thousand years and at least four continents.

There has also been much confusion and heartache caused in trying to equate the Hare with a bird who could legitimately give birth to eggs. Obviously, the Hare no more physically gives birth to an egg than the shadows on the moon were really been created by a bad tempered American native warrior hurling his old granny up into the sky in a testosterone-fuelled fit of pique. The academic floundering of rational and intelligent adults attempting to explain how a Hare could possibly lay an egg begins to look a bit childish and laughable. Sadly, I would suggest that they have totally missed the point. The archetypal Hare 'laying' or otherwise producing/gifting eggs is the spiritual embodiment of the energies of the newly unfurling spring season and is the vehicle – the messenger – who channels these energies in the form of the egg, universal symbol of life, birth, rebirth and new growth.

COMMENT FROM JOAN: SPRING 1964

I said that I became a slave, all in the April green of that morning. A more correct description would be that I became a bondswoman. I walked up the hill at the side of the house – my very own hill – and found myself in a golden world of daffodils and faint budding silver birch; long, long hazel catkins and pussy willow – the kind that is called 'palm' in this part of Lancashire.

I looked and drew deep breaths and looked again. I have heard it said that the purest form of prayer is just thankfulness, and as I stood looking at all this dancing gold in the new-washed sunshine of a spring morning, I felt that my heart would burst with thankfulness for the boon of the feelings I was experiencing.

How could I transform all this with flame-throwers, bulldozers and unfeeling machines? I could not. I must tidy it somewhat and preserve the scene as near as possible as it was. This I am doing, yes, still labouring patiently at the task because no one told me that later in the season, mixed among the daffodils would be well rooted bracken and rosebay willow herb. Yes, they are beautiful too, seen in the distance, the only way they can be seen at my five feet, two inches of height when the 'weeds' in question tower above me at six feet tall!

MELANGELL AND THE HARE

In the early Christian persona of Saint Melangell we perhaps have a protector of pre-Christian belief in the guise of the Hare, potent messenger of the moon and representative of new life.

The story goes that Melangell was a Sixth Century Welsh saint of Irish descent who was forced to make a vow of chastity and flee across the Irish Sea to Wales when her father – an Irish king – tried to force her to marry against her will. Melangell eventually found sanctuary in a remote spot in the hills of Powys where she became a hermit, living in isolation without seeing the face of any man for fifteen years.

One day, it so happened that the Prince of Powys – whose name was Brochwel Yscythrog – was out hunting near her hermitage when his dogs roused a hare and chased it, forcing it to take refuge in a thicket. The prince thought the dogs had the hare at his mercy but when he caught up with them he got a shock. The hounds all stood at bay around the hare which sat defiantly glaring at the dogs from the folds of the dress worn by a young woman of great beauty who was deep in prayer. All around the dogs howled and bayed but they refused to go any nearer to the hare who sat staring boldly at them from the shelter of the woman's dress.

The prince then spoke to the woman who told him her story, of how she was a hermitess who lived nearby and had dedicated herself to God. Melangell explained how she had arrived and lived a life of great hardship and dedication to God, how her bed had been the hard cleft in a nearby rock, how she had vowed chastity and how he and his huntsmen were the first men she had seen in fifteen years.

Brochwel was so impressed by the woman and her story – not to mention the amazing effect she seemed to exert on his animals – that he gave her the land in that small isolated valley to keep and use as a sanctuary for all life, where hunting of any kind would no longer be permissible and where she could live in peace ever after.

In return, Brochwel asked Melangell to build him an abbey on the site, which she duly did, and where she became its abbess, living there for many years and dying at a great age.

As a higher proportion of fish tended to find its way onto domestic Lenten menus, I have decided to include two 'fishy' recipes for lesser-known water inhabitants. Both recipes originate from fond memories of when my parents were children back in the 1930s and were found in the early pages of my mother's manuscript cookery book.

Snigs
1952

Small, young eels – about 12 - 18 inches long

Method

- *Skin and remove heads of eels.*
- *Cut into six inch lengths and cook in hot deep fat – serve at once with chips or alone with bread and butter.*

There is no fish quite so rich and succulent or quite so satisfying after a day's fishing – and what a mouth-watering smell if you are at the wrong side of the lake. Jim likes them but thinks that either name is discouraging.

When my mother was a child, she used to go away every weekend with her family, camping in one of the three caravans which her father had built himself. He was a keen fisherman and they would drive up to the Lake District or down into Herefordshire or further south along the banks of the Severn or the Wye. My mother was free to explore the many wild places she found herself in while her father fished, but her parents always knew that she would soon be home if she smelt the snigs cooking. I remember when I was a teenager, one of our postmen discovered that my mother loved snigs and when he had been fishing, he would pop a parcel of them through our letterbox along with our mail!

Ray Knobs
1955

For the first time this spring I have tasted this uncommon fish. I spotted it on Preston market and often having heard Jim speak of them in Fleetwood in his youth, I eagerly bought some. The fishmonger advised me to boil them, as other parts of the ray, but Jim said to batter them. I battered and fried them in deep hot fat – just a flour and water batter – they were delicious and very filling. Jim was most pleased. Not knowing what part of the ray the 'knobs' come from we presume it to be the tail. (1964: I have just discovered it's the eyeball surround.)

KAYLEE'S AFTERNOON ADVENTURE
(A story for sharing with children)

Kaylee was confused. She had felt so important and grown-up when she told Annie and Jacob that there really was *no* Easter Bunny. She knew it for a fact because she had heard her dad talking to Mr Bennett (who lived further down their road) about it… how it always made her dad smile when he sneaked out with mum's shopping bag full of gaily coloured chocolate eggs and crept about their garden hiding them under or besides every flower he could find. Even the renegade daisies growing in his little front lawn were awarded one of the smallest Easter confectionaries. It made the garden look quite pretty as the shiny reds, golds, blues and greens of the metallic sweet wrappers glinted back at him. But it was a real pain if the weather was wet! "The kids do nothing but moan and complain and nag about it until the rain stops!" dad had chuckled.

Hearing all this, Kaylee was absolutely bursting to tell all her friends and even the little tots who lived at Number Fifteen. At the fine age of eight and a half, Kaylee was one of the eldest children in Primrose Road – except for the Big Girls and Boys who went away on the bus to the secondary school in the next town, but she didn't count *them* because they never had anything to do with the younger children and only laughed and teased them.

Kaylee was quite puffed up with importance as she described her father's antics to her wide-eyed audience and got rather cross when some of the children refused to believe her. Some of the little ones even burst into tears. There were no games played out in the quiet road that Saturday afternoon as small children dispersed in various states of anger and upset.

Then there came a succession of knocks at Kaylee's front door and her mum's polite and then anxiously apologetic tones repeated several times before she finally called out Kaylee's name.

What a hullabaloo there had been! Mum wanted to know why Kaylee had spread such stories to the other children upsetting them all and then was admonished with "Well, if you're such a big girl, you should know better than to go spoiling the fun for everyone else!" Kaylee felt that she couldn't do right whatever she did.

Finally, with tears scalding her own blazing red cheeks she slunk off into the back garden, but after a few minutes she decided that she would do something really naughty – she'd show them all – and with that thought firmly fixed in her head, she disappeared behind her dad's little wooden shed at the bottom of the garden and eased her way along between the wooden panelling and the bushes until she reached a part where the hedge was a bit thin and straggly. Here she squirmed under the prickly branches. She was free!

Beyond their back garden and the hedge lay an old disused quarry. It hadn't been worked for many years and the council kept suggesting that it should be redeveloped as a new housing estate. Most of the piles of waste had grasses growing over them and they looked lovely to climb and sit on. There were several big pits, too, where the stone had been taken out and which were now filled with water – it was quite a pretty place of lakes and pools and little hills and knolls. But all the children were forbidden to go there. It was far too dangerous, their parents told them, and by and large, the youngsters kept away, except for the Big Girls and Boys who Kaylee sometimes saw walking there; she didn't know if they ever got into trouble or not. Well, today she was a Big Girl too – her mother had told her so – so she was going to explore and have an adventure of her own.

The little girl wandered about a bit. She felt grumpy and cross and all spikey, just as we all do when we know we have done something wrong but don't want to admit it. Even worse, she was beginning to feel a bit nervous because she wasn't sure which direction to take to get back to her own hedge and so home again. Eventually, she sat down feeling very disconsolate, and very quietly began to cry. This was turning into the worst day of her life!

Presently, Kaylee became aware that she was not alone. Slowly, she turned her head and found that a very large rabbit was staring straight at her from the other side of a little gorse bush. Its eyes were very bright and it was so close that Kaylee could see its whiskers twitching.

"Why are you crying?" the animal finally asked her. Kaylee was so surprised to hear the rabbit speak that at first, she just stared back at it in amazement.

"Rabbits can't talk!" The girl finally gasped.

"Quite right," the animal agreed, "But then I'm not a rabbit."

"What are you then?" Kaylee queried, her tears quite forgotten.

"I'm a hare. Look, my ears are much longer than a rabbit's and my back legs are much bigger and more powerful because I can run, oh, so *very* fast… and my fur is quite different too." Kaylee was trying to take all this in when the hare spoke again, "And anyway, I'm not even an ordinary hare – I am the Easter Hare. It isn't the Rabbit who hides all the chocolate Easter Eggs for you children, it is me, the Hare, who has been guarding these special eggs and giving them away for many, many years.

"Why do you do it?"

"Because, the Lady Eostre, Queen of the Springtime asks me to do it."

"But why does *she* do it?"

"Because she rules the Spring," replied the Hare with some asperity, "Eggs represent birth and new life and that is what springtime is – the time when everything comes back to life and regrows - lambs are born, the trees burst into leaf, the grass starts to grow again and flowers bloom, and the days grow warmer and lighter." The Hare saw that Kaylee was still looking somewhat astonished and unconvinced so he continued more gently, "Everyone used to have real hen's eggs and people would colour and decorate them. It was a time for everyone to celebrate, but now it is just for the children. Times change and we have chocolate eggs now..." the Hare trailed off a little sadly.

"But my dad hides our eggs around our garden – I heard him say so myself with my own ears... and dad wouldn't tell lies!" Kaylee exclaimed indignantly.

"Of course he does," the Hare agreed, "But you don't think that I can get around to every single child's home or garden, do you? And then what about all the big public Easter Egg hunts? I'd never do it – I'd be running around with baskets of eggs until Christmas and then I'd be in trouble with Father Christmas because I'd be in *his* way." The Hare watched the little girl and could see that she was still struggling to understand.

"Look," he continued more gently, "No one can do everything themselves, it just isn't possible. So, we in the magical world get some of you humans to help us. They don't know that they are helping us, of course. They think that they are having these ideas all on their own, but it is me who guides them to buy and then hide the chocolate eggs. There are so many children now that most years it takes *me* all my time just to seed these ideas into the grow-up's heads."

"So, dad *does* hide our eggs, but they are really from you?"

"Yes," replied the Hare.

"Then I was right all along, and mum was wrong. But she was right, too, and I hadn't got it quite right either." Kaylee looked as perplexed as the Hare was beginning to feel. "I think that you have some explaining to do," he said kindly. Kaylee went on to explain everything that had happened that afternoon. By the end of her tale of woe, the Hare was grinning from ear to ear. "Yes," he chuckled, "You were all definitely right... and wrong!" Then the Hare looked thoughtful for a moment. "Don't you worry, m'dear, everything is going to be just fine. The really important thing now is to convince the little children that there really is springtime magic, and that their eggs really do come from My Lady, Eostre, via me. I have an idea! Just to prove that I am real, go home and when you next see all your little friends, tell them that on Easter Sunday morning, when they go out to hunt their eggs, they will be sure to also find a chocolate Hare each, wrapped in shiny gold foil with a little gold tinkly bell hanging around its neck... we magical creatures rather like high fluting music and tinkling bells. It is very important that all you children go on believing in the magical miracle of the Spring and the time of everything springing back to life."

Kaylee looked rather doubtful, but she didn't like to argue with the Hare; she had had more than enough of doing and saying the wrong thing for one day. Now the Easter Hare was offering to help her find her way back to the gap in her hedge. As she walked down the slope towards it, she turned to the animal besides her to thank him... only to find that she was on her own – the Hare had completely vanished.

"Did I dream it?" Kaylee asked herself. "Oh, I give up!"

However, Kaylee did as the Easter Hare had asked; she went and explained to each of the younger children how she had made a mistake and had actually spoken to the Easter Hare who was really behind it all, even if their mums and dads also helped him out. Some of the older children frankly didn't believe Kaylee and laughed at her. Some of the little ones were goggle-eyed and became terribly over-excited.

Kaylee did surprise her parents by asking if they could hard boil some eggs and decorate them for breakfast on Easter Sunday morning, before they had their Egg Hunt. "What a nice idea!" Kaylee's dad smiled enthusiastically. "I remember my mum telling me how they used to do that when they were children – I'd forgotten."

Whatever anyone thought, or did or didn't believe, that year *every* child was delighted to discover a chocolate gold foil-wrapped 'Hare' among the rest of their Easter Eggs; even some of the grow-ups were give one as well. Only Kaylee wasn't surprised. At last, she knew the truth, but she wasn't going to say anything to anyone!

It was only when she sat down to breakfast that Easter Sunday morning that she received her own very special surprise, for there of the table was a whole bowl of hard boiled eggs and on each one of them was a beautiful coloured picture of the Easter Hare. Mum had no idea where they had come from and thought that dad must have put them there as a surprise but dad was just as baffled as everyone else.

Kaylee smiled to herself. She knew where the specially decorated eggs had come from. Carefully, the little girl gently took the top off her egg so as not to break the part of the shell with the picture on it – she was going to keep *that* for ever and ever – but she had such a Springtime song in her heart as she did so.

"Thank you, Easter Hare, and Lady Eostre… I really *do* believe in your magic now, and when I am grown up, I shall always be happy to help you!"

Decorating Eggs

If you would like to decorate some eggs for yourself, like the ones Kaylee had, here are some simple tips to help you get started.

For hard boiled eggs

First decide on how many eggs you would like to decorate and hard boil them by putting them in a pan, covering them with water, placing them over a heat source, bringing them to the boil and then simmering for ten minutes. Remove from heat, drain and allow to cool.

Once they are cold there are many ways in which you can decorate them:

- **MARBLED EGGS:** place a teaspoon of vegetable oil into a bowl of dye and stir gently to disperse oil bubbles. Gently roll each egg in the bowl for a few seconds. Pat off excess liquid with paper towel and set on cooling rack to dry. Once completely dry, use dry cloth to completely wipe away excess oil residue.
- **NAIL POLISH EGGS:** Swirl some nail polish into water and then dip egg into it.
- **PRESSED FLOWER EGGS:** either of the above – or even plain hard boiled eggs – may be further embellished by gluing tiny pressed flowers to the eggshell for a dainty and very appealing natural look.

- **PAPER PUNCH EGGS:** Use craft punches to cut shapes from different coloured paper. Fold the shapes down the middle and attach to solid coloured (or plain) hard boiled eggs with craft glue.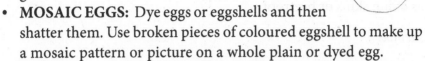
- **MOSAIC EGGS:** Dye eggs or eggshells and then shatter them. Use broken pieces of coloured eggshell to make up a mosaic pattern or picture on a whole plain or dyed egg.

 TRIPLE DIPPED EGGS: You might wish to achieve a more modern, geometric look by submerging a hard boiled egg in dye. Once dry, re-dip just a part of the egg at an angle for a longer period of time. Repeat process at a third angle.

- **BRIGHT EGG VOTIVES:** For this, do not boil your eggs – blow the egg out of the shell and dry completely. Gently break the shell with a spoon, removing the top third. Dye the rest of the eggshell and once dry, place a tealight inside it. These make good breakfast or dinner table decorations as well as spring/Easter themed decorative lights to dot around a room – ensure they don't fall over by standing in empty metal tealight container.
- **COLOURED PENS:** these can always be used for quick, easy results – perhaps when all the family wants to have a quick go at decorating an egg or you have very young children.

Making Natural Dyes

Ingredients

These can be made from things you might find in the kitchen such as onion skins or beetroot.

Method

- Place a quart (1 litre) of water and two tablespoons of white vinegar in a pan and bring to the boil. Add whatever ingredients you are using for colour and lower heat, and simmer for thirty minutes.
- Leave to cool and then strain.
- Place eggs in liquid dye for thirty minutes. Remove eggs from dye with tongues and pat dry with paper towel.

Ideas for dyes

Pink – four cups chopped beetroot simmered for thirty minutes
Orange – four cups onion skins simmered for thirty minutes
Yellow – Three tablespoons turmeric, simmered for thirty minutes
Light blue – three cups red or purple cabbage, simmered for thirty minutes
Dark blue – four cups of blueberries, simmered for thirty minutes

All of these ingredients above then need to be strained and once cool, the eggs to be dyed placed in the liquid dye. If a deeper, more vibrant colour is required, leave the eggs in the dye for longer or even overnight.

Chapter Ten

How does your garden grow?

"And the Spring arose on the garden fair,
And the Spirit of Love fell everywhere;
And each flower and herb on Earth's dark breast
Rose from the dreams of its wintry rest."

Percy Byshe Shelley

Action follows thought. Perhaps you are one of those sorts of people who have been sitting inside all winter, plotting, planning and dreaming of all the things which you might do once the days grow longer and the weather improves. Or maybe you are the kind of person who simply wakes up one day to a symphony of birdsong, blossom on the trees, warm sunshine and the certainty that spring has already well and truly arrived. Whatever, there comes a point when the call and allure of the outdoors becomes too strong to ignore and, donning stout shoes or wellington boots and a waterproof jacket, we venture out into the lanes and woods, the parks and forests. For many of us, the first point of contact after the vegetative state of Midwinter celebration and the cold, dark days following it are our gardens.

THE GIFT OF HEALING

This primeval pull to get close up and personal with the land is deeply instinctual. The benefits of working with and over the soil are manifold, not least because it usually culminates in something beautiful to look at and/or delicious to eat. Plants also help to clean our air, whether that be in or outside our homes. We gain great satisfaction and pleasure from the tiniest achievement, not to mention healthy exercise and a host of other pluses such as improved health.

Microbes in soil called *Mycobacterium vaccae* are inhaled by gardeners which cause cytokine levels to rise in the body resulting in the production of higher levels of serotonin, which in turn helps us to feel less anxious, more relaxed and to sleep better. Two and a half hours of working on the land at a moderately intense level of activity each week can improve cognitive function and also seriously reduce the risk of many illnesses such as colon cancer, heart disease, obesity, osteoporosis, rheumatoid arthritis and type 2 diabetes.

Furthermore, science tells us that our planet has magnetic fields and that walking or standing barefoot on any natural surface (soil, grass, sand, etc.) allows us to connect to these natural energies of the earth. It results in an exchange of energies between us as individuals and the planet we live on, which neutralises and cleanses our body.

According to a study published in the Journal of Environmental and Public Health, we draw electrons from the earth which helps to lessen our aches and pains. There is also another study which demonstrates through the use of an electroencephalogram how going barefoot in the natural world can change the activity in the brain. Other studies suggest that walking barefoot on the earth can provide health benefits such as improved glucose control, regulation of the heartbeat and a strengthening of the immune system.

It has been suggested that wearing leather-soled footwear does not create such a barrier to these energies, whereas synthetic soled shoes cuts them off from our feet entirely, and that a rise in certain modern illnesses is perhaps due to the mass introduction of such synthetic footwear. Whether this is so or not, the fact remains that until very recently (the past two hundred years) humanity has traditionally lived on and with the land in agrarian communities, allied to the natural rhythms and cycles of the seasons. Our Twenty-first Century life is largely de-nurtured and unnatural and, as a species, we are seriously beginning to pay the price. If these simple, basic actions of connecting to the natural world can help us to heal and improve our health in ways often denied us by modern mainstream medicine, might we have avoided a lot of our ailments if we hadn't become so disconnected from the earth in the first place? The burning question now is how to reverse the detrimental trends and repair the damage?

Like everything else in existence, plants resonate at various energetic frequencies. Growing them, having soil and plants – the natural living world – in our lives, simply by being near them, can exert tremendous beneficial influences on all those who come into contact with them. Therefore, whatever your circumstances, I would strongly recommend growing something. It might only be a few pots of herbs on the kitchen windowsill of your tiny flat, or several tubs of flowers on your balcony or outside your front/back door, but the difference to your life will be incalculable.

THE SEED FAIR

Thoughts produce ideas which alternately lead to inspiration and enthusiasm as we dream with the Earth in her slumber throughout the cold months. Thoughts are very like seeds. They germinate and begin to grow. For some, the coming of spring might simply be a case of maintaining what has already been formed and achieved in the garden; for others it might be a case of a complete make-over and change. Some of us might be lucky enough to have just acquired a garden for the first time, and some of us might not have a garden at all.

For me, my annual gardening activities begin with seeds which I collect and save from plants in my garden throughout the year. You can do this with any plant, including all your vegetables. Just allow one or two plants to flower and go to seed. I especially love the frothy yellow blooms produced in spring by the last of my broccoli. Against a background of blue forget-me-not 'weeds' they are an utter joy to behold. Just be aware that if your plants originally came from hybrid seed, they won't grow back true to the type you harvested them from.

Also, make sure that your seeds have fully developed before you harvest them or they won't be able to grow the next season. This usually means leaving the seed heads or pods until they are brown and dry. On the other hand, don't wait too long or the heads might have begun to open and broadcast themselves to the four winds before you can reap the benefits.

Some seeds are relatively large and can be collected by hand and placed on paper tissue in an open basket to dry somewhere warm but not too hot. Other seeds are tiny and difficult to handle and have to be collected by gently placing a paper bag over the seed heads whilst still in situ, gripping or tying the bag tightly before carefully cutting the stems with the other hand. Upend the bag and shake it until most – or all – of the seeds have detached themselves from the seed heads and fallen into the bag. Sometimes it might be a good idea to hang the upended bag somewhere for a few days to allow all the seeds to fall from their casings gradually. Then place them somewhere warm and dry in the open for a few hours to ensure that the seeds are completely dry. Finally, place in an airtight container and label with the date and name of the seeds and store in a cool dark place until you are ready to replant them. Why throw your crop of fresh seed onto the compost heap or into the rubbish bin and then pay for more seed which someone else has grown? This way you can save a considerable amount of money each spring or use it instead to buy alternative treats or experiments for the garden.

You may have been pouring over seed catalogues since January or been seduced by the racks of packets of seeds at your local garden centre and even displays of seed packets in many of the supermarkets. I find them all very enticing and exciting and I have to confess to succumbing to all of them at one time or another!

My favourite time and place to buy seeds – and plants – is at our local 'Seed Fair' in Conwy which takes place every year on the 26th March. The Seed Fair is allied to the Honey Fair which dates back over seven hundred years to when King Edward I of England granted the town a Royal Charter. It included the right for beekeepers to sell honey within the walls of Conwy every 13th September from midnight to midnight, without being charged for doing so. It is unclear when the Seed Fair actually began, but it was certainly in existence by the year 1835 when seven fairs occurred annually in Conwy, featuring wool, butter and horses, as well as seeds and honey. By the 1980s the fairs were in decline, but when members of the Aberconwy and Colwyn Beekeepers Association (now known as Conwy Beekeepers) stepped in and decided to take over the organising and promotion of the Honey Fair, prospects began to improve. The opening of the road tunnel under the River Conwy in 1991 freed the town from much heavy traffic and meant that the fairs could once more be held in the main streets of the town without causing too much disruption – although many of the local shop owners still protest vociferously.

I think that part of the charm of any market is that it is held in the open air – subject to the perfidious weather – and that it is in the heart of its community, in other words, the central streets of whichever town, village (or city) it serves. The first time I visited the Seed Fair I was captivated by its variety and charm but disturbed that there were relatively few stalls actually selling seeds. There was a very good selection of vendors offering a great variety of plants – some of them most unusual or comparatively rare – but not so many seeds. I strongly believe that if you wish to see something done, or done differently, it behoves you to do something about it yourself. In my usual enthusiastic fashion, I therefore decided to try to reverse this trend and spent that summer and autumn collecting, drying and saving my own seeds from the garden to packet up and offer for sale at the Seed Fair the following spring.

My husband, son and me duly drove the 30 miles up the coast and arrived in Conwy around 7:30 a.m. on a very cold and frosty March morning. We were in good time to be given a reasonable spot and to set up my table. Inevitably, I had also decided to take a variety of plants to offer for sale too – otherwise you need an awful lot of packets of seeds to make a truly decent display. I had also prepared a few other 'pocket money' items to sell, such as plant labels cut from recycled plastic milk containers. We were somewhat bemused to find ourselves on the middle of the main street which slopes to a greater or lesser degree and which therefore caused my tabletop to slope too. I had to employ a little ingenious subterfuge to prevent certain items from gradually working their way to the edge of the table and disappearing on to ground. (My husband made me a set of wooden blocks to place under the table legs so levelling the table up – and the next year we bought a table with adjustable lengths of leg and our problems were sorted!) Then there was the wind. One corner in Lancaster Square can be quite savage and sometimes almost takes one's breath as well as the stall canopies away, let alone the produce. Even the slightest breath can disturb or remove information cards and price labels. I had attended fairs of a different sort with my collector's miniatures for over twenty years, but they had all been held under cover. This was a completely different ball game! As always under these circumstances, a good dollop of common sense mixed with a sprinkle of humour makes for a successful day.

It was successful, too. By the time the first customers came strolling along the street just after nine o'clock, the sun came out and began to warm us up. It also lifted my spirits. I could hardly believe that I was helping to take part in an event and on the very same spot where people had laid out their wares and stamped their cold feet and blown on their frozen fingers for dozens of generations. Following in the footsteps of my ancestors – the druid and historian in me responded deeply to that realisation. I revelled in simply being there; also in the fact that it is a fairly traditional fair selling home produce – no piped music or electric lights or plastic products – except, perhaps, on one of two charity stalls, but that is a different thing and understandable – after all, some of our forebears lived in the Stone Age and the Iron Age and now we live in the Plastic Age.

I had great fun that day, meeting and talking to dozens of lovely, interesting people; enjoying the other stalls and buying treats for my own garden; beginning my Christmas shopping for the following Midwinter and just simply absorbing the sights, sounds, smells and atmosphere. We had so much fun that after that, we regularly had a stall at both Seed and Honey Fairs until relatively recently when, owing to pressure of work and the inevitable aging process, standing outside for the best part of ten hours in sometimes near freezing temperatures or in arctic wind and rain began to get more challenging than was comfortable.

However, I do still attend the Seed Fair regularly. One nurseryman comes all the way down from Preston in Lancashire, only a few miles from where I used to live, and I always like to buy some spring bulbs, onion and Shallotte sets and more unusual varieties of seeds from him. It is also where we purchased the Bramley Apple and the two currant bushes for Cae Non. Then there is another fellow who always has the healthiest sweet pea plants, and several other stalls where it is possible to find unusual herbs – an absolute must for my medical herbalist son!

Contrary to the criticisms of the irritated shop keepers, we also take the opportunity to visit the shops. Edwards the prize-winning butcher sells delicious sausages; Hinton's Bookshop is always worth exploring – as is Yesteryear's Toyshop where I like to keep abreast of what the toy industry is actually offering to children by way of doll's houses and accessories. Our favourite watering hole is the café and bookshop on the High Street. Here we meet up with friends and on cold rainy days, gossip an hour or so away with our hands wrapped around the most delicious mugs of frothy hot chocolate. On warm sunny days we can sit out in the bustle of the street, or in the suntrap of a little courtyard at the back. The fairs in Conwy have always been a good time to do business or socialise. If we need a breather from all the busyness, we take a stroll around the mediaeval town walls – Conwy is one of my favourite places!

With Silver Bells and Cockle Shells

Our gardens can be as individual as the homes we live in. Much depends on the size, shape, geographical location and soil type. Even in this day and age, it is surprising that some people still opt for the pocket handkerchief of grass surrounded by borders of flowers, or, horror of horrors, just concrete it all over. There is such scope to join with the land and express your mutual individuality and character. A garden is also an extension of your home. Many of us need space outside to fulfil various functions. You might need somewhere to store recycling bins, erect a shed for extra storage, a safe space for the children to play, somewhere to dry your washing and last but no means least, somewhere to relax, eat outside on warm days and possibly entertain on celebratory ones.

- To begin re-designing your outdoor space, simply draw the shape of it. Mark in the features which cannot be moved or changed or that you wish to keep – such as boundary walls or fences, gates or doors, steps, garages or outbuildings. Then begin playing with ideas of what you might wish to include – trees, water features, seating areas, firepits, storage units – and then add details of plants, drawing them as blobs with the colour of pen that their flowers will bloom into to get an idea of how the colours will fit together. This is not to submit to the best small garden competition at the Chelsea Flower Show. This is your 'outdoor room' designed and built and grown to reflect you and suit your needs. You might wish to grow flowers, or fruit and vegetables, or have decking or a paved terrace... the possibilities are endless. For those of you who don't actually have a garden, please be patient. I will return to suggestions as to what you might be able to do instead later in the chapter.

- To begin with I am going to suggest a fairly small and manageable project which can be adapted to your needs and preferences in many different ways. Or perhaps it will stir your mind and inspire you to come up with your own unique design.

- Below is a star design (See *Fig 1*) which measures five feet six inches long by just four feet wide. It provides seven beds and can be sited wherever you like - in the corner of a garden, or in the middle of a lawn as a centre-piece and adapted for a whole variety of uses. You might like to plant a dwarf or semi standard fruit tree or fruit bush in the centre and surround it with a variety of fruit and veg.

- Or you may wish to fill in between the points of the star (as I have done with the dotted lines) and give yourself a maximum of twelve beds. The central hexagon can be left as a bed or paved or gravelled to provide easier access within the circle of beds… or somewhere to stand a small garden chair or stool so that you can sit literally in the midst of your garden glory and unwind.

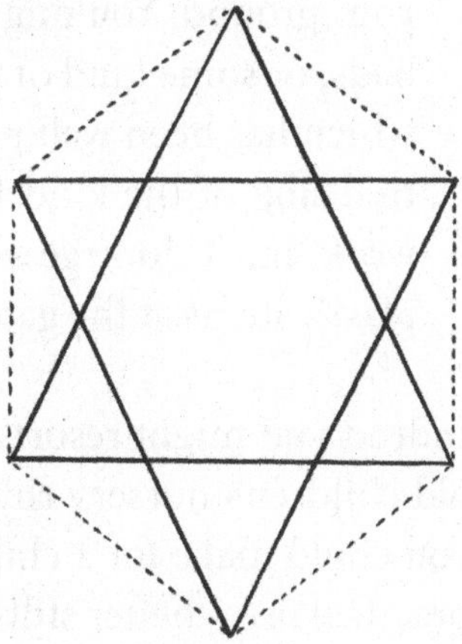

Figure 1

- Perhaps you have a little more space or feel the need to be even more adventurous. Looking at the larger design in *Fig 2*, add an extra set of points. This would still only give you twelve beds, but a larger multifaceted feature. Or you might prefer to give yourself the second row of star points but then surround the whole with a boundary of some sort - the same as you have formed the rest

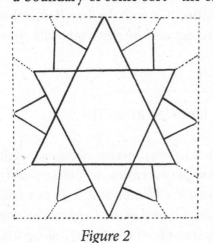

Figure 2

of the design with or perhaps a low fence or simply an edging border of lavender or other aromatic herbs. This can then be subdivided again (see the dotted lines in *Fig 2*) which would give you a potential 24/25 beds in an area only approximately five feet six inches in length and five feet two inches in breadth. If you have the space and the inclination, you might wish to double the dimensions making an overall design of eleven feet by ten feet six inches. This is still not huge but gives you a lot more scope as to the variety and amount you grow there.

- How you arrange access to the centre – perhaps by devoting one or two triangles to acting as a pathway – is up to you. It is also for you to decide what you wish to use to mark out the design on your ground. You might wish to use reclaimed bricks to edge the beds, or some kind of paving stones or slate slabs, or even timber which has been well preserved. Some kind of miniature wooden trellising of the kind found in shops and garden centres would work, but I do urge you to use something natural and leave all plastic items at the gate.

Indeed you might resort to the 'silver bells and cockle shells' of the old children's nursery rhyme – just think what a pretty little garden you could make for a child – a place of beauty and magic as well as practical use – better still, get them to help you in the making of it so that they feel fully invested in the activity from the very beginning. If you have older children or teenagers, get them to do it for you, perhaps just do the marking out for them first. But remember that in cases such as these, be prepared for it to look nothing like you originally anticipated or planned. It will be unique. On the other hand, they might amaze you with what they create and it might be even better than your original intention. Go with the flow. Remember that this is obviously a family project and be generous with your enthusiasm and praise.

COMMENT FROM JOAN: SPRING 1964

In like manner I have unexpectedly discovered masses of colour which, on closer inspection, in turn became purple crocus, celandine (lesser), campanula, lily of the valley, primroses, iris, bleeding hearts. In fact, both wild and once garden flowers that have survived years of neglect have now become hardy and thrived, surviving even the all-enveloping couch grass.

Every time I see this horrible type of grass scourge I remember that Nicholas Culpepper, the 17th Century herbalist, wrote that one field of this grass was worth three such fields of carrots to any physician. My mind then contemplates with horror that I am the unfortunate who has the equivalent quantity scattered with a liberal hand all over my land. I must say that he must be correct when he tells you to watch a dog who will go straight to it to cleanse its system. All five of my Alsatians (German Shepherd dogs) do just this, following each bunch of roots to the bitter end, and you know how quickly (wonder if that is why it is called Quick Grass?) and by what devious and torturous ways the scourge spreads. Usually through and towards any drop-in-the-ocean patch I have cleared, digging like beings possessed, on and on like gigantic surface whales, my canines will pursue them through lovingly tended flowers and vegetables.

At such times, I have wondered if the dogs could be trained to hunt for truffles as pigs are in France. Mind you, I haven't any idea if truffles are to be found here, though one of the farm children told me that they had 'piggy nuts' about the size of a crocus in their wood, since when I have hugged the thought to myself, but have never put the theory to the test. In any case, though the farmer is one of the most kind and helpful people here, I think that even he would draw the line if he saw trees uprooted and damage like to that in the wake of a hurricane wrought by my pack of over-enthusiastic hounds.

Not that it would surprise me to discover that even truffles are to be found close at hand. When I first came here, I had ideas of transforming the dreams of a lifetime into reality; definite, but yet - up till then – ideas of silver birch, beech hedges, lilac and running, falling water. Well, that first year here was a revelation. Every day I met my husband with excited announcements, "Jim, what do you think, I've found a silver birch... an old, scented rose... more apple trees..." Like the secret garden in the book of the same name by Frances Hodgson Burnett, the garden never ceased to surprise and delight me.'

A BOUQUET OF CHOICES

When I was a youngster, my vegetable garden would have vied with the Romans in its military precision and grid-like design of square and rectangular beds and borders. However, since I grew older, I have to confess that I have grown to love watching my garden randomly develop and choose how and where – and with whom – the plants within it wish to live and thrive. I delight in finding self-seeded plants happily moving in to other areas than where they were originally situated and for many years my greatest joy – and the best nursery bed that I have ever had - has been to observe and harvest all the baby seedlings which have endlessly tried to colonise the slate chipping paths in my herb garden. Just like us, plants and trees know where they are going to feel happiest living… and who they would most like to have for neighbours. Some plants actually keep others free of pests or encourage growth by providing nutriment for the soil which will enable their neighbour to grow more prolifically. It pays to watch, observe and take note of what your garden is trying to tell you.

Having taken things into consideration such as the type of soil (clay, sand, etc.) or acid or alkaline your garden might be, and whether it is dry, wet, sunny or shaded, etc, one has to begin somewhere and put your own stamp on your space, even if you rapidly change your mind as you see what flourishes where and what droops and fades. This can sometimes be quite daunting, so I have a few suggestions which you might like to consider.

Bearing in mind what part of the British Isles or the world you live in, and what attributes your plot possesses, you might like to ask yourself three questions. What do you want to grow? What do you need to grow? What do you need/want to use your garden for? You might need to grow as much of your own organic food as possible, but that still doesn't preclude you from making it look beautiful and making a feature of it. You might feel drawn to propagating your own herbs for culinary use or medicinal purposes or have a bit of a problem spot which is too shady, too damp, or too dry.

I am not going to try and explain how to grow things – there are a plethora of wonderful books, magazines, films and blog posts on how to do anything and everything for you to delve into and enjoy. I have included some useful links, addresses and titles at the end if this book which might be helpful in starting you off, refreshing your memory or otherwise inspiring you. In each of the sections below, I have suggested a small selection of possible plants to start you off – go and look them up and find more of the same, and thoroughly enjoy doing a little detective work of your own.

CULINARY HERB GARDEN: A basic selection of leafy growth which can be used in your cooking is always an added bonus. There are so many to choose from but you could start with these – one for each of the twelve smaller beds in my design.

Sage, thyme, chives, oregano, marjoram, lemon balm, parsley, coriander and dill. Mint is essential, but don't just plant it straight into the ground unless you don't mind having it colonise everywhere else in a few years' time – it can be awfully invasive, so plant it in a container and either sink it partially into the ground (to retain moisture and prevent the wind blowing it over) or simply stand it on the soil. Basil is a must for so many dishes but, depending on where you are trying to grow it, it might not do for you… remember that it is a Mediterranean plant and does not thrive in cold damp conditions, so choose somewhere sheltered and sunny for it. Borage can be a bit floppy and untidy but does provide beautiful blue flowers for adding to summer salads and long cool drinks. The leaves also make a good tea to help bolster flagging spirits. Rosemary will grow larger into a bush if allowed so might make a good central feature. Sweet cicely makes a slightly unusual and aniseedy addition to salads but its true gift is that it intensifies flavour. Add it to soups, stews and casseroles and reduce your use of salt; add it to sweet dishes such as stewed fruit and you will be able to greatly reduce your use of sugar.

MEDICINAL HERB GARDEN: Be sure to plant mint, especially peppermint (*Mentha x piperita*) for its soothing action on the digestive system, comfrey (*Symphytum officinale*) for muscle aches and pains, St. John's Wort (*Hypericum perforatum*) to heal nerves, and melissa (*Melissa officinalis*) as a soothing carminative for both ragged nerves, sleepless nights, and upset stomachs. Garden favourites like lavender (*Lavandula angustifolia*) and rose (Especially *Rosa x Damascena*! Rosemary (*Rosmarinus officinalis*) is a must in a sunny garden for its ability to de-fog muzzy heads – and improve the digestion! Marigolds (*Calendula officinalis*) are a lovely flower which will brighten any flower bed from spring right the way through to early winter and are very useful as a 'do it all' herb with a special affinity for skin conditions. Lastly, we mustn't forget thyme (*Thymus vulgaris*) for its clearing effect on the lungs, and its ability to fight infection, or sage (*Salvia officinalis*) for its cooling, drying qualities beloved of ladies going through the change – and those who love stuffing with their Sunday roast!

SCENTED GARDEN: In this case I am referring to the foliage rather than the flowers and therefore have all-year-round appeal. The leaves of many plants contain aromatic essential oils which release a scent when picked, brushed against or crushed. If you have some ground which you frequently walk past or a seat where you often sit, surround it with a bouquet of natural perfume: eau de cologne mint, southernwood, lemon balm, mint, cotton lavender (*Santolina chamaecyparissus*), sage, pelargoniums, myrtle, rosemary, eucalyptus, lemon verbena, bergamot/bee balm (*Monarda didyma*), lavender and sweet woodruff (*Gallium odoratum*). If you wish to attract cats to your garden or amuse your own feline friends, you might also like to plant some catnip – there are several kinds but the one to really get our furry friends in a tizzy is *Nepata cataria* – but you might need to protect it with wire netting as it can be totally rubbed away by over-enthusiastic animals! And if you fancy something a bit spicy, why not add a curry plant? Just be careful what you place it next to so that the two scents don't dramatically clash.

THE EVENING GARDEN: If you are an ultra-busy person who works for long hours during the daytime, you might wish to consider planting an evening or night garden where you can sit in the twilight with a glass of wine and unwind amongst the heady scents of fragrant foliage and allow the cares and stresses of the day to melt away.

For starters you might have night-scented stocks (*Matthiola longipetala*), night-scented jasmine (*Cestrum nocturnum*), perennial white stocks (*Matthiola perennis 'Alba'*), evening primrose (*Oenothera*), tuberose (*Polianthes tuberosa*), tobacco plants (*Nicotiana sylvestris*), night phlox, honeysuckle, petunias or pinks (*Dianthus*). There is also a variety of wisteria which is said to have the strongest scent in the evening, and this is *Wisteria floribunda*. Of course, all these plants have different needs of habitat and various colours of flowers, shapes of foliage, heights and so on – which gives you lots of room for interpretation in your initial garden design. And there are a lot more to choose from… this is only the start!

A DAMP GARDEN: There are also plants which love damp or wet ground – or which you might want to use to enliven around the perimeters of a tired pond: astilbe, great burnet, marsh marigolds and candelabra primulas are all good for this, as is Rudbeckia (*fulgida*), lobelia (*cordinalis*) and *Trollius europaeus*. Something like a Japanese painted fern (*Athyrium niponicum var pictum*) would help to create dramatic structure and a Coronus 'Midwinter Fire' would bring lots of colour, especially in winter at the most drab time of the year.

THE SHADY GARDEN: Like everything else, the concept of shade is more complicated than you might first imagine. Your garden might be in slight shade for most of the day, in which case it would be classified as 'lightly shaded'. Or it might be in sunshine for part of the day but in shade for the rest which would be classified as partial shade. Dappled shade is patchy light and dark caused by the sun filtering through overhead foliage. Plus, your soil might be dry (because it is beneath trees and receives little rain) or it might be damp as a result of the amount of shade it is in. Life is never straight forward!

For dry shade you could start off with snowdrops in spring, and move on to wood anemones, Japanese anemones, euphorbia, hellebores, lily of the valley, lily turf (*Liriope muscari*), pheasant grass (*Anemanthele lessoniana*), Hydrengia (*macrophylla*) and ivy leaved cyclamen (*Cyclamen hederfolium*). Our common or garden ivy is easy to grow and very good at completely disguising ugly fences or walls and also provides excellent cover for a whole host of insects and, if allowed to grow more thickly or bush a bit, our smaller birds. And don't forget the impressive variety, majesty and structure of the fern (*Dryopteris*) which are really easy to grow, need little or no attention and are very good at covering unsightly patches.

THE SHADY VEGETABLE OR FRUIT GARDEN: Most fruit and vegetable plants enjoy sunshine, but that doesn't mean to say that they will not grow without it. Swiss chard, brassicas, (cabbage, broccoli, Brussel sprouts, etc.), beetroot, carrots, leeks, kale, broad beans, loose leaf lettuce and mizuna, radishes and kohlrabi will all tolerate a shady garden and give you something back.

As for fruit, gooseberries, rhubarb, blackberries, currants (black, white and red), raspberries, pears, damsons and plums will also tolerate a fair amount of shade. So, do not be put off. Have a go!

THE DAMP SHADY GARDEN: have a look at Camelias, hellebores, pulmonaria, fritillaria and box for starters – then allow your imagination to take over! You can always fall back on our friends the ferns – heart's tongue ferns are more unusual.

THE EDIBLE FLOWER GARDEN: You might wish to combine the functionality of edible flowers with the beauty of colourful blooms in which case, try planting a selection of primroses, violets, pansies, calendulas, chives, daisies, basil, chervil, nasturtiums, dandelions, lavender and borage. Don't forget the lilac and roses either. My mother used to love decorating her spring and summer salads with flowers and bemused guests would sometimes have to admit that they weren't sure whether the dish was part of the meal or simply the table decoration.

However, finding a theme for your garden doesn't have to stop here. You might wish to specialise in a Mediterranean garden, or a seaside garden (especially if you do, indeed, live near the coast). You could create a smaller garden of miniature succulents or a rockery of alpines. You might plump for the higgledy piggledy nature of a cottage garden where flowers, herbs, veg, fruit and wild flowers are all mixed up growing in happy companionship and abundant array. Or you might choose to devote your garden to one, two or three colours. How about a pink and blue garden? Or one which is just green, grey and white? Or a gold and purple garden? Or a garden which spans every shade from white through all the pinks to scarlet and almost purple/black? Or you might decide on a bird garden, a moth and butterfly garden – or a wildlife space which attempts to cater for as many different species as possible. The possibilities are endless, so enjoy.

BALCONIES, WINDOWSILLS, HANGING BASKETS AND PLANTERS: There are several books-worth of possible information in those six simple words. I hope to cover these possibilities in more detail in my next book, along with ideas for recycling plastic into useful garden containers. Suffice it to say that it is possible to grow a remarkable amount utilising these types of containers and spaces. Pots – even quite large ones – can stand on windowsills for tomatoes, cucumbers and peppers, or in grow bags on balconies or on the floor next to a glass door or low/floor-length window. All the smaller herbs – medicinal and culinary – can be grown in pots on windowsills too, as can smaller flowers, and don't forget the veg and salad which can be propagated from scraps (see previous Chapter Six) or from seed in small trays. Brackets can be put up on outside sunny walls to support window boxes or hanging baskets and vertical expanses of wall might be utilised to support your entire herb and salad garden. Just remember to keep them all well-watered as they will pick up heat from the wall and dry out more quickly.

HERBS IN A WITCH'S GARDEN

In a little hard-backed notebook, carefully covered in floral wrapping paper, my mother wrote out for me her own 'Language of Flowers' and many other snippets of interest about our domesticated gardens. One of the things she mentioned was the ability to recognise a witch by some of the herbs growing in her or his garden. These, she affirmed, are absolutely necessary to a wise man or woman's calling:

- Hellebore
- Rosemary
- Lavender
- Sage
- Comfrey
- Rue
- Wormwood
- Marjoram
- Vervain

Below is a quick and easy recipe which might be just the thing to pop in the oven after some hard work out in the garden.

Cheese and Onion Pie

early 1950s

Ingredients

Short crust pastry
1 medium onion
¼ - ½ lb (125 – 250g) of cheese

Method

- *Line a shallow pie dish with pastry.*
- *Boil onion until tender, lift from pan and chop finely and arrange in pie dish.*
- *Slice cheese and place over onion, cover with rest of pastry, decorate and cook in a hot oven until pastry is brown.*
- *A very simple dish which is exceptionally tasty for high tea of supper. We usually had one at home when Mummy had been baking, rainy Saturday afternoons.*

- *You might wish to add a few veg to the onion and cheese – perhaps a few mushrooms or a handful of cooked peas – and serve with a green salad.*

THE HERITAGE SEED LIBRARY AND GARDEN ORGANICS

Lawrence Hills was a freelance journalist and horticulturalist and passionate about promoting the potential of the herb comfrey as a natural fertiliser and the benefits of organic growing as a whole. In 1954 Lawrence rented a smallholding in Essex where he could experiment with comfrey. He encouraged other growers to share his research, particularly into 'companion planting' for pest control.

In 1958 Lawrence created a membership organisation to support the research into comfrey and organic growing. He named it the Henry Doubleday Research Association after the 19th Century Quaker scientist and horticulturalist who was responsible for developing the Boking cultivar, which is actually a hybrid between our own native species and Caucasian Comfrey and has become so invasive. (Henry Doubleday is not to be confused with his cousin of the same name who also lived at the same time and was an enthusiastic entomologist and ornithologist and author of the first catalogue of British butterflies and moths).

The Henry Doubleday Research Association changed its name to Garden Organics and its main purpose was to conserve and protect the seed of thousands of European varieties of vegetables which were endangered by the new European Union regulations. They formed the Heritage Seed Library. Seed is grown and harvested by the Garden Organics Heritage Seed Library team at their headquarters at Ryton Gardens in Sussex. These then become available to members, some of whom decide to become Seed Guardians themselves, which means that they are gardeners who have chosen to take on the extra work and responsibility of growing seed for redistribution through Garden Organics.

The Seed Library currently holds approximately eight hundred varieties which in the past have been donated by members and other members of the public or passed to Garden Organics by seed companies who are no longer maintaining them. Each year, around one hundred and fifty varieties from within their collection are chosen for inclusion in the Heritage Seed Library Seed Catalogue. Members can then choose up to six free packets of seeds and a seventh 'lucky dip' variety so that everyone can try out lesser known and more unusual varieties.

There are four main benefits to growing Heritage Seed Library Seed. First of all, it supports the conservation of unusual vegetable varieties for future generations. This is even more important now as the companies who produce the chemical fertilisers skew their products to work best with limited mainstream varieties. Secondly, it helps to increase biodiversity in gardens. It also gives gardeners the ability to save some of their own seed, unlike many common varieties which are F1 hybrids which cannot come true to type when re-sown. Lastly, it helps to maintain genetic biodiversity which may be useful to plant breeders of the future.

Garden Organics is now the largest organic gardening and horticultural organisation in Europe. Their website contains lots of information and eco-friendly alternatives for use in our modern lives. They also have an extensive seed and plant catalogue which anyone can buy from.

My mother must have discovered The Henry Doubleday Research Association sometime in the mid to late sixties. I well remember that she became very excited when the Heritage Seed Library was formed, and until her health became challenged, she was proud to be a Seed Guardian. When she finally passed away, I took over where Joan left off — although I have never acted as a Seed Guardian… yet, but there is still time. Perhaps as I grow older and become a little less caught up in work and family, I shall take the plunge. I have to admit that with so many strange events occurring in our natural world – as well as on our human plane – we might very well be in desperate need of such resources in the not too distant future.

SEED VIABILITY: Not all seed will regrow if you keep them for longer than a year after they were harvested. On the other hand, some varieties of seed will keep for many years and will still burst forth with exuberance once they come into contact with their preferred growing medium once more. In the same little notebook where I found the information about a witch's garden, I came across this amusing but very useful verse which might help us all to work out if our seeds are too old or not.

Written in the style of Thomas Tusser (1524 – 1590) who in 1558 wrote a poem of the same name which the poem below is based on:

A HUNDRED GOOD POINTS OF HUSBANDRIE

One acre composted is worth acres three,
At harvest thy barns shall declare it to thee.
You have in your drawer since Candlemas Day,
All the seed packets you daren't throw away,
Seed catalogues cometh as year it doth end,
But look in ye drawer before money you spend.
Throw out ye Parsnip, 'tis no good next year,
And Scorzonera if there's any there,
For these have a life that is gone with the wynde,
Unlike all seeds of ye Cabbage kind;
Broccoli, cauliflower, sprouts, cabbage and kale
Live long like a farmer who knoweth good ale,
Three years for certain, mabe five or four,
To sow in their seasons they stay in ye drawer.
Kohl-Rabi lasts with them and so does Pai-Tsai,
The winter 'cos lettuce' to sow in July,
But short is the life of ye Turnips and Swedes,
sow next year only enough for your needs.
Mustard and Cress for when salads come round,
Sows for three seasons so buy half a pound.
Radish lasts four years, both round ones and long,

Sow thinly and often, they're never too strong.
Last year's left Lettuce sows three summers more,
And Beetroot and Spinach beat easily four,
But ordinary Spinach, both prickly and round,
Hath one summer left before gaps waste ye ground.
Leeks sow three Aprils, and one hath gone past,
And this is as long as ye Carrot will last.
Onion seed keeps 'till three years have flown by,
But Sets are so easy and dodge onion-fly.
Store Marrows and Cucumbers best when they're old
Full seven summer's sowing a packet can hold.
Six hath ye Celery that needs a frost to taste,
So hath Celeriac before it goes to waste.
Broad beans, French ones, Runners grown in May,
Each hath a sowing left before you throw away.
And store Peas, tall Peas, fast ones and slow,
Parsley and Salsify have one more spring to sow.
then fillen ye form that your seedsman doth send,
For novelties plenty, there's money to spend.
Good seed and good horses are worth the expense,
So pay them your poundes as I paid my pence.

Lawrence D. Hills,
first printed 1963

Chapter Eleven

Easter

"Loveliest of trees, the cherry now
Is hung with bloom along the bough'
And stands about the woodland ride
Wearing white for Eastertide."

A.E. Houseman

The celebration of Easter lasts just one week, beginning with the Christian feast of Easter (Sunday) and ending a week later on Easter Saturday. This is known as Holy Week. However, confusion soon arises due to the secular misuse of the term Easter Saturday which instead refers to the day know liturgically as Holy Saturday or Easter Eve, the day on which Lent officially ends, the day before Easter Day or Easter Sunday. Further complications arise from there being a national holiday on Good Friday, the day before Lent ends and two days before Easter Day. The uncertainty deepens because the celebration of Easter can be held anywhere from late March to the third week in April. The next logical question is to ask why this should be so?

WHEN IS EASTER?

According to the Bible, the death and resurrection of Jesus Christ occurred at the time of the Jewish Passover which was celebrated on the first full moon following the March Equinox. This soon led to

Christians celebrating Easter on different dates because by the end of the 2nd century, some congregations were celebrating Easter on the day of the Passover, while others were celebrating it on the following Sunday.

In 325 CE, the Council of Nicaea established that Easter would be held on the first Sunday after the first Full Moon occurring on or after the March Equinox and if the full moon fell on a Sunday, Easter would be celebrated on the following Sunday. However, the actual date of the March Equinox also varies, between the 19th – 22nd of the month and also depends on the time zone but for the Christian church, the date of the March Equinox is always set on the 21st March. Up until the Middle Ages, many of the Christian saints days were also calculated in this way.

Using the lunar cycles to calculate something like the date of a festival is called Menology, which literally means 'knowledge of the moon'. The Christian church's 'moveable feasts' literally change their date from year to year, because they are determined by lunar cycles, not solar ones, causing them to drift erratically through the months of the canonical calendar.

In the Twentieth Century there have been a number of suggestions made as to how the date of Easter could be made more regular. In the United Kingdom, the Easter Act of 1928 was established to allow the date for Easter to be fixed as the first Sunday after the second Saturday in April. However, this law was not implemented, although it still remains on the U.K. Statute Law Database.

More recently, in 1997 the World Council of Churches proposed a reform of the Easter calculation to replace an equation-based method of calculating Easter with direct astronomical observation. This would have solved the Easter date difference between churches that observe the Gregorian calendar and those that observe the Julian calendar. The reform was proposed to be implemented in 2001, but it has not yet been adopted.

Personally, I think that it would be something of a shame if the date for Easter was 'regularised'. I find that part of the charm of the celebration is that it might be held at a stormy end of March or in a near-summer heatwave in April. The same goes for the suggestion of celebrating Christmas Day on the nearest Sunday to the 25th December – although I haven't heard this one repeated for a while. Why does everything always have to be the same, just because it makes it more convenient for the authorities planning school term times and businesses plotting their work? Variety is the spice of life and long may it continue to be so.

Easter Biscuits
early 1950s

In my childhood this recipe was variously referred to Easter biscuits, breakfast biscuits and Aberffraw Cakes (this last having the addition of the traditional imprint of a large scallop shell on each surface). There are numerous ways in which this recipe can be varied and it might be a little plainer than more modern recipes – a lot of food was fairly plain after the Second World War and some was still rationed – but the twist in the tail of this treat is a teaspoon of brandy!

Ingredients

4 oz (110 g) butter
2 oz (60 g) currants
4 oz (110 g) sugar
2 egg yolks
egg white
10 oz (285 g) flour
1 teaspoon brandy
caster sugar

Method

- Cream fat and sugar and beat in the egg yolks.
- Add the brandy and fruit.
- Work in the flour with a very little milk if needed to bind the mixture into a paste softer than pastry dough, but possible to roll out.

- *Prick all over surface with a fork and cut into rounds with a fluted cutter.*
- *Bake on a greased tray in a moderately hot oven, 15 – 20 minutes.*
- *After 10 minutes, briefly remove from oven and brush very sparingly with white of egg and then dredge them with castor sugar. Return to oven to finish baking.*
- *When cooked, remove from oven and allow to cool for couple of minutes before transferring to a wire rack to go cold.*

Jim and Eileen adore these biscuits eaten instead of toast and marmalade, or, indeed, at any time.

WHAT IS EASTER?

In a nutshell, the concept of sacrifice, resurrection and salvation rooted in the spring season has appeared and reappeared many times and in many places throughout the history of mankind. There are numerous festivals and celebrations which take place throughout the spring season which focus on the symbolic death of winter, or the old year and old ways, sweeping the way clear for a new cycle of seasons. In various cultures at some point in the year, the vegetation or sun god is slain and reconceived by the mother, the goddess, to enable a new wave of growth and nutriment to be brought forth – both literal and spiritual – which will ensure the continuance of mankind.

Parallels between the masculine deities Isis, Horus and Mithras and the feminine deities of Ishtar and Inanna (among others) may be drawn here. The cult of the agrarian goddess, Cybele, possibly originated in modern-day Anatolia, Turkey. She, and her Phrygian son/lover, Attis, god of vegetation, bear closer inspection.

Christians celebrate Easter as the resurrection of Jesus Christ after his crucifixion. It is the oldest Christian holiday and the most important day of the church year, with the religion being based on the events surrounding it. The celebration was usually referred to as *Pascha* or the month of *Paschal* (Greek/Latin) or simply Resurrection Sunday. It was only in mediaeval times that the (questionable) pagan goddess' name of Eostre (Easter) began to be used.

In Germany, Easter was given the same name as the season of the sacred pagan king's sacrifice, *Hoch-Zeit*, meaning 'High Time'. In English, Easter also used to be called the 'Hye Tide' which is where we get the colloquial description of any festival holiday as being a 'high day and holiday' or having a 'high old time'.

HOT CROSS BUNS

In the Old Testament, we are told that the Israelites baked sweet buns to gift to their idols. Perhaps this is where our tradition of making and eating Hot Cross Buns originates from? They certainly appear to have a long history. Loaves which had been stamped with a cross and dating from the First Century CE have been found at Herculaneum. There is also a suggestion that the Anglo-Saxons made them in honour of the goddess, Eostre. In the Fourteenth Century, a monk in Saint Albans is said to have distributed these sweet treats to the needy.

In 1592, Queen Elizabeth I decided that these fragrant buns smacked of too much Popery and banned their consumption except on specific special days. The embargo was eventually lifted and by the 1700s the sweet, spicy, fruit buns were once more being sold on the streets of English towns and cities, accompanied by the cry of 'One a penny, two a penny'(one large or two small buns for one penny) and where the old nursery rhyme originates from. We have written records that both Samuel Pepys and Dr Samuel Johnson enjoyed 'cross buns'. 'This is the season at which all good Christians devour hot cross buns for breakfast' the Figaro magazine of London boldly declared in 1836 – all good Christians who could afford them, that is.

In Christian tradition the cross on the top of the bun is said to represent the cross on which Jesus Christ died and the spices the precious ingredients with which his body was afterwards embalmed.

Originally, the cross would probably only have been cut into the top of the dough of each bun before it was baked. One wonders if all buns were so decorated at one time as there used to be an old saying – certainly in my part of the North West of England – that marking the top of one's dough would prevent the devil from stopping the bread rising and spoiling the bake. Logically, however, if you cut the top of dough before leaving it to 'prove', it releases the surface tension and allows it to rise freely. Just a thought.

Whatever, one thing is certain, we British love our Hot Cross Buns. In 2019, Tesco's alone sold seventy million of them by the end of the Easter weekend. If you would like to try making your own, here is our family recipe. But be warned, making them yourself in greater quantities than the supermarket packs can lead to over-indulgence! Last Easter I sent up a batch of eight pounds of bun dough which yielded ninety buns. Admittedly, I gave around half of them away to friends and neighbours, but that still left plenty for the family and I to gorge on. On Good Friday afternoon I ended up sitting on the sheltered porch of my North Welsh home — blue skies... lush grass... birdsong in joyful symphony... blossoms and blooms all around me and the lively excited sounds of the village on spring holiday. The family had brunched on very sticky hot cross buns, dripping butter, with pots of tea and coffee to wash them down. My Easter had truly begun and all was well with my world!

Hot Cross Buns

Ingredients

1 lb (500 g) strong white bread flour
6 oz (170 g) mixed dried fruit – home-made candied peel is good
        to include
4 oz (110 g) sugar - can use more but be aware it can inhibit rise of
        bread dough
2 teaspoons ground mixed spice
Pinch of salt
Tablespoon of veg oil
½ pint (280 ml) hand-warm water
1 ½ oz (40 g) fresh yeast – if using dried yeast use a little more
        than is stipulated for a pound loaf

Method

- Heat your oven to 180°C.
- If using fresh yeast, crumble into jug or bowl and add a little of the sugar with the half pint of water and set somewhere warm to give it time to activate – you will know that it has done this when it froths and bubbles.
- Mix first five ingredients together in a large bowl.
- Make a well in the middle of the ingredients and add the oil. If using dried yeast, sprinkle the yeast in as well and add the warm water. If using the fresh yeast, add the water. Sugar and yeast mixture to the centre of your dried ingredients.
- Mix well; using a little extra flour on your hands knead the dough for a few minutes.
- Form into a ball, cut a cross in the top of the dough (cuts surface tension and helps it to rise) cover with a clean cloth and leave somewhere warm to prove (rise) until it has at least doubled in size.
- Knock back and lightly knead again. Either roll out to ½ inch thick and cut or separate into balls, knead and roll flat. Should make 10 – 12 individual buns.

- *Place on greased baking tray. Paint with beaten egg. And carefully cut a cross in the top of each bun with a sharp knife.*
- *Bake in oven for 20 minutes or until the buns are golden brown and the base sounds hollow when tapped with your knuckles.*
- *Remove from tray and leave to cool on a wire rack.*
- *Can be eaten fresh from the oven or sprinkled with water and reheated in a hot oven for five minutes. Delicious split in two and eaten with lashings of butter or toasted and buttered.*
- *A simple glaze can be made from a little milk and sugar warmed and dissolved together and then painted on the top of each bun – makes them shiny and sticky and even sweeter! (However, don't add this if toasting as the sugar will simply burn.)*

EASTER BUNNIES AND EGGS

When thinking of Easter and the significance of bunny rabbits and chocolate treats, don't forget the ancient and widespread beliefs in the magical egg-laying hare and its connection to springtime and renewal – the egg itself also being a symbol of new life, birth and rebirth. It is not a difficult step to take from there to the Easter Bunny, especially in view of the suspicion and reverence which the hare was held in. A gentle furry bunny rabbit is much easier to associate with than the mystical, magical hare which defied people's beliefs and presented them with questions and dilemmas.

The Orthodox Church used to have a tradition of fasting from eggs in Lent, so coloured hard-boiled eggs were used as a way to celebrate breaking the fast on Easter (Sunday) morning.

Interestingly, the eastern Orthodox tradition teaches that after the resurrection, Mary Magdalene travelled to Rome to complain about how poorly justice had been served under Pontius Pilot during the trial of Jesus Christ. We are told that because of her high social standing, (which does not quite equate with how the Christian Church portrays her), she was admitted to the court of Tiberius Caesar where she also informed the assembled court that Christ had risen from the dead, and to help explain his resurrection, Mary Magdalene supposedly took an egg from the table where a feast was laid out. Much as I have a very great deal of time for Mary Magdalene, in view of the wealth of evidence about the egg being such a widespread symbol of new life, it sounds very similar to all the other traditions and practices which the Christian Church has appropriated and subsumed over the centuries.

The Persians (modern-day Iranians) use the Gregorian calendar for civic administration but they still begin their solar New Year at the Spring Equinox and still follow an old custom of giving each other coloured eggs on the occasion. In Eastern Europe the colour of life is red. When I was a child, I well remember holidaying in Greece just before Easter and being amazed that there were no chocolate Easter eggs. Instead, the shops in Athens were full of red, silk-covered cardboard eggs of all sizes, from small ones just two or three inches tall to massive creations two feet high. Pictures of flowers and chicks were stuck on the outside of the egg which broke into two equal halves, revealing sweeties or chocolates and other token gifts. My mother purchased several more modest eggs for me and I have them still, stored away in the loft, but I do not know if they are still a Hellenic tradition in the Twenty-first Century.

As with so many of our Midwinter and Christmas traditions, we have to look to the north and the Germanic people to possibly find some answers to the question of where the Hare, Bunny and the Egg of more modern tradition sprang from. Easter eggs were first recorded as long ago as 1280 in Germany when children were told that the Hare laid the Pasch eggs and children built little nests in their gardens ready for the Hare to leave its blessings.

In the Eighteenth Century, German Anglican immigrants told a mythical story about *Osterhase* who gave gifts of candy and coloured eggs to good children. As the Christian Orthodox Church used to have the tradition of fasting from eggs during the period of Lent, coloured hard-boiled eggs were used as a way to celebrate breaking the fast on Easter morning. Later the German Lutherans created a version of the Easter Bunny who judged whether children had been good or bad during the season of Lent, with well-behaved youngsters receiving a treat as a reward. It is not difficult to see why the more sanitised and less pagan symbol of a cute rabbit should be heavily supported and promoted by Christian communities. However, such deep-seated impulses are incredibly difficult to eradicate.

In Austria on Palm Sunday, (the Sunday before Easter weekend), catkins are brought into the church and blessed and then taken home and kept outside the house until Easter Sunday. (In my part of North West England, the old folk would still refer to catkins as 'palm'.) The first child to carry the catkins into the house at dawn on Easter Sunday is rewarded with the first Easter eggs.

After attending church, the children hunt for eggs which have previously been hidden in the gardens in large numbers. In the afternoon there is a ritual visit to the Grandmother or another older female substitute, (possibly representing the 'grandmother moon' figure that is connected to the hare?). To get there, the family processes led by a child dressed in a cape with the head and ears of a hare and carrying on their back a small water butt (representing the water/moon correspondence?) filled with coloured eggs. Once the family have arrived at the grandmother's house, they are treated to a cake baked like a flattish nest (similar to a hare's 'form') and filled with more coloured eggs.

After tea, the children play a game whereby the 'Hare-child' gives the eggs in the water butt to the other children, but distributes them as whimsically, capriciously and unfairly as they desire, giving free rein to favouritism and leading to much rough and tumble and dashing about. There is then yet another egg hunt conducted around the grandmother's garden.

There is also a game sometimes played where one child holds a coloured hard-boiled egg while another child tries to pierce it by stabbing at it with a silver coin. If the coin lodges in the egg, both are claimed by the attacker. (Again, possible moon imagery of the silver disk equating with the silver coin.)

EASTER BONNETS AND HATS

It is an old belief that one must have new clothes to greet the fresh season of spring. When people only possessed two or three sets of clothes in total, this was possibly a vital necessity. Old working clothes from the previous year would be torn and threadbare and one's 'best' outfit would be worn and at the very least require remaking or refurbishing. Easter marks the height of the Christian church's annual celebration and occurs in deepest springtime. What better way of taking part in the festivities but by donning one's very best – or newest – clothes and strutting one's stuff through the community on the way to and from church? The tradition of a new hat – or as the fashion then demanded, a new bonnet – is one of long duration, and so it was that the ladies of the time would treat themselves to a new bonnet, or at least last year's embellished with new decorations.

You might decide to buy a hat to match a new spring outfit. Alternatively, you might wish to get creative, experimental or even outrageously silly and have a go at making a real Easter bonnet yourself. The actual hat is not so very important; it is the wealth and combination of decoration with which you decorate it which really makes the difference. You might find a reasonably priced straw or summer hat to buy on the hight street – charity shops are very good sources of such items. Or you might decide to buy a hat which you can later remove the decorations from and wear throughout the rest of the summer – a cotton sun hat is good for this.

Alternatively, you can have a go at making a proper bonnet yourself. A lot of expense is not necessary. It only requires three pieces to construct a genuine 'bonnet' and it is possible to cut them all from one large cardboard cereal box which can be painted or covered in white paper or thin material.

How to make an Easter Bonnet

Method

- Measure from where your ear meets your head, straight up over the top of your head, down to where your other ear meets your head. This gives you the size you need to measure out as in *Fig 1*. You can then draw the edge of your bonnet brim – as in *Fig 2* – any size or shape you wish. Cut this shape out carefully.
- Draw a second line one inch from the edge of the bonnet, as in *Fig 1*. With a pair of scissors, make diagonal cuts in to this line and carefully fold back each piece along the line.
- Cut a strip of cardboard which is the same length as the inside of your bonnet brim at *Fig 1* and 6 inches deep. Diagonally trim about 1 ½ inches (4 cm) off each short end so that it resembles the shape in *Fig 3*.
- Draw a line along one long side one inch in from the edge and make diagonal cuts to the line, or cut out triangles. Carefully fold back each flap to the line.
- Dab glue on each of the folded flaps of the long rectangular shape, and bend it round, sticking it to the smallest piece of cardboard (*Fig 4*) to form the body and back of the bonnet.
- Finally, dab glue on the tabs of the bonnet brim and attach to the body of the bonnet. You may have to hold in place for a few seconds and then leave to set completely for a few minutes.
- You are then ready to decorate your bonnet. Paint or cover your bonnet with paper or material – or, if made from coloured card, leave it bare. You may use any (or all!) of the suggestions for decorations listed. Sew or glue them around the inside of the brim which will provide an amazing festive frame for your face, and/or pile them over the back body of the bonnet.
- Finally, ribbons can be stapled to the outside edge of the bonnet at *Fig 5* so that you can tie it in place on your head.

Have fun and enjoy!

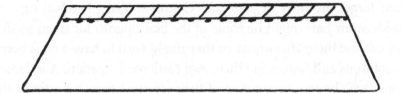

Figure 1

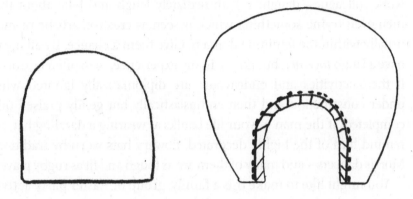

Figure 2   *Figure 3*

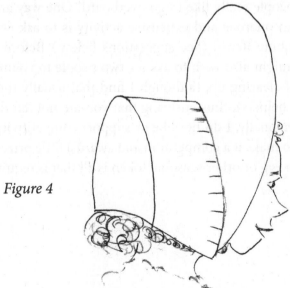

Figure 4

Don't forget the men in your life! Cotton sunhats, baseball caps or seaside straw hats might be some of the best options for them so that they can use them afterwards, or they might wish to have a go at being adventurous and fashioning their own cardboard creation. And ladies, please don't be too disparaging of their efforts. I fear that a lot of the gentlemen in our lives are instantly put off from trying things out because the women in their lives (mothers, wives, girlfriends, partners, work colleagues, daughters) immediately laugh and joke about their men even trying something which is seen as creative, artistic or more usually within the feminine domain. Give them a chance. By all means have a laugh *together*, but not *at*. In my experience, men often fare better if their activities and endeavours are diplomatically ignored whilst under construction and then enthusiastically but gently praised once completed. If the man in your life baulks at wearing a dazzling hat, just remind him of the highly decorated, flowery hats worn by traditional Morris dancers – and many of them are as tough and fit as rugby players!

You might like to make this a family, group or Easter party activity and have everyone make or at least decorate their own hat. If this is the case, make sure that you have plenty of cheap/reasonably priced things to offer as decorations – it takes a surprising amount and some people really like to go overboard! One way around this becoming an onerous and expensive activity is to ask everyone to bring/contribute items. (See suggestions below.) Before you even begin, you might also wish to ask for two people to volunteer to be in charge of clearing up, (although I find that usually there are no shortage of helpers), thus ensuring that you are not left doing it all yourself. Personally, I do not like or support competitivity, but you might like to make it a competition and award a little prize – a single small cream egg or other seasonal token is all that is required.

IDEAS FOR DECORATING BONNETS AND HATS:

- Silk flowers
- Buttons
- Old broaches
- Paper flowers
- Lace
- Tissue paper

- Real flowers
- Wool
- Small toys
- Ribbons
- Beads
- Cardboard cut-outs

- Easter chicks
- Easter eggs
- Old silk ties or scarves

If you really are not very dextrous with craft projects, or have very young children, keep it simple. Roll lots of large and small balls of coloured crepe or tissue paper and glue them decoratively in place. You would be surprised how effective – and attractive – this can be!

NOTE: If using cloth or straw hats which you want to ordinarily wear later, sew or staple your decorations to your hat so that they can easily be removed again without damaging it.

EASTER THEN AND NOW

My mother made it her policy to spend every Bank Holiday relaxing at home in the shady woods besides the gurgling stream, along the cool banks of the river. She would holiday or travel at other less fraught and busy times of the year. After spending so many weekends as a child away fishing with her father and much of her youth exploring the roads of Lancashire, the Lake District and North Wales on the back of a motorbike she sought peace and stillness. As she regularly pointed out, why should we spend several hot, fraught, fume-filled hours on packed roads to get to some already overcrowded beauty spot when we already lived in one? Now living in North Wales, we still do not have to travel to enjoy the rivers and mountains of Snowdonia and the coast which is only three miles away.

Then again, it also depends on which weekend Easter falls – if it is early and comes at the end the end of March, the weather might still be cold and wet, and indeed, as a child, I do remember one or two Easters when I was very little which were abysmally rainy when I would haunt the windows of the cottage, constantly seeking a tell-tale sign of the weather possibly clearing up so that I could go out and hunt my eggs. Traditionally an activity for Easter Sunday morning, I recall sometimes only getting out to retrieve them by Sunday teatime and on one occasion having to postpone it altogether until the next day! When my son was a child, Easter Sunday was inevitably cloudy, dark and grey, but at least it remained dry. Even now, there have been a couple of Easter Sundays when we have retreated from unseasonably cold weather and ended up having an egg hunt around the house and sitting in front of a roaring fire playing 'Monopoly'! Such are the vagaries of the British climate.

Do not allow older children to harvest their chocolate treats too easily either. Make them use their young enthusiasm and intelligence. Organise an Easter egg treasure hunt with written clues and eggs to find with them. One year, I actually buried some of the eggs in the garden, much to my son's irate bewilderment – he wasn't simply going to stroll around and find the Easter bounty *that* easily!

By and large, all is safely gathered in by Easter Sunday lunchtime, the intense anticipation and magic of a visit from the Easter Hare coming only second to that of Father Christmas! For when I was very little, my mother quite rightly told me that it was the magical Hare who seeded the springtime garden with chocolate emblems of renewal – eggs being the symbol of rebirth and new life - but to be careful not to be too curious on Easter Sunday morning for if I looked out and spotted the Hare doing its rounds, then like Father Christmas, it would not reward me with any of its sweet bounty. When I became worried that the wet weather would spoil the chocolate, I was assured that the Hare ‚seeded' the eggs and that they would only magically develop and grow into eggs once the sun came out.

With the rain stopped, clouds cleared away and the sun shining, I would bravely set off around the garden with my little straw basket, which, (due to the Easter Hare's extreme generosity, I would often have to return to the cottage to empty two or three times – and with my father carrying the larger eggs for me) before they were all safely retrieved.

An egg hunt in the garden at Drybones was quite mind blowing! Cadbury's chocolate cream eggs, tiny chocolate eggs and copious quantities of brightly wrapped Quality Street chocolates would be carefully placed all around and about any flowers and we had many golden trumpeted daffodils, dainty pale blue forget-me-nots, sweet lemon-petalled primroses and pink and purple primulas around the garden as well as carpets of wild flowers. But Easter Hare was joyfully generous in its bountiful distribution and the Wild Wood was particularly well favoured, for here I would find little shiny jewel colours winking and glinting at me from many of the trees – any crook or fork where a sweetmeat could be perched, wedged or balanced and the whole effect was as to enter a Fairyland of Sweets... beflowered glades where birds trilled and water chuckled and chocolatey treats could be spied and found all around.

It is just as well that I was not a greedy child or else I should have either rapidly become extremely sick or obese – or both! As it was, I rationed myself to the deep enjoyment of one egg and a couple of chocolates each day and usually only ate the last by the beginning of July.

I say that I wasn't a greedy child – and I was always slim – but I enjoyed a healthy interest in my food and, as with other special occasions, Easter was a lovely time of seasonal dishes and a coming together of family to share them.

On Good Friday, my mother always got up hours before the rest of the family and had hot cross buns fresh and piping hot from the oven for when the rest of us came down to breakfast. Served with lashings of butter and the lids coated in a sticky sugary syrup, the fragrantly scented, spicy fruit buns were a delightful indulgence! My mother would percolate coffee for her and my father – I preferred beakers of hot steaming tea. We still adhere to this delightful little family custom, except that I now bake the buns beforehand and simply reheat them in the oven before serving. Somehow, this sweet treat for breakfast signals the beginning of a 'special time' and brings the family together at the start of it, whatever other activities we go on to participate in together or singly.

It is a local tradition in our part of Lancashire that tens of thousands of people from the surrounding areas of Chorley, Adlington, Horwich and Bolton take a walk up Rivington Pike – one of our prominent hills and an old beacon site — on Good Friday. From the summit there is a splendid view of the Lancashire plain, both across the fertile flatlands towards the sea at Southport and away towards Bolton and Manchester in the south. They little realise that they are responding to the call of thousands of previous generations of people who had always taken to the hills at this time in celebration of their pre-Christian gods. I never made the climb on Good Friday (although went frequently at other times of the year) but my parents used to make the annual pilgrimage with their friends and family when they were younger.

As a child Good Friday dinner always came in the form of a traditional High Tea but with fish rather than cold sliced meats – and more often than not, it was Prince's tinned salmon, but no less tasty for that. In fact, my grandfather, (who regularly used to catch salmon fresh from the Severn or Wye, would come home and deposit his catch on the kitchen table and go and open himself a tin... he said that it was tastier! Philistines, all of us! We still follow this old habit, now, with crusty home-made rolls, lots of sauces and salad dressings and something creamily extra special for dessert.

When I was little, at least until I reached the age of about nine or ten, my father went into the office on Saturday mornings, including that of the Easter weekend. But at Easter it only seemed to heighten the holiday feeling as he often returned home early, bringing little treats of flowers or a magazine for my mother and a comic or sweeties for me.

Personally, it has always been the relaxed and laid-back atmosphere of Easter which has impressed me most – even at an early age –

unlike Christmas which is ultra-exciting but full of more obligatory traditional activities. Easter was and is more free and easy – possible, and permissible to relax in the early spring sunshine or garden hard from dawn to dusk or tackle outdoor spring cleaning jobs, any of which would be unthinkable on other high days and holidays. Nor did my parents tend to invite guests at Eastertime either, although people would sometimes come and find us and end up joining us in our impromptu woodland feasts on a disparate collection of woollen rugs and old garden chairs. Sometimes my mother would get talking to holiday makers walking through the woods outside our gate and simply invite them in to join us, which must have seemed like a children's story come to life for them. In more recent years we tend to throw open house on one of the days over the Bank Holiday weekend and gather up any friends or family who are available for a barbecue in the garden or a cold buffet inside.

One of the few things that *had* to be done over the holidays was, of course, attending mass at church on Sunday morning. Sometimes my mother would accompany us but as I grew older, she went to church less and less. My father was a Roman Catholic but that is not how my mother had been brought up. It was usually just my father and me. There is an old belief that those who didn't wear new clothes on Easter Sunday would have 'something nasty' dropped on them by the crows. I would always have a pretty, new dress to wear and a newly trimmed hat or bonnet with a little square straw basket trimmed to match. In this I would carry my baby version of a prayer book and my handkerchief. The crows certainly never got the chance to drop anything on me as my mother always dressed me so beautifully that I never gave this awful possibility any serious consideration.

Coins for the church collections were usually passed to me just as the ushers began moving down the aisle with their collecting plates.

I have to admit that going to the steeple house has never held any appeal for me and when I was a little girl I quietly hated having to leave my games and play to get primly dressed up and go and sit still for an hour indoors listening mostly to people speaking in a language that I couldn't understand, as Latin was still used in the Catholic church services at that time. Nor did being in the presence of God seem to make any of the congregation very happy – they all sat or stood or knelt to pray with such solemn and serious expressions on their faces. Even when they came out of church at the end of the service, most hurried away in silence, making me wonder why they had bothered to go in the first place. It did vaguely cross my mind that perhaps they had been naughty and were afraid of God punishing them. At that tender age I felt pretty humbled by Him myself and always very intimidated when faced with The Church!

But as I understood it, the lovely baby who had been born on Christmas morning had, a few short months later, miraculously grown into a handsome young man and then suffered and died – *again* – and was now reborn and reunited with his friends which seemed a lovely thing to rejoice in and I was so very happy for him. Also the pools of softly coloured light reflected from the stained glass windows which moved across the floor and pews and sometimes garishly coloured the backs of ladies hats or gentleman's heads were lovely to watch and afterwards I always felt extra *good* and righteous for having done the right thing... and my father was always pleased that I was a good girl and accompanied him. It is always so seductive to know that you have 'done the right thing' and that you are in everyone's good books for doing so, but far from a sufficient reason for trying to shape one's spiritual values and practices! Now my 'church' is a simple and unconsecrated Meeting House, or the open woods, beaches and mountainsides of my Welsh home where I am no longer afraid of God but in harmony with the divine energy of All That Is and deeply in love with Life.

Easter Sunday morning was (and still is) a time for serving boiled eggs for breakfast, but with the added excitement of never knowing how they were going to be decorated. Sometimes my mother would colour eggs with onion skins to produce golden patterns on their shells. Other times, she would put edible dyes in the cooking water, although cochineal always turned them a purply colour rather than the red of the Greek orthodox tradition that she was attempting to achieve. And then, of course, there was always the mysteriously uncoloured plain white egg that found its way into my eggcup at some point during the meal... one which I quietly struggled to crack while my parents – apparently – became increasingly annoyed with my frustrated attempts, abjuring me to "Come on, Gilly, get *on* with it!" until they couldn't keep their faces straight any longer and dissolved into gales of laughter at my indignant struggles... that old china egg has played tricks on many unsuspecting people over the years!

It was the picnic-type teas out in the Wild Wood that made the most impact on me when I was very young. My mother had built a wooden seat – a simple affair constructed from two huge logs and a good stout wooden plank – beneath the branches of a stand of mountain ash overlooking the river. A small sunny glade opened up before this seat – a sheltered sunny space of coarse tufted grass with cushions of soft leaf mould between. Here my mother would spread a cloth and my father would carry out the big cream and blue wooden tray stacked with my mother's pink and white Mason's pottery – cups and saucers, plates, cutlery, napkins, complete with large square teapot. I realised as a child that food and drink – but especially tea – when eaten or drunk outside, always tasted different and better than when consumed in the house. I have never been able to work out why, or recapture that scent and taste of my childhood, but it remains with me to this day.

There would then be a second tray containing all the goodies to eat – fat sandwiches bulging with salad; lettuce, tomatoes, cucumber and chives and any other fresh edible leaf available at that early season; or succulent slices of cold beef (left over from the roast at lunch) with crunchy pickled onions; golden custard cream biscuits and sugary dark bourbons, and pink blancmanges in little conical glass cups. But it was the homemade cakes which were always my favourite... featherlight sponges coated in pristine white icing, the top encircled with luminous ruby red glacé cherries and oozing homemade scarlet raspberry jam, squidgy dark chocolate cake with pale green mint icing and the rich fruity simnel cake sporting the proscribed eleven marzipan ,apostles'. These were lazy and long drawn out affairs when my father would stretch out on the grass, shirt sleeves rolled up and top button undone to expose his very pale winter skin beneath, and my mother would recline in one of our padded garden chairs and I was left to the wooden bench. If Uncle Ricky had joined us, then he would keep my father company on the ground. Much conversation and laughter along with edible consumption ensued and I was happy to quietly listen or drift off into my own fantasy world, content that my family was happily disported around me and that all was well with the world.

Quick Chocolate Krispie Nest Cake

This is a quick and easy recipe which a friend gave to me a few years ago but it has become a firm favourite with all the family. It is good for busy people or if you suddenly need an extra Easter cake. The ingredients can be formed into one large nest or spooned into small paper cases. Children can easily make this too, just be careful while they melt the chocolate and keep a sharp eye out for finger and spoon licking!

Ingredients

4 oz (110 g) unsalted butter
4 heaped tablespoons golden syrup
8 oz (220 g) chocolate – preferably dark or dark and milk mixed
6 – 8 oz (170 – 220 g) mixed cereal – cornflakes and rice krispies
Chocolate mini-eggs

Method

- *Line a round cake tin with greaseproof paper.*
- *Place the butter, syrup and chocolate in a pan inside a larger pan with a couple of inches of water in the bottom (to prevent mixture from burning) and melt slowly – or place in large pan and melt carefully over a low heat stirring continuously to prevent sticking and burning.*
- *Mix the cornflakes and rice krispies and add to the chocolate mixture, stirring gently but well until all cereal is thoroughly coated.*

- *Tip into prepared cake tin making a wide dent or well in the top of the mixture to resemble a large nest or spoon into individual small cake papers.*
- *Chill until firm.*
- *Fill top of 'nest' with mini eggs – little fluffy yellow chicks can also be dotted among the eggs or around the edge of the 'nest'.*
- *If making small cakes, while the mixture is still soft, gently press one or two eggs into the top of each cake – can also add a chick to some – and leave to set.*

ALL THINGS WHICH ROLL

Easter Monday was especially marked by the hard boiling of yet more eggs, but this time they were not to eat but to symbolically roll – a representation of the rolling away of the stone from the entrance to Jesus' tomb. Again, when I was very small my mother would carefully decorate large bowls full of eggs, but as I became more dexterous I took over most of the decorations myself. Our problem at Drybones was having no suitable slope down which to roll them! It really required short smooth grass, which we didn't possess in the garden, and the farmer's fields were far too rough and shaggy to use... our eggs would easily have become lost! In more recent years when the weather has been too inclement to be out of doors we have rolled our eggs across the dining room carpet instead, but somehow, it isn't quite the same... one needs the uncertainty and *frisson* which automatically comes with the natural world. It has been a long-standing tradition for people to gather on Easter Monday on Moor Park in Preston to roll their eggs and enjoy lots of other games, but we never went, having no particular desire to seek out the crowds.

In Hallaton in Leicestershire, there is a procession on Easter Monday (Monday deriving its name from 'Moon Day' and reflecting the connection between the moon and the hare). It is led by a person carrying the bronze effigy of a hare on a pole, followed by a woman dressed in red with a basket of loaves and two girls bearing the large 'Hare Pie'. These days the pie is made from beef and measures about eighteen inches by thirty inches. There are also three Bottle Bearers holding small wooden bowls. They process from the public house to the other end of the village by the church where the minister delivers a short address and then distributes the pie and loaves to the waiting crowd. Not surprisingly this part of the festivities can get quite chaotic! The crowd then surge up the steep hill to Hare Pie Bank where 'Bottle Kicking' takes place – each little barrel is thrown in turn into the crowd and the inhabitants of the villages of Hallaton and Medbourne attempt to wrestle them over the boundaries of one or the other villages. The contents of the captured cask are drunk by the victors.

Charles J. Billson suggests that this may be a relic of an ancient springtide celebration in which the spirit of winter is carried to the outskirts of the community and ritually destroyed, as in the many football matches of Lent. Historically football matches were played on the Isle of Anglesey over the Easter period, which similar to the Lenten matches, involved hundreds of players, lasted for many hours and frequently involved danger to life and limb. Such was the widespread rural tradition.

COMMENT FROM JOAN: APRIL 1964

"Jim, what do you think, I've found a silver birch!"
A beautiful, graceful, tall, upstanding member of the species it is too. I will just add that being in full view up the hill, I can't see how I missed it, but then there was so much to get to know… being on the hill and surrounded for most of the year by herbage taller than myself I never paid much attention to saplings round about and had a hazy idea of moving them into the boundary hedge.

Now five years on, I have a well rooted copse of silver birch; trunks just turning from that new glossy chestnut brown to the silver that gives them their name, and underneath from late April through May to June is a heavenly scented profusion of bluebells. The whole could not have been more to my liking if I'd striven for it. The bondwoman has striven since, keeping down the brambles and bracken between the trees, and just this year I can see that after a slight bi-annual tidy round, the trees themselves will keep the undergrowth under control. Unfortunately, there seem to be an uncommonly liberal quantity of tiny rooted seedlings provided annually... I might have to start a forest!

Chapter Twelve

April

"Then summon April forth, and send
Commandment through the flowers;
About our woods your grace extend,
A queen of careless hours."

Hilaire Beloc

"Goodness, Gilly, you've got soot smeared all across your face. Just look at yourself in the mirror," my mother admonishes.

"Well, *I* can't see anything," my young self peers cautiously into the round dining room mirror.

"April fool!" my parent laughs in reply.

APRIL FOOL

On the first day of April, it is the old custom across Britain, Scandinavia and Europe and as far east as the Lebanon, to spend the morning playing tricks and practical jokes on people. It is known as April Fool's Day. Such inane tasks as sending a youngster for a long stand, a drop of pigeon's milk, some memory powder or a bar of black soap are indulged in. A common practical joke used to be to send some unsuspecting soul to deliver a note which read, "Send the fool further!" In Scotland they celebrate 'hunting the gowk' (a word which means cuckoo, symbol of a fool) when folk are sent on phony errands. This is followed by Tailie Day which involved pranks being played literally on people's tails, derrieres, bottoms, such as secretly pinning fake tails to them or attaching 'kick me' signs to them without their knowledge.

What gave rise to such an idiotic and farcical practice? No one seems to really know, and it is possibly an amalgam of many origins. It has been suggested that it had something to do with celebrating the end of Lent, but I feel that the date for this changes too frequently and widely to hold true. More likely is the general chaos of moving the beginning of the new year from the 25th March to the 1st January; it is possible that the 1st April would have come at the end of the old new year celebrations, similar to Twelfth Night and Mischief Night. One also has to take into consideration the spring festival of the Celtic god of humour, Lud, which involved a great deal of japery, coming as it did at the end of winter's privations. A similar festival was celebrated by the cult followers of Cybele in ancient Roman, *Hilaria* being the Latin for joyful, when participants dressed in disguises and mocked their fellow citizens.

In France, people slow to adhere to the new date for the start of the new year became the butt of jokes, paper fish being placed on their backs and referred to as *Poisson d'Averil* ('April fish') said to symbolise young, easily caught fish and therefore a gullible person. In 1508 the French poet, Eloy d'Amerval, gave the first written account of these 'April Fish'.

In 1686, John Aubrey gave the first British reference to the celebrations naming it 'Fooles holy day', and in 1698, several people were memorably tricked into going to the Tower of London to 'see the lions washed'. The popularity of April Fool's Day in the British Isles grew throughout the Eighteenth Century and continues today, although just how many people actually still take part in it is debateable. Amazingly, well known institutions have also been known to have a joke at the general public's expense. For instance, in 1958, the fledgling BBC TV broadcast a documentary presented by Richard Dimbleby reporting on the Swiss farmers who were experiencing a record spaghetti crop – it even showed people harvesting noodles from trees. Just after the millennium there was a radio report that the London Eye was to be laid on its side to make a carousel, which created a public outcry, until everyone realised what day the report had been broadcast!

Whatever the derivation of 'April Fooling', it must only be indulged in before twelve noon. After midday, the victim may justifiably turn on his tormentors and cry:

'April Fool's gone past,
You're the biggest fool at last!'

DUTY CALLS

One particularly important childhood memory for me was when, at the age of ten years old, I was taken to buy my first proper adult bicycle. It was a reward for helping my father to look after our home and our animals while my mother was in hospital for a week and then taking over and looking after her and everything else for a fortnight while my father returned to work and my mother convalesced in bed. At the time this was quite a task. We had six Alsatian dogs and several cats to care for, plus we ran two open fires, used paraffin lamps for lighting and our household water had to be pumped – by hand – from the well outside the back door. Also, my mother was not the easiest of patients and I was left trying to tempt her with as many little snacks and light meals as were in my child's limited repertoire. Never had the stairs seemed so steep or the top corridor to my mother's bedroom so long as they did those dark, tiring weeks of March, 1966 when I first tried my hand at becoming a housewife.

I have to confess that there was a certain satisfaction at bringing cleanliness and order to everything and seeing everyone fed, watered and comfortable. I had watched and helped my mother do it often enough... for some unfathomable reason it took me much longer though!

However, I did enjoy our weekly shopping day when my father ran me to town in the van and then became my beast of burden while I spent the afternoon marching briskly from shop to shop, competently making my purchases and leaving my poor father to pay the bills and struggle after me with numerous bags and baskets. We always went to the General Post Office first to post our mail and buy extra stamps to see us through the week (both my mother and I have always been inveterate letter writers). Then we visited the market before the best fruit and veg had been sold from the greengrocers stall, bought crumbly Lancashire cheese and slabs of golden Cheddar at the cheese stall, and cakes and biscuits from another stall (if they weren't being baked at home), then went on to Macfisheries for fresh plaice to fry for tea, Thornley's Pork Butcher's for bacon and sausages, Melias for the rest of our meat order and finally Booths for the rest of our groceries. We would finally finish up at the library to change our books. I always accompanied my mother on similar errands when I wasn't at school; sometimes she still had the bulkier items to get after I had descended from the school bus and could help her to carry them. I had also learned to 'market' and barter for things while we were away in Greece and Sri Lanka the previous year, so Lancashire shop keepers needed to watch out when I entered their portals. Years later, my mother told me that when she began to do the weekly shop again for herself, some of the shopkeepers complimented her for having such a competent little girl, and also commented on her bewildered and breathless husband.

My parents were so impressed by my general domestic performance that they generously deemed me worthy of such a big present. It was actually Easter Saturday when my mother (on her first trip to town after leaving her bed) and my father took me to the bicycle shop right in the middle of Chorley, almost directly opposite to where we had once lived and my mother had kept her toy shop and doll's hospital. We spent some time looking at the various makes and models, but I eventually chose a smart new Raleigh with a cherry red frame, black mudguards and a shiny silver bell.

Everything I have ever owned has always had to have a name and my bicycle was no exception. The little child's bike which I had ridden since the age of five – initially with little back stabilizer wheels on until after a year I learned to balance properly without them – was called 'Molly' after my older cousin's horse. My mother suggested that I follow in her footsteps and name it 'Giggleswick the III' (she had owned 'Giggleswick I and II' in her younger days before she progressed on to motorbikes). I rather liked the idea of calling my bike such a jolly, giggly name, so 'Giggleswick' it became.

I loved my bicycle. When I changed schools from Juniors at the convent in Leyland to Secondary in Chorley, I was able to cycle there every day – a refreshing change from the mile and a half walk and two bus journeys twice a day… I was even able to pop home for my lunch! Into my teens I cycled everywhere and when I met my first boyfriend, we would spend every weekend exploring all the local lanes, villages, moorland rides and hills within a thirty mile radius and I got to know my area extremely well! When I moved to North Wales, 'Giggleswick' came with me too and in fact, has only just – finally – gone to the great bicycle heaven this last spring, after giving me well over fifty years of loyal service.

Guess what I want for Christmas?

IT'S NOT MY FAULT!
by Carys Bateman

(A story to share with children – but a lesson to be learnt by us all!)

Benji sat and scowled at the bed of brightly coloured flowers, bobbing their heads in the warm spring breeze. He had lost his temper in the house but that wasn't his fault, Felicity shouldn't have interfered with his game and Jacob should have left his things alone too. So, it wasn't *his* fault, it was all *their* fault! Mummy was being unfair to take their side and make him go out and run in the garden. He was sick of always being the one in trouble. With that thought, Benji glared at a particularly sunny daffodil and hit it with his stick, swiping a wide swathe in the pretty garden bed. Glaring again, he began to dig with the pointed end of his stick, pushing out the bulbs and upending flowers until what had been a round flowerbed full of colours now looked bare, with clods of earth and broken flowers strewn all over the lawn and gaping holes in the ground. Benji looked at the mess he had made and gulped in shock. Now Mummy would be really cross and he would end up having to go to bed early and… *it wasn't his fault!*

"Oi!"

Benji looked around him, the voice was sharp and a bit squeaky and sounded really angry. Although he looked left and right and then twisted around, Benji couldn't see anyone so he picked his stick up again, ready to dig out more flowers.

"I said 'oi!, you spoilsport. You too big to answer?"

Now Benji was puzzled. He wasn't a big boy; he was small for his age. Then he felt his eyes bulge out as his jaw dropped open, for there before him was a little man made out of sticks and bark. Benji rubbed his eyes, thinking he must be imagining things, but the little man was still there.

"H-hello," muttered Benji, still in shock. "My name's Benji and I am not too big to talk to you, I just didn't think you were real."

"Huh," said the stickman, a little mollified. "In that case I will let it go. My name is Twig and I want to know why you have made all this mess? Don't you realise that the bees need the flowers for pollen so they can make lovely honey? And look how dirty you are. Why were you so angry with the flowers? They haven't done you any harm."

So Benji explained how his brother and sister had been picking on him and how Mummy had told him to run around in the garden to get rid of his frustration and how he had just, well, hit the flowers without thinking.

"It sounds to me like you do much too much of that, rushing about and hitting things, just because you are fed up," Twig said.

"It's not my fault," said Benji, rushing in with his usual excuse.

"Oh? Then who hit the flowers if it wasn't you? Who dug holes and damaged bulbs if it wasn't you? Who threw stones at the cat next door, if it wasn't you?" Twig didn't look angry now, he just wanted an answer.

"I didn't hit the cat," blustered the boy. "It ran away."

"But she was very frightened and as she is only just a little more than a kitten, she is now scared to come outside when she hears children. So, who's fault was it?"

Benji hung his head in shame. He remembered how the cat had let out a yowl and shot across the fence. She was a pretty little calico one too and Benji had enjoyed stroking her when he wasn't so angry. With a deep sigh he raised his head and looked directly into the strange bark-like features of this little man.

"Mine," Benji admitted, feeling ashamed and squirmy inside. "I can't make it right though and now my Mummy and Daddy will be mad at me and..."

"Hold on, son," said Twig. "If you really want to put things right, you can but it will take a lot of hard work and you will have to say sorry to the cat. Can you do that?"

"Yes, I don't like saying sorry but... but it is my fault, isn't it?"

Twig smiled up at the boy and nodded his head. "Now it is time to put things right with a little bit of magic and lots of luck!"

With that, Twig took a handful of sparkly earth out of his scratchy jacket pocket and said a few words over it before running to Benji and throwing the stuff at him. With a cry of surprise Benji found himself shrinking down, down, *down!*

A moment of dizziness and then Benji gave a shout of delight, he was exactly the same size as Twig, who looked even more like a walking bunch of sticks close up. With a nod of satisfaction, Twig gave a whistle and the cat from next door crept over the fence. Benji felt a bit scared seeing the cat was so big now, but he went forward bravely.

"I am very sorry for throwing the stone at you and I am very glad it missed you. Please don't stay away from the garden as I love petting you and I promise never to do that again. Is there any way I can make it up to you?" he finished anxiously.

After looking at him gravely, she cleaned her paw before she spoke.

"You may stroke me when I come to you, but you must not be rough. And if you happen to find any salmon in your fridge, you should bring it to me."

"He can't do that, Cally, that would be stealing but he will be able to stroke you gently. Right, boy?"

Nodding his head, Benji agreed.

"We don't have salmon but we sometimes have tuna. When we do, I will ask Mummy to see if I am allowed to give you some, would that be alright?"

"Oh yes," purred the cat. "That would be very nice indeed!"

Everyone was satisfied with this and the cat accepted a hug and went on her way. Twig looked at Benji and smiled.

"That was a really good start, youngster. Now let's get busy!"

Through the afternoon, Benji worked harder than he ever had. With a little broom, he swept up the soil that his carelessness had strewn everywhere. Then he went and picked up the bulbs, the broken flowers and other debris. As he was very small now, this was hard work and he got very hot and sweaty. Once everything was piled together, Twig held Benji's hand and waved his other one in the air.

Up they swirled; Benji, Twig, the flowers and the dirt. Twirling and tumbling about, over, under and through. Then, with a bump, Benji landed on the ground, his normal size, almost clean and looking at the flowerbed which was now back in its colourful state. A small pile of weeds was stacked at the side and Benji wondered if he had been asleep and dreaming all that had happened. Then there was a small whistle and he looked down and saw Twig.

"You worked very hard without grumbling, young man. Well done, you! As a reward I have taken the few weeds out of this patch. Look at them carefully and if you see any elsewhere in a flowerbed, take them out. Now, I want you to ask your Mummy or Daddy if they will let a patch of the garden grow wild; if you sow some seeds, you will have a lovely lot of wildflowers by next spring. Also, ask if you can have a bird table and put food out for them. Perhaps you could even make a house for a hedgehog. Use your energy to make things instead of breaking and you never know, you may see more magic in the garden like me!" With that, the little man twirled around and disappeared with a quiet '*pop*'.

"Benji! Benji! You can come in now if you promise to behave," his Mummy called from the kitchen window.

"Mummy! Come and see what I have done!" he called back. With a sigh, his mother closed the window and went out to him, expecting to see a real mess. Instead she was delighted with the little bit of weeding he had done and even more in how excited he was with plans for the garden. Dazedly she found herself promising that he could have a wildflower garden, he could have a bird table and he was definitely allowed a hedgehog house!

Later, Benji tried to tell Felicity and Jacob all about Twig but neither one of them believed him. Benji didn't mind, he knew that Twig was real and that they would meet again very soon. So, he went off happily to talk to his Daddy about how to make the garden an even better place for the birds, butterflies, bees and even, yes, even magic!

NO FOOLING!

One of the first freshly grown springtime crops to be harvested from any garden is rhubarb. It first begins to push its way up through the cold earth some time in February. It is possible to force the growth by placing some protection over the top of a crown, but I prefer to allow it to grow at its own pace. This means that we get to harvest our first bunch of sticks sometime in April which creates much joy within the family as it is ceremoniously cut, brought into the kitchen, lightly stewed with a little sugar and then consumed with lashings of whipped cream.

There is something very special about harvesting and enjoying foods in their season. Yes, it is very useful to be able to purchase fresh raspberries at Christmas, strawberries at the end of January and blackberries in March, but it takes away all the anticipation and thrill of waiting for the new crop to be ready and the first dish of the season to appear on the table. Being sent out to pick the first crisp green peas, the first whiskery globular gooseberries, the first pie's worth of juicy dark currants have always been special treats and annually looked forward to. Nothing can compare to the taste of freshly dug new potatoes, cooked and served with a big knob of butter – food fit for a king. In fact, the taste of homegrown and prepared food is quite unlike and far superior to anything that can be found in any shop or supermarket.

Rhubarb fool is one of our regular springtime desserts. This recipe below dates from the early 1950s. With sugar still rationed after World War Two until September 1953, I am sure that my mother could have made good use of some sprigs of Sweet Cicely to intensify the flavour and reduce the acidity, but she only learnt of it's wonderful taste-enhancing properties a couple of decades later, when my mother added it to the original recipe some time in the 1970s.

Rhubarb Fool

Ingredients

1 lb (500 g) rhubarb, washed and cut into 1 inch long pieces
Sugar to taste, but 3 – 4 oz (85 – 110 g) if not sure
A small bunch of sweet cicely leaves
Half a pint (280 ml) of cold custard
Whipped cream and glacé cherries to decorate

Method

- *Place pieces of rhubarb, sweet cicely and sugar along with a little water into a heavy bottomed pan and stew gently until tender.*
- *Sieve to a fine purée (these days just purée in whatever electrical device you have to hand – so much easier!) removing sweet cicely leaves if too tough to break down.*
- *When cold, stir in the custard until thoroughly mixed, spoon into pretty glass dishes and decorate with a spoonful of whipped cream and half a glacé cherry.*

Nothing could be simpler or quicker, but I assure you, truly delicious!

HARBINGERS OF SUMMER

Ever since I was a very little girl, I have always looked out for the return of our swallows and the call of the cuckoo, both harbingers of summer. There has always been something magical and extremely significant in watching the graceful acrobatics of the swallows, dipping, swooping and diving for insects over the sunny fields and limpid river on summer evenings. The singular sound of the cuckoo's call is no less so – how typically British is a late spring woodland redolent with the call of myriad birds, punctuated by the distinctive double note of the audacious cuckoo.

Swallows return to Britain (and Europe generally) to breed, usually arriving in the U.K. around the middle of April and leaving our shores sometime in September or early October at the very latest. Traditionally the 15th April has been referred to as 'Swallow Day' to mark their return, but much depends on the weather and where you live. Birds from different parts of Europe fly to different destinations in Africa. Swallows from the British Isles tend to end up in the far south, travelling down through western France and eastern Spain and across Morocco before crossing the Sahara Desert and the Congo rainforest, finally reaching their other home in South Africa and Namibia. Flying low, feeding on air born insects as they go, these intrepid birds cover approximately 200 miles (320 km) each day. At night they roost in huge flocks in reedbeds at traditional stopover spots. The whole journey takes them about six weeks. Amazingly, making this epic journey around the globe twice yearly, a swallow can live for up to sixteen years.

Many species of bird do not spend the entire year in one place but migrate to other areas of the globe, flying north for the summer to breed when their winter home becomes too hot or otherwise inhospitable, or flying south to avoid the harshest winter weather, or from east to west and vice-versa for similar reasons. Most of them travel many thousands of miles so it is a double joy to have these tenacious little souls arrive back to spend even a few short months with us.

The cuckoo makes a similar journey with first sightings (or more accurately, soundings) from the 14th April onwards when they traditionally arrive back in the Scilly Isles and South West England and rapidly repopulate the rest of the U.K. with their unmistakeable 'cuck-coo' call. However, this date might be somewhat inaccurate now as it has been remarked that the cuckoo has been arriving around five days earlier which is attributed to global climate change.

Like the swallow, the cuckoo comes to Britain to mate and produce its young. By late June or July, the adult cuckoo has already left our shores to make its return flight south, the chicks following sometime in August. These birds are brood parasites and do not raise their own young. Instead they lay eggs in the nests of other birds – primarily dunnocks, meadow pipits and reed warblers who inhabit the edges of woodland, edges of reed beds or moorland. The female cuckoo will wait until the host birds have left the nest – or will sometimes scare them away on purpose – and while they are gone, will swoop in and lay a single egg which the adoptive birds then raise, thinking that it is their own. The chick takes about eleven days to hatch and will then push any other eggs or fledglings out of the nest to ensure that it receives the undivided attention and care of the adoptive parent birds. The young cuckoo leaves the nest after twenty days or so but continues to demand care from the host birds for a few more weeks. I have no idea why the tradition has sprung up that the cuckoo is symbolic of being daft or a bit short on sense and intelligence – it seems to me that as a species, they have everything worked out very well indeed!

Needless to say, like so many of our other native birds, the welfare of the cuckoo is under threat due to loss of habitat and the way this also affects their host species. Deforestation is another contributing factor, as is hunting these vulnerable birds whilst on their migration routes when millions are netted and destroyed each year. Since the early 1980s numbers of cuckoos have dropped 65% and it is estimated that there are only around 55,000 breeding pairs left in the U.K. Therefore, I was truly delighted to hear our usual cuckoo calling from across the valley this spring, and then to hear a second cuckoo calling in the woods further up the valley around the old quarry.

There are numerous widespread superstitions and beliefs about the cuckoo, particularly those involving good and bad luck and where you are and what you are doing when you first hear its call. Some advise you to bury money on the spot where you are standing, or to turn the money over in your pocket, or to turn around three times where you stand.

Various April dates are referred to as Cuckoo Day – the 14th April is a popular one – and some places hold Cuckoo Fairs. In Marsden in West Yorkshire there is an annual festival celebrating the arrival of spring which largely features the cuckoo. There is also the Downton Cuckoo fair in Wiltshire which marks the 'opening of the gate' to let the cuckoo through – and presumably the start of summer with it. Heathfield Cuckoo Fair in East Sussex is perhaps the most explicit and obvious as they abide by an annual tradition which depicts an Old Woman (the same Old Woman of Winter?) releasing a cuckoo from her basket, whereupon it 'flies up England carrying warmer days with it'!

Why not try looking out for all the 'firsts' in your area? Keep a small notebook or jot them down in your everyday diary. When do you see the first swallows? When do you hear the first cuckoo? You can extend it to other little natural events right the way through spring; when do you see the first snowdrop, the first catkins and daffodil in bloom, the first bumble bee and ladybird and so on. Which tree comes into leaf first? When does the blackthorn blossom appear, or the fruit trees burst into flower? It is a good way to encourage yourself – and others around you, especially youngsters – to notice what is happening in the natural world. The passage of time and the turning of the seasons becomes relevant to you personally and is a habitual marker of natural events in which you are uniquely involved, if only as an observer.

COMMENT FROM JOAN: APRIL 1960

We were just looking at the sycamore tree – where the honeysuckle grows, by the see-saw in the wood. The sycamore leaf buds were covered in greenfly. Never thought about them being on trees before. Will pop one or two of our many ladybirds up there next time I see them.

While looking at the sycamore we heard sheep bleating and in the meadow across the river we saw a flock of sheep and their lambs. There were three sheep on the face of the cliff-like part of the bend if the river just across from our back door. Two had twin lambs, the other ewe one single one and the baaing had been the ewes warning the lambs away from cliff or river, or both. One set of twin lambs were black faced. What a high proportion of twins and triplets are born these days.

Noticed that the ground frost has got the three Balsam plants I bought on Tuesday, so I won't have to worry that they might be the Indian Balsam which covers the riverside to the extent of being a weed and a nuisance. The asters, antirrhinums and verbena plants seem to have weathered alright. Must get ready to go into town now – wish it would rain then I needn't worry about the grass and woods firing – it's chilly enough in all conscience!

DID YOU... ?

Did you see to catkins quiver
in the merry breeze?
Did you mark the speckled buds
in the hedgerow trees?
Did you see a black-faced lamb
skip over King Cups bright?
Did you see the sky awash
with a blue and silver light?
Did you hear the swelling birdsong
Trilling so sweetly clear?
Finest of all symphonies
to be heard throughout the year.

Did you mark the daffy buds
nodding their bells of gold?
Did you hear the blackbird shrill
calling so clear and bold?
'Tis April again my dearest love,
come out, I'm waiting here;
Be with me in this fresh delight
at the springing of the year.

Agnes Gore-Green

A CAUSE FOR CELEBRATION

As the month of April rolls on, the natural world really goes into overdrive. The fruit trees, especially the apple, burst into blossom by the end of the month and many also come into leaf. The possibility of night time frosts remains but is less likely or to be as severe if they do occur. The warmer, lighter days are definitely here and we can begin to engage in all manner of summer-orientated pursuits... sports, walking and trekking, open air fetes, markets and festivals, picnics and camping. School children are able to leave heavy coats at home and lighter clothes appear out of the wardrobe from their winter incarceration. The summer holidays which were planned long ago in the autumn or winter have suddenly become a reality as we begin to count down the weeks. The children may have only just returned to school for the start of the summer term, but even here, the pace and atmosphere has changed and there is more emphasis on sport and spending time out of doors, with the bonus of being able to look forward to the long summer holidays.

There are lots of little mini occasions to celebrate if you need an excuse to focus your entertaining skills or jolly the children along a bit. If you wish to have an alternative focus to Easter, you might choose an event such as Hanamatsuri on the 8th April which is a flower festival celebrating the birth of Buddha. The royalists amongst you who follow the activities of the Royal family might wish to do something to mark the Queen's birthday on the 21st April. For those of a literary persuasion, there is William Shakespeare's birthday to celebrate on the 23rd of the month – and for those who do not enjoy his plays there is also the fact that he died on or around the same date fifty-two years later in 1616. Or alternatively you might wish to mark Saint George's Day which falls on the same date.

Locally for us is Saint Beuno's Day on the 21st. Beuno was a Welshman from Gwynedd who was reputed to have wonderful healing skills, frequently using the water from the well at Clynnog. Beuno settled on land on the Gwynedd coast at Clynnogfawr given to him by King Cadwallon where he built a church near the sacred well which became known as Saint Beuno's well. There are many churches and healing wells on the pilgrim routes to Bardsey Island at the far end of the Llyn Peninsula. Saint Beuno's church is remarkably large with an ancient and venerable air and I am very fond of it. The little well with its protective walls was vandalised some years ago but has since been renovated. Wearing my druid hat, we have sometimes been known to go there at Gwyl Ffraid/Imbolc or for healing rituals, planting spring bulbs and wild flowers and being blessed by the clear fresh water.

April is also the month when a number of events have taken place which intimately reflect on our modern lives too. It was on the 12th April 1606, when the Union Flag (often erroneously referred to as the 'Union Jack') became the official flag of the United Kingdom. Closer to us now, it was on this same date in 1961 that the Russian, Yuri Gargarin made the first human flight into space – forward just eight years and humanity landed on the moon – how is that for fast progress? On the 14th April 1931, the Highway Code was first issued and on the 18th April 1934, the first laundrette was opened in Fort Worth Texas, while on the 25th April 1953, DNA was discovered by James Watson and Francis Crick. From the sublime to the possibly slightly ridiculous, on the 7th April 1827, the first matches were sold, which might not seem very important to you in the Twenty-first Century but it made a heck of a difference to a world which heated and illuminated itself by the naked flame.

EARTH HOURS AND DAYS

I love the whole concept of both Earth Hour and Earth Day and feel that support for and participation in both should be wholeheartedly endorsed. I am frequently amazed that so many people still do not know of their existence.

Earth Day is the oldest of the two events and began back in 1970 to demonstrate support for environmental protection. It takes place annually on the 22nd April and now includes events co-ordinated globally by the Earth Day Network in more than one hundred and ninety-three countries. This is something which affects every single one of us, whether we care to admit or accept it or not. Go on-line and read of their events and ethos. How might you join in with such vital awareness and activity? What can *you* do to begin to make a difference?

Earth Hour is a favourite occasion for all my family. For us, personally, it is so endearingly reminiscent of the way we were brought up and have experienced so much of our lives at Drybones. Another annual event held on the last Saturday of March it is global movement organised by the World Wide Fund for Nature to celebrate sustainability and show support for strategies which will help to solve the problem of global warming. Importantly, it is a grassroots movement, uniting ordinary people to take action on environmental issues and protect our planet.

It all began in Sydney in 2007 when everyone was asked to simply switch off all their electric lights and appliances – or at least as many of them as possible – for just one hour, between 8:30 p.m. and 9:30 p.m. Thirteen years further on and it is widely adhered to around the world, with the lights also being doused on such famous international iconic buildings as the Eiffel Tower in Paris, the Sydney Opera House in Australia and the Houses of Parliament in London. As well as individuals and communities, businesses of all sizes and council or government run properties also join in.

We simply switch off the whole house at the main junction box for an hour (usually longer as we don't like to break the spell!). Even the freezers go off; they won't catch any harm for a short while on a chilly March night. I have to say that the peace and stillness which descends over the whole establishment is remarkable. None of us ordinarily notice the disturbance which electrical currents cause just running through our walls to our sockets. Try it and see for yourself.

The most amazing effect we observed one year involved Jim, my father. He had been severely ill with Parkinson's Disease for some time and spent most of the time dozing in his chair, his waking hours a tangle of painful confusion and difficulty even in speaking clearly. This particular Earth Hour, only a few minutes after we had thrown the main switch, my dad opened his eyes and began to talk quite lucidly and clearly– mostly about things in the past, but not entirely. We were able to ask him questions, which he answered and miraculously, it was suddenly like having my original parent back again. We were all astonished… and deeply touched that we had been given this one wonderful evening. But it also made us think seriously about the possible effects which electricity has on any and all of us.

We always fill the room with candlelight, brew a pot of coffee and sit down in the gently flickering shadows to talk to each other. It has become something of a family institution that this evening is spent solely in each other's company with no other distractions greater than pouring extra cream in our coffee. Other evenings we might play games or listen to the radio or do craft and handiwork, but on this one night of the year, we sit and give each other our undivided attention.

Many other families play games and enter into all manner of activities… anything so long as it does not require electricity. I have heard numerous stories of bitterly complaining children and teenagers who have deeply resented being asked to turn off their various devices of electronic communication. But come the end of the designated hour, the cry has gone up, "Oh, must we turn the lights on again *just* yet?" You really don't have to wait until Earth Hour to 'switch off'. Simply turning everything off, pouring yourself a glass of wine and putting your feet up for an hour by the light of a solitary candle will do wonders for your stress levels and de-stressing capabilities.

How to make a fir cone gnome for spring

You will need

1 fir cone
2 x 7 cm lengths of coloured pipe-cleaner – springtime colours
      (pale blue, pink, lemon, yellow, light green)
Small piece of coloured felt
15 mm wooden bead
Length of coloured wool or thread
Blue and red pens, markers or paints – gel pens are really useful for this
Scissors
Glue

Method

- Cut two lengths of coloured pipe cleaner and bend as shown (see *Fig. 1*) to form:
  a) a pair of arms with curved 'hands' at each end, and
  b) a pair of 'legs', bent at the knee with feet.
- Place a dab of glue in bend of arms and attach to pine of fir cone, near top. (see *Fig. 2*)
  Place another dab of glue in bend of legs and attach to spine of cone near base.
- Paint or draw features on bead to form face. (see *Fig. 3*)
- Glue head onto top of cone (see *Fig. 4*). Usually there is a spike sticking more or less straight up from the cone which you can slide the head onto through the hole in the bead. This provides a stronger connection and acts as a 'neck'.
- Cut out piece of coloured felt as shown (see *Fig. 5*). Run glue lightly down one straight edge and roll around your finger to form a cone and stick other straight edge down firmly over glue.
- Spread some glue on top of the bead head and stick the hat on (see *Fig. 6*)
- If you want your fir cone gnomes to hang up on a Valentine, spring or Easter branch, or in your window or from the edge of a shelf, tie

a loop of coloured cotton, wool, narrow ribbon or embroidery thread loosely around the cone where the arms are fitted (see *Fig. 7*). They will then dangle nicely! Or you can perch them among a vase of flowers. Alternatively, you don't have to hang them up at all - you can sit your gnome(s) anywhere, on tables, shelves, windowsills... or on your springtime log decoration.

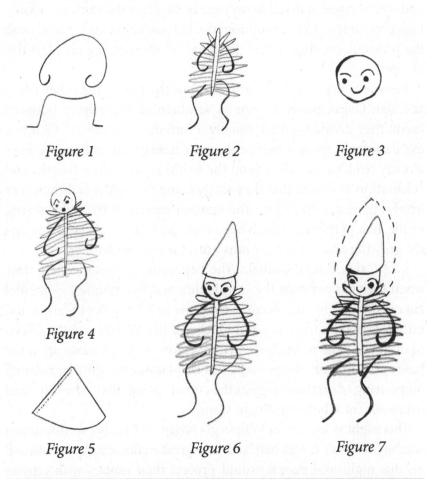

Figure 1   *Figure 2*   *Figure 3*

Figure 4   *Figure 5*   *Figure 6*   *Figure 7*

Share a photo of your gnome with me (and other readers) by posting it to my Author page on Facebook (Gillian Monks Author) or Instagram using the hashtag #gillianmonks – I can't wait to see where the little fellows get to!

CALLING THE TYLWYTH TEG

The month of April rolls on and as it nears its end, we approach the ancient festival of Beltane, the beloved festival of May Day and all the traditions of the maypole, dancing and flowers which are associated with it. It is a fire festival of fertility and the beginning of summer and will be covered in full in my next book about the summer season. However, in true Celtic tradition, the Beltane activities begin at dusk the previous evening, as the daylight dwindles on the very last day of April.

Beltane is the second great festival of the year – the other being at Calan Gaeaf, better known as Samhain or Hallowe'en. Between them, they divide the year equally. From dusk on the 31st October, the dark, cold, winter half of the year holds sway and, as we have already read, people all around the world go to endless lengths and celebration to ensure that they safely come through it and then very firmly mark the end of it. The counterbalance is the light, warm, fertile, half of the year which begins on the 1st May and lasts through the growing and harvest months until the end of October.

Like Calan Gaeaf/Samhain, the beginning of summer is a time when the veils between the worlds thin and the manifest elemental energy of new life takes form in the guise of all manner of fairies and little folk, led by the King and Queen of the Woods and the Green Man. It is a time when these primeval forces are let loose upon the land and humanity temporarily has no place in the shifting swirling outpouring of earthy energy as the cup of spring fills to the brim and overflows into the fecundity of summer.

This night is known as Walpurgis Night and is also an important witches' festival. It was believed that great malevolence was abroad on this night and people would protect their houses with crosses made from rowan wood and elder leaves. Talismans such as objects made from rowan or iron, yellow flowers, salt or holy water were also used for personal protection. The period from sunset on the 30th April to sunrise on the 1st May was the most feared in terms of the actions of faeries, witches and supernatural forces.

There are certainly times when the elemental energies of nature are so potent – either through the activities of the weather or the shifting of the seasons and pulsing of Earth – that it is wise for humanity to withdraw and leave it to its own devices. There have been times when my son has set out for an evening stroll into the woods around the cottage, only to reappear at the front door a few minutes later saying, "The woods are rather busy tonight and my presence is not wanted there." This is the atmosphere of May Eve. It is a wild night, an ungoverned time when boundaries dissolve, restrictions are lifted and absolutely anything goes. Perhaps this is necessary to get our half of the planet (either in the Northern or Southern Hemispheres) over the hump of such a massive change in focus and frequency.

On evenings such as these, I like to call and welcome the energies of the Tylwyth Teg to come and bless and protect my home by conducting some of their fairy revels around my garden. I set out a plate or tray containing home baked bread spread with local honey, a crystal wine glass of home-made may blossom wine and a dish of milk. I play bells or my singing bowl in the garden allowing their chimes and high frequencies to call out to and attract these other higher energies and I sing to them and send out my love. On magical nights such as these – as with any other situation or time of the year – you yourself can determine what you surround yourself with, what you attract to yourself. I do not countenance the dark energy and presences which can abound at this time but choose to openly and thankfully offer hospitality to all good and loving beings of a positive and more enlightened nature.

OPENING THE DOOR

This is the time to open the door to a new order, a new season, a new period of growth and progress. Allow the tentative hopes of late winter and the cautious endeavours of spring to burst forth into full blown, joyous celebration and activity under the young summer sun. Now is the beginning of the time for which we have all been plotting, planning and dreaming throughout the past six months or so. We are no longer held back by force of weather or circumstance; we are free to launch into any new adventure or endeavour our heart desires. Does this realisation not make you feel a bit giddy and wild? Perhaps it is exactly the same for the natural world which is why, for a short period of time, it appears to be so ungoverned and out of control.

We have travelled the past three months together – just three short months, but what a huge change there has been in the world during that time. From the frozen dead wastes at the end of darkest January, through all the unfolding and opening of new life throughout spring to this, the very threshold of summer.

Spend this evening preparing to open the door to your own personal summer season of golden light and bright new possibilities. Cleanse your body by bathing mindfully, perhaps using essential oils or flower petals to energise the water. Clear your mind of all repetitive, negative thoughts and concentrate your vision on the literal and metaphorical new dawn which is about to occur. If you wish, set out a platter of sweet offerings to attract the fair folk of your homeland and leave it by your outer door. Ask for their blessings. Invite all that is good, kind and gentle to accompany you through this opening into the sweet summer woods and fields beyond.

May you have beautiful memories of shy, ephemeral, transient springtime and a bold, joyous entry into shimmering, dazzling summer.

Let the new season begin!

Calendar of Springtime

Feasts, Festivals, Celebrations and Events

In this section I have listed some of the many festivals, celebrations and individual special days which occur around the world during our spring months. They make interesting reading. Not only do they demonstrate how widely and similarly different cultures celebrate the end of winter and the birth of spring but they also provide us with lots of fresh ideas of how we might like to celebrate the turning of the seasons too.

Conversely, some of the events have nothing specifically to do with the time of year. World Book Day and the celebration of our wetlands, meteorology and World Radio Day are some of these which bring a fresh relevance and change of focus into our daily lives. If you are looking for some occasion with which to enliven and jolly a hum-drum, drab time of year, here you might find just the thing to provide some impetus and new perspective.

Remember, there is no reason why life has to be all work, dull, boring or stale. But it is your choice. You choose whether your days are mediocre or exciting, simply by what you choose to fill them with and how you choose to view it.

Also remember that many of the older celebrations reflect our traditional agrarian culture, ancestry and the origins of our society today. They might come across as twee, amusing or quirky now, but they are buried in our genetic psyche and will resonate satisfactorily at a deeper, emotional level which we might be totally unaware of.

If you want to instigate activities and celebration into your life, and the lives of your family members, work colleagues or friends, don't try to do it all yourself! The fact that you have had the idea, made the suggestion and are prepared to be the driving force behind it all does not mean that you have to actually *do* it all. A large proportion of the fun in anything is the planning the preparations for it. It is unrealistic to expect yourself to fulfil every function – that way leads to exhaustion, disillusionment, disappointment and resentment. And will be all your own fault! You will also be denying someone else a part of the satisfaction and enjoyment.

Choose what you would like to have a go at or celebrate and then suggest it to others. If their response seems cool, then either drop the idea and choose something else – or find a different set of people to suggest it to! If it is something you feel really strongly about, go ahead anyway. Perhaps when people are actually exposed to or involved in an activity, they might end up enjoying much more than they thought they would.

Whichever, ask, delegate, co-opt or even coerce people into helping you! Ask for volunteers if possible so that people can choose the tasks they feel happiest, more experienced or best equipped to carry out. If that doesn't work, give specific tasks to people. Either way round, regularly check that they have no problems or do not need help. Encouraging children of all ages and abilities to take part in both preparations and the celebration itself is a wonderful way of nurturing feelings of self-worth and satisfaction, engendering responsibility, reliability and the value of community activity and introducing new skills for them to learn.

Life is for living and enjoying. Perhaps you and your friends or family might like to take it in turns to organise an evening in or a day / night out. Perhaps that may entail making costumes, masks or hats, or cooking food to share. Give someone the opportunity to choose, suggest, organise… and shine.

Most importantly, have fun and enjoy!

January

25th January
SAINT DWYNWEN'S DAY: Welsh celebration of love and lovers

31st January – 2nd February
FEBRULIA: Dedicated to Vesta, goddess of fire and hearth

31st January – 3rd February
FEAST OF ISIS: Egyptian Mother Goddess, patroness of magic and healing

End of January – beginning of February
LESSER ELUSIAN MYSTERIES: The return of Persephone to her mother, Demeter symbolising the return of life back to the land, the end of winter and the beginning of spring

February

1st February
IMBOLC / GWYL FFRAID, BRIGHID: Celebration of the beginning of early spring… healing, poetry, the hearth and smithcraft

SAINT BRIGIT'S DAY

OLD SAINT BRIDE'S DAY (Isle of Man): Kirk Bride fair held formally on this date. The old woman of winter is reborn as Bride, the young maiden of spring

DISTING-TID: Norse Imbolc, included dwarves who were legendary miners of metal and masters of smithcraft. Ploughs were blessed at this time.

2nd February
CANDLEMAS

JUNO FEBRUATA: Virgin mother of Mars who brought love to the world. Candles were lit in her honour

PANAGIA ARKOUDIOTISSA (Crete): The Goddess in the form of a bear is deeply engrained in our psyche. In Crete they celebrate the Virgin Mary of the Bear and at the cave of Acrotiri, near ancient Kydonia, there is a festival in honour of Panagia (Mary) Arkoudiotissi – 'she of the bear'

WORLD WETLANDS DAY

3rd February
GYRO NIGHT: Celebrated at Papa Westray, Orkney, the effigy of a female monster is burned upon a bonfire, representing the burning of the old spirit – or woman – of winter

SAINT IA'S DAY (St. Ives, Cornwall): hurling the Silver Ball, community ball game

3rd – 4th February
SETSUBUN: Japanese Bean Throwing and Lantern Festival. Some ancient cultures believed that the departed soul lived on in a bean. Therefore, the spirit of winter might still be residing in a bean and by tossing it away it signifies symbolically that winter is being sent away – dismissed. Lanterns are also lit at this time to encourage return of light and warmth.

5th February
SAINT AGATHA'S DAY

First week in February
SAPPORO SNOW FESTIVAL (Japan): Began in 1950, features

spectacular snow and ice sculptures which annually attract millions of people from around the world.

8th February
CHINESE LANTERN FESTIVAL

13th February
FALGUN (Bangladesh): Marks the arrival of spring

WORLD RADIO DAY

14th February
SAINT VALENTINE'S DAY: Celebration for those who are in love.

FEAST OF VALI: Loyalty, kinship, solar festival of end of winter and the growing strength of the Sun – the survival of the community

FEAST OF JUNO (Roman): Queen of the Heavens, consort of Jupiter, Great Mother, goddess of Earth and Moon, protectress of women. With Jupiter and Minerva, Juno was a member of the Capitoline triad of deities traditionally introduced to the early Romans by the Etruscan kings. She was connected to all aspects of the life of women, particularly married women, and as Juno Lucina, goddess of childbirth, Juno's role as female comforter led to her becoming a guardian of the very female principle of life, the principle female divinity of the state.

15th February
APHRODITE: Greek goddess of love, beauty, vegetation and flowers

LUPERCALIA (Roman): Cleansing, purification, fertility and love

17th February
SAINT FINAN'S DAY: Seventh Century bishop of Lindisfarne who wanted to preserve the distinction of early Celtic Christianity and challenged the Catholic attempts to dominate it.

21st February
INTERNATIONAL MOTHER LANGUAGE DAY

Sometime in late February or very early March
CARNIVAL / MARDI GRAS: Last few days before beginning of Lent

SHROVETIDE: Last few days before beginning of Lent

EGG SATURDAY: Shrove Saturday – the last Saturday before the beginning of Lent. In some parts of Europe, eggs are used up on this day, as an alternative to using them up in pancakes before the start of Lent

COLLOP MONDAY: Shrove Monday, the last Monday before the start of Lent when joints (collops) of bacon were served with eggs

NICKANNAN NIGHT (Cornwall): Evening of Shrove Monday, youngsters create havoc in local communities

SHROVE TUESDAY / PANCAKE DAY: Last day before the beginning of Lent, when pancakes were eaten to use up the last of the eggs before the Lenten Fast

FARSANG FARKA (Hungary): Covers the period from the 6th January (the end of the Twelve Days of Christmas), and culminates in colourful and loud celebrations, rich feasting, masquerade, and costume balls during the last three days before the start of Lent. It is also a time when 'Old Winter' was ritually burned. Traditionally a time for weddings as agricultural workers are not very busy at this time of year.

KURENTOVANJE (Slovenia): Celebration prior to the fasting season of Lent, it begins eleven days before Ash Wednesday and ends on Shrove Tuesday, with parades, parties, open air performances and a general rite of spring. the main figure of the festivities are the

Kurenti, daunting messengers dressed in sheep skins with huge bells tied around their waists, large boots on their feet, fearsome hats and masks and big wooden clubs, their main task being to frighten away winter. This increasingly popular festival was originally organised by cultural historian, Drago Hasl, who brought together various old customs from the rural areas to prevent them from disappearing in the onslaught of modern Twentieth-Century life and presented this new festival to the world in 1960.

ASH WEDNESDAY: First day of Lent

HOLI: Hindu festival to celebrate the end of winter and beginning of spring. Time to celebrate the new year and the joyous colours of springtime. Cleansing, forgiveness, new beginnings. Bonfires, singing and dancing, chaos, laughter and jest, hospitality, treats.

29th February
LEAP YEAR DAY

March

1ˢᵗ March
SAINT DAVID'S DAY: feast day of patron saint of Wales

WHUPPITY SCOORIE (Lanark, Scotland)

MATRONALIA: Roman feast of mothers and the renewal and reawakening of nature

BABA MARTA DAY (Bulgaria): In folklore she is a cranky old woman who symbolises the stormy and unpredictable weather of winter and who must be appeased to avoid more bad weather and the delay of the onset of spring. Red and white bracelets and favours are gifted and worn.

BEER DAY (Iceland)

3rd March
SAINT NON'S DAY: Mother of Saint David and healer of mental disorders

HINAMATSURI: Japanese Doll Festival

5th March
SAINT PIRAN'S DAY (Cornwall): Patron saint of tin miners

WORLD BOOK DAY

8th March
INTERNATIONAL WOMEN'S DAY

9th March
COMMOMWEALTH DAY

BUTTER LAMP FESTIVAL: Tibetan Buddhist

14th March
DITA E VERES (Albania): A time when pilgrimages were made into the mountains where prayers were offered to the Sun God for a fertile year and a good harvest.

15th March
WORLD CONTACT DAY

17th March
SAINT PATRICK'S DAY: Feast day of patron saint of Ireland

MOTHERING SUNDAY (U.K.): Fourth Sunday of Lent, three Sundays before Easter

19th March
FALLES or **FALLAS** (Valencia, Spain): To welcome the spring this event takes place over the last four days before the 19th March when there are street parties of fiery satirical entertainment which begin with processions to honour Saint Joseph and end with the incineration of ninots, papier-mache figurines stuffed with fire crackers.

20th March
INTERNATIONAL DAY OF HAPPINESS

WORLD SLEEP DAY

21st March
SPRING / VERNAL / MARCH EQUINOX: Equal balance between daylight and darkness around the earth

MARZANNA (Poland): Marzanna are large straw dolls which embody the spirit of the winter weather and season. They are paraded through the towns and then literally drowned in the nearest large body of water – river, pond, lake – to symbolise the 'death' of winter.

CIMBURIJADA (Bosnia): In the city of Zenica they hold a festival of scrambled eggs on this day, the egg being a symbol of new life, as the new season of spring begins. Massive quantities of scrambled eggs are cooked in huge pots and given out to the crowds for free.

NOWRUZ: National New Year festivity celebrated in Iran, Afghanistan and the Kurdish regions or Iraq, Turkey and Syria and throughout central Asia. A springtime celebration, its activities symbolise rebirth and the link between humanity and nature.

WORLD HARMONY DAY (Australia)

INTERNATIONAL DAY OF FORESTS

22nd March
WORLD WATER DAY

23rd March
WORLD METEOROLOGICAL DAY

25th March
LADY'S DAY

EARTH HOUR: usually the last Saturday in March

April

Late March through April
EASTER: Christian celebration of resurrection, new life and salvation

PASSOVER: Jewish celebration of exodus and freedom from slavery

DAFFODIL SUNDAY: First Sunday in April. In the Victorian era families picked daffodils from their gardens and gave them to those less fortunate such as hospital patients.

1st April
APRIL FOOL'S DAY

2nd April
WORLD AUTISM AWARENESS DAY

6th April
CANDLE AUCTIONS: A candle would be lit and a pin stuck in it about 2 ½ cm from the top. People would start biding for a piece of church land to let to the poor for a year. The person bidding when the candle burned down enough to allow the pin to fall became owner of the land.

TARTAN DAY (U.S.A. and Scotland)

7th April
WORLD HEALTH DAY

SAINT BRYNACH'S DAY: Little is known of this Welsh king and saint but a cross dedicated to Saint Brynach stands at Nevern, near Newport, Dyfed, traditionally the perch of the first cuckoo to reach mid-Wales.

10th April
SIBLINGS DAY: Annual holiday in some parts of the U.S.A.

13th April
PERSUIT OF HAPPINESS DAY

15th April
SWALLOW DAY

16th April
CUCKOO DAY

SAINT MAGNUS' DAY: According to the Orkneyinga Saga, Magnus had a reputation for piety and gentleness, which the Norwegians viewed as cowardice. He refused to fight in a Viking raid in Anglesey, Wales, because of his religious convictions, and instead stayed on board the ship during the Battle of Menai Straits, singing psalms. He was later granted the Dukedom of Orkney, to rule in partnership with his cousin, Haakon, who later had him murdered. (I applaud him for attempting to use peaceful ways in such a bloodthirsty and violent period in history and have a personal affection for him for not using violence upon my adopted home!)

19th April
PAN CELTIC FESTIVAL

21st April
SAINT BEUNO'S DAY: Early Welsh saint of Gwynedd who had a wonderful reputation for healing

22nd April
EARTH DAY

23rd April
WILLIAM SHAKESPEARE'S BIRTH... AND DEATH

SAINT GEORGE'S DAY: Feast of patron saint of England

24th April
SAINT MARK'S EVE: Celtic celebration, especially in the Isle of Man and Brittany; a mystical evening when a channel of communication was opened between this world and that of the dead. A time of divination.

25th April
SAINT MARK'S DAY: Continues the divinatory theme. Also heralded the start of the crayfish season in Brittany and the traditional time to sow crops of barley.

29th April
INTERNATIONAL DANCE DAY

30th April
INTERNATIONAL JAZZ DAY

WALPURGIS NACHT / BELTANE EVE

THE BOOGG (Switzerland): A popular celebration which dates back to the Sixteenth Century and takes place once the first flowers of spring begin to bloom, definitively marking the end of winter, usually sometime in April. The figure of a snowman (old winter) whose head had been stuffed with explosives, is set alight. In more modern times, the rate at which the Boogg burns is seen as a predictor of the coming summer weather. The faster the fire reaches the head of the snowman, the better the conditions are expected to be. If it explodes in the first 6 – 10 minutes, the summer will be dry and sunny. An explosion after 10 – 15 minutes of burning forecasts a rainy summer.

BLOEMENSCORSO BOLLENSTREEK (Netherlands): At the end of the month of April a twelve hour long parade travels from Noordwijk in Southern Holland to Haarlem. The region's most anticipated spring event, this flower parade is constructed from bulb blooms - daffodils, hyacinths, tulips, etc. – which cover the elaborate floats which wander through the streets along a twenty-four-mile (40 kilometre) route.

HANAMI (Japan): Cherry Blossom Festival which takes place sometime between late March and early May, depending on how early the spring is. A centuries-old tradition of hosting parties and celebrating beneath the flowering trees.

May

1ˢᵗ May
BELTANE: Celebration of beginning of early summer.

ACKNOWLEDGEMENT

I could not do what I do, or be what I am, without all the loving support of the people who surround me, My deepest thanks go to my family; my wonderfully patient husband, Holger, who unquestioningly looks after the rest of the household whenever I am shut away writing, and my son, Dafydd, and his partner Jess, who are now also my editors and publishers and who provide endless loving support, listening ears and cups of tea!

My thanks also go to my dearest friend, Alison, who, whilst also working on getting her own book *Dementia Diary: A love story to the end'* into print, generously took the time to read, edit and offer her advice on my manuscript. (She also came to my rescue by drawing a girl in a bonnet and a plate of Glamorgan Sausages when my own meagre artistry failed me!)

I would also like to offer my loving thanks to Annie and John who bravely suggested some radical changes which I didn't necessarily abide by but deeply appreciated all the same - their loving support has been unfailing throughout and means a great deal to me.

However, during this unprecedentedly difficult and challenging time of Covid-19 and the pandemic there are many other 'ordinary' but absolutely wonderful people who have also helped to keep everything going on my behalf, often at great risk to themselves. For instance, the people who work to grow, process and supply my food, who keep my utilities functioning, the movement of deliveries and communication freely flowing and the country generally ticking over. All these unsung heroes who have given selflessly of themselves and who have all contributed to my being able to safely and happily secrete myself away and free my mind and spirit to simply dream, plot, plan and write, I send out a huge 'thank you'.

Lastly, but by no means least, a massive 'thank you' to you, my wonderful readers, without whom my work would be futile. You all bring me such inspiration, joy, satisfaction and pleasure. I always love to hear from you! If you have any comments ideas or suggestions, or you simply would like to say 'Hello!', please do get in touch with me at gillian@gillianmonks.com.

COMPETITION WINNER

I decided to run a competition for a children's short story to include in my next book because I felt that it might help to inspire a budding author to see their work in a professional publication. As the spring progressed, it dawned on me that it might also help many aspiring authors to focus on something positive during the Covid-19 pandemic emergency and consequent lockdown and isolation. It was huge fun to receive all the very varied submissions and I really fell in love with many of them. Choosing a winner was a very difficult task, but when Carys's story, 'It's Not My Fault!' arrived in my in-tray only a couple of weeks before the competition closed, I was in no doubt and knew in my heart that I had found exactly the right story for my book.

As Carys says herself: *"I have always been a voracious reader. I learnt how to swim the ocean deep with mermaids, explored enchanted woods with pixies, found new worlds riding on the back of dragons. I even trekked over snow covered mountains to return a ring to a volcano. I have been writing for a few years now and love the fact that my stories tell me what happens. I used to think I was in control until I started to write…how wrong I was!"*

I very much look forward to reading more of Carys' work, and as she has one novel already finished and another two on the go, it hopefully won't be long before I am able to do so. Look out for more from this talented lady – I wish her much success.

ANSWER TO QUESTION ON PAGE 171: Easter

Bibliography

- Amber K and Azrael Arynn K: '*Candlemas, Feast of Flames*' GT4995.C36 K36 2001*
- Cater, Karen: '*Spirit of the Hare in Folklore, Mythology and the Artist's Landscape*' - ISBN 9780955647536*
- Chainey, Dee Dee: '*A Treasury of British Folklore*' - ISBN 9781911358398*
- Collins, Tony: '*Encyclopaedia of Traditional Rural Sports*' - ISBN 9780415647472
- Day, Brian: '*Chronicle of Celtic Folk Customs*' - ISBN 0600598373*
- Druit, Ann; Fynes-Clinton, Christine; Rowling, Marije: '*All Year Round, A Calendar of Celebrations*' - ISBN 0781869890476*
- Gascoigne, Margaret: '*Discovering English Customs and Traditions*' - ISBN 0747803773
- Grimassi, Raven: '*BELTANE: Springtime Rituals, Lore and Celebration*' - ISBN 1567183836*
- Jenkins, J. Geraint: '*Life and Tradition in Rural Wales*'
- Owen, Trevor M.: '*A Pocket Guide to the Customs and Traditions of Wales*' - ISBN 0708311180
- Owen, Trevor M.: '*Welsh Folk Customs*' - ISNB 0863833470
- Parry-Jones, D.: '*Welsh Children's Games and Pastimes*'
- Simpson, Jacqueline: '*The Folklore of the Welsh Boarder*' - ISBN 0713431636
- Walker, Barbara: '*The Woman's Encyclopaedia Of Myths and Secrets*' ISBN 0062509268/ ISBN 006250925X
- Waterson, Meggan: '*Mary Magdalen Revealed*'
- White, Julie, and Tallboys, Graeme K.: '*ARIANRHOD'S DANCE: A Druid Ritual Handbook*' - ISBN 0954053125*

LINKS AND FURTHER INFORMATION

- 'Identification of an Immune-Responsive Mesolimbocortical Serotonergic System: Potential Role in Regulation of Emotional Behavior' by Christopher Lowry et al., published online on March 28, 2007 in Neuroscience: http://www.sage.edu/newsevents/news/?story_id=240785
- Mind & Brain/Depression and Happiness – Raw Data 'Is Dirt the New Prozac?' by Josie Glausiusz, Discover Magazine, July 2007 Issue: https://discovermagazine.com/2007/jul/raw-data-is-dirt-the-new-prozac
- A Hundred Good Points of Husbandrie by Lawrence D. Mills, by courtesy of Thompson and Morgan: https://www.thompson-morgan.com/
- Read more at Gardening Know How: *Antidepressant*
- *Microbes In Soil: How Dirt Makes You Happy*: https://www.gardeningknowhow.com/garden-how-to/soil-fertilizers/antidepressant-microbes-soil.htm
- scottishpaganfellowship.co.uk
- www.britannica.com
- www.historic-uk.com/cultureUK/St-Valentines-Day
- www.earlybritishkingdoms.com
- www.timeanddate.com
- http://www.healthwithfood.org/health-benefits/microgreens-nutrition.php
- http://www.agniinstitute.org/microgreens
- http://www.cuesa.org/article/raw-truth-about-sprouts-and-microgreens
- http://www.gardeningknowhow.com/edible/vegetables/vgen/regrowing-vegetables-in-water.htm
- www.ferndalegardencentre.co.uk
- www.bridgeman.co.uk
- www.craigiehallnursery.co.uk
- www.jacksonnurseries.co.uk
- www.farmyardnurseries.co.uk

- www.marshalls-seeds.co.uk
- www.suttons.co.uk
- www.chilternseeds.co.uk
- www.gardenorganic.org.uk
- www.gardenersworld.com
- www.theenglishgarden.co.uk
- www.dobies.co.uk
- www.britishfoodhistory.com
- www.historytoday.com

Feeding and Care of Wild Birds

- www.rspb.org.uk
- www.woodlandtrust.org.uk/blog/2018/02/feedong-winter-birds
- www.britishbirdlovers.co.uk/bird-food/10-tips-for-feeding-birds
- Catholic Encyclopaedia: www.newadvent.org
  https://www.churchofengland.org

$\mathcal{L}$

$\mathcal{M}$

$\mathcal{N}$

WITH A LOVE FOR BOOKS

With a large range of imprints, from herbalism, selfsufficiency, physical and mental wellbeing, food, memoirs and many more, Herbary Books is shaped by the passion for writing and bringing innovative ideas close to our readers.

All our authors put their hearts into their books and as publishers we just lend a helping hand to bring their creation to life.

Thank you to our authors and to you, dear reader.

Discover and purchase all our books on

WWW.HERBARYBOOKS.COM

HERBARYBOOKS